D1233411

The London & South Western Railway in the 20th Century

J. N. Faulkner, MCIT
and
R. A. Williams, MCIT

DAVID & CHARLES
Newton Abbot   London   North Pomfret (VT)

British Library Cataloguing in Publication Data
Faulkner, J. N.
The LSWR in the twentieth century.
1. Southern England. Railway services.
London & South Western Railway, 1900–1923
I. Title   II. Williams, R. A. (Ronald Alfred)
385′.09423

ISBN 0–7153–8927–0

Photoset and printed in Great Britain
by Redwood Burn Limited, Trowbridge, Wiltshire
for David & Charles (Publishers) PLC
Brunel House Newton Abbot Devon

Published in the United States of America
by David & Charles Inc
North Pomfret   Vermont 05053 USA

Contents

INTRODUCTION

Volumes 1 and 2 of the *History of the London & South Western Railway* by R. A. Williams appeared in 1968 and 1973, and many readers were looking forward to the appearance of the third volume to complete the story. Circumstances prevented its publication at that time, but it became possible to return to the subject in time for the celebration of the 150th anniversary of the London & Southampton Railway.

Although the present book deals with the history of the London & South Western Railway during the 20th Century, many of the projects completed had their origins prior to 1900. For the sake of today's readers who do not possess the earlier volumes, some brief historical introductions have been included. Conversely, some 20th Century developments had already been described in Volume 2 and their stories are repeated to provide the full picture for the new readers.

Locomotive matters have been dealt with very briefly, as a detailed history can be found in the two volumes produced by the late D. L. Bradley for The Railway Correspondence & Travel Society. No detailed histories or descriptions of the new branch lines built have been included as most are already covered by the many published works, large and small, on local railway history. The present book has concentrated on the major achievements of the LSWR which have received less attention—the reconstruction of Waterloo, improving the main line, suburban electrification, and the development of Southampton Docks. The railway historian must not overlook that a railway company is a business, so due attention has been given to the LSWR management, its staff relations, its profitability, and finally the difficult negotiations which preceded the formation of the Southern Railway

J. N. Faulkner
R. A. Williams
January 1988

CHAPTER 1

THE NEW WATERLOO

THE OLD STATION

'We got to Waterloo at eleven and asked where the eleven-five started from. Of course nobody knew; nobody at Waterloo ever does know where a train is going to start from, or where a train when it does start is going to, or anything about it.' The Three Men in a Boat were not the only travellers to get lost in the old Waterloo. Fifty years of piecemeal development found the terminus formed of three separate stations—Central, the original 1848 building; South, added in 1878; and North, dating from 1885. To add to the confusion, the 18 lines in the station shared only ten platform numbers.

Our imaginary tour of Waterloo commences with the South station, opened on 16 December 1878 and known as 'Cyprus' following the British annexation of that island. It had its own booking office and concourse facing a long island platform, not numbered, flanked by lines 1 and 2, used for suburban services to Kingston, Hampton Court, Guildford and Epsom. Between the South and Central stations was the cab yard serving the main line departure platforms, reached by an evil-smelling tunnel from York Street, with exit via a ramp down to Waterloo Road. At the outer end, above the cab tunnel, was a small locomotive shed and turntable.

The Central station was the original terminus opened on 11 July 1848. The buildings alongside the main departure platform 1 housed the booking office, refreshment and waiting rooms, with offices above for company officials. *The Times* in August 1899 criticised the congestion and confusion on this platform, which it considered a danger to the public. Platform 1, served by road 3, was used for such principal departures as the 11.00am to Plymouth and the Southampton Docks boat trains, but also for the 5.38pm local to Kingston.

Road 3 was double-sided with the narrow platform 2 beyond, which had road 4 at its outer face. This was used for other important main line departures, as well as for some local trains. Road 5 was the through connection to the South Eastern Railway at Waterloo

Junction, opened on 11 January 1864 and used only by (LNWR) passenger trains from 6 July 1865 to 31 December 1867. Since then the link had been employed for transfer and special traffic—for example, Queen Victoria travelled this way from Windsor to Woolwich on 22 March 1900.

Road 6 alongside platform 3 was used for main line arrivals, but also for departures to Basingstoke, Alton and Portsmouth, which were often formed from incoming trains. In 1902 the platform was widened to reach the former middle road 5, and line 6 was removed for most of its length. Double-sided road 7 separated platforms 3 and 4, beyond which was the arrival cab road with similar access and exit to that on the departure side. The long tracks 4, 5 and 6 were an obstacle to movement across the station, only partially relieved by a drawbridge over the through line and a footbridge from platform 1 to platform 3 and beyond. All these original platforms were spanned by a low wooden roof.

At the outer end of platform 4 was dock road 8, used for parcels and horse-and-carriage traffic. The next four platforms, 5–7, served by roads 9–12, comprised the first Windsor Line extension opened on 3 August 1860, and used mostly for main line arrivals. Facing these was a small concourse with the Windsor Line booking office and the main parcels office.

The North station was the most recent addition, opened in stages during 1885 and dubbed 'Khartoum' after the Sudan campaign of that year. Intended for Windsor Line traffic, the North station was covered by a substantial iron roof and its concourse was backed by a range of new general offices, opened on 1 July 1886. The Windsor Line face of platform 7 was served by road 13, the island platforms 8 and 9 by roads 14–15 and 16–17 respectively and platform 10, mainly used for milk traffic, by road 18. The North station platforms were provided with iron railings and gates, but elsewhere the platforms were open, and Waterloo was the haunt of idlers and petty criminals.

Beyond the North station were carriage sidings, the hoist to the Waterloo & City line and a small locomotive yard. On the south side of the station stood the Necropolis platform and beyond it all lines converged to six tracks to cross Westminster Bridge Road. West of that bridge, on the down side, was another small locomotive yard dating from 1892. The tracks outside the station were spanned by the gantry carrying the 220-lever 'A' signalbox; shunting movements were also controlled by the 'Crows' Nest' box in the roof of the Central station and by the North Yard box in the Windsor Line sidings.

Waterloo was unique among the major London termini in not having a station hotel. There were abortive plans by a private syn-

dicate during 1898–1901 to build an hotel near the junction of Waterloo Road and York Road, linked to the station by a covered way, and
intended to be called the South Western Grand Hotel.

In this chapter the authors have followed the company's references
to works being on the north or south side of the station, but the
directions are west and east respectively.

PLANNING, PARLIAMENTARY AND PROPERTY

The old station was both inconvenient and inadequate; the 1,049 train
movements on August Bank Holiday 1899 were close to its capacity.
Already on 9 December 1897 Archibald Scott, the former general
manager and now a member of the board, had called attention to the
need to plan for a further extension on the south side of the station.
Here 6½ acres of squalid and crowded property provided the only
available site for expansion. Powers to acquire this land were sought in
the company's 1898 Bill, but were deleted because of opposition from
the local authorities. During 1898 every meeting of the LSWR board
examined plans and models of the new station, sending each back in
turn for revision. On 21 July the concept of a complete reconstruction
was accepted, and on 13 October a special committee was appointed to
prepare plans and to handle negotiations for a further Bill in 1899.

This committee recommended taking powers for additional land on
the north and east sides of the station (some of which was never
required), but it was necessary to go back to Parliament in 1911 for
authority to acquire land in Mepham Street alongside the SECR
viaduct. The LSWR purchased from the Waterloo & City Railway its
property in York Road, near the hoist, and planned to roof over the
shunting yard on the south side of the station, for which the W&C was
paid £35,000 and had its rent reduced.

The political groundwork for the 1899 Bill was more thorough, and
negotiations were held beforehand with the London County Council
(LCC), the Lambeth Vestry and the church authorities. The LCC was
placated by an LSWR contribution towards road improvements,
while the vestry was given assurances as to the rehousing of the 1,750
inhabitants to be displaced. After agreement had been reached with
the London Necropolis Company (LNC), no further opposition was
offered to the Bill, which received Royal Assent on 9 August 1899.

The Necropolis station was situated in a key position in relation to
the enlargement of Waterloo. It had been built in 1854 on the south
side of the line to the east of Westminster Bridge Road. In 1878, in
order to gain access to the new South station, the LSWR had removed

the station's outer wall and second track, but in return had granted the LNC a 999-year lease of the remaining land. Prolonged negotiations were concluded by an agreement on 16 May 1899, by which the LSWR was to build a new Necropolis station beyond Westminster Bridge Road to designs prepared by C. B. Tubbs (the LNC architect), to give the Necropolis company a 999-year lease of the new site at a nominal rent, to provide new stock for the Brookwood funeral train and to end various restrictions on the availability of mourners' tickets. The LSWR would also pay the LNC £12,000 compensation for disturbance.

Adjacent to the existing boundary of the South station stood All Saints church and school, which would have to be demolished. As most of the parishioners were to be rehoused, it was agreed to amalgamate the parish with that of Saint John, Waterloo Road. The former vicar would be paid an annuity until he obtained an equivalent benefice, the remaining congregation was to be housed in a chapel of ease in York Road, and a combined school for the two parishes was to be built in Exton Street—all this at LSWR expense.

The LSWR was compelled by statute to provide alternative accommodation nearby for the labouring classes displaced. Plans for these dwellings were subject to the approval of the Lambeth Vestry, the LCC and the Home Office, which also fixed the scale of rents. The first site was acquired at Boniface Street, near the foot of Westminster Bridge, where Stangate Buildings were ready for occupation in September 1901. The major part of the rehousing was carried out on the former Maudslay engineering works site in Westminster Bridge Road, purchased in September 1899. The estate was named Campbell Buildings, in honour of the LSWR chairman; the five blocks of flats to house 1,450 people were completed between June 1902 and May 1904.

Various housing bodies, such as the Peabody Trust, had offered to erect and manage these dwellings on behalf of the LSWR, but the company preferred to keep control in its own hands. Including the blocks near Vauxhall, the total outlay came to £255,802 on which net rentals brought the modest return of $2^3/4$ per cent. All these estates have now been swept away by redevelopment.

CONSTRUCTION 1900–1910

The Necropolis station was the obstacle to enlargement of Waterloo, and it was here that work commenced. As soon as the 1899 Act had been passed, a start was made on the new LNC premises and the

Construction of new South station Waterloo 1904–5. In the foreground are the Waterloo & City Line sidings, with rolling stock and shunting locomotive. *National Railway Museum*

Waterloo station concourse summer 1913, showing new platforms 1–6 and remains of old Central station roof. *Commercial postcard, courtesy G. Gundry*

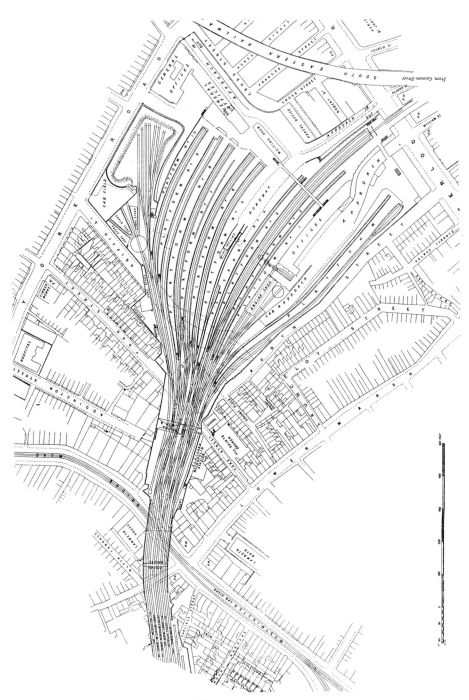

Waterloo station in 1900

£43,494 station came into use on 16 February 1902. Fronting West-minster Bridge Road was the LNC office block with an archway leading into the station courtyard. At second floor level were the two platforms, the northern one for first class mourners, the other for loading the coffins and for third class and parish funerals. The Necro-polis branch joined the down main line near 'B' signal box, while the space between the Necropolis station and the main line was occupied by carriage sidings and a remodelled locomotive yard and turntable.

The enlargement to be made to the terminus was known as the New South station. On 28 February 1900 W. T. Foxlee, who had been engaged as new works engineer, submitted plans for the enlargement, followed by details of the staging of the works to maintain the flow of traffic. Meanwhile,the property on the south side of the station was acquired and in February 1903 it was reported that the area had been cleared.

Detailed plans for the sub-structure were approved on 23 July 1902 and the first of many contracts for building work on the station was concluded with Perry & Co (Bow) Ltd on 9 October. The board decided on 30 April 1903 that the additional south side accommo-dation was to be completed in such a manner as to form part of a complete scheme of reconstruction; in March 1905 it was agreed that the new roof should be extended over the top of the old station as work proceeded. With work to rail level approaching completion, tenders for the roof were approved on 28 June 1905 and the first column was erected in November.

During 1906 deliveries of steel for the roof fell behind schedule and the chief engineer's hopes of completion in 1907 were not fulfilled. The roofing over the concourse was the subject of separate contracts approved in March 1908. Eventually, platforms 1 to 3 in the new South station came into use on 24 January 1909 and the old South station was then closed. Two locomotive spurs served platforms 1–2 and 3–4 respectively, but these were removed after electrification. The new South station was completed by platform 4 on 25 July 1909 and platform 5 on 6 March 1910.

Roadways from Westminster Bridge Road and Lower Marsh pro-vided easy access to the new platforms and a doorway adjacent to platform 1 enabled VIPs to depart inconspicuously. Although the new roadways were not opened for public use until 18 December 1911, the new platforms were invaluable for handling special traffic, such as the 1909 Territorial Army manoeuvres, the funeral of King Edward VII in 1910 and the coronation of King George V in 1911.

Construction of the office block behind the concourse was deferred several times before receiving final approval on 7 January 1909. It was completed on 7 November 1910, with its lighting and heating provided from the W&C power station. Passenger amenities included a cloakroom and a gentlemen's basement lavatory, stated by *The Railway Magazine* to be 'perhaps the finest in England.' A spacious new booking hall came into use on 11 June 1911.

The building of the new South station was accompanied by widening of the immediate approaches to the terminus. A new 24-chain down local line was brought into use on 4 July 1900, providing an additional exit from the old South station across Westminster Bridge Road. Powers were obtained in the 1899 and 1902 Acts for extra land on the north side of the station to widen this bridge for eleven tracks, also to allow room for the reconstruction and lengthening of the main line platforms. The widening over Westminster Bridge Road was carried out during 1906 to 1908 to provide eight running lines into the terminus. The board on 11 June 1909 approved the continuation of the north side widening as the next stage in complete reconstruction. Here a new Windsor Line locomotive yard came into use on 1 March 1914. It now remained to connect the widened approach lines with the new and reconstructed platforms as they were brought into service.

A chronology of the main stages in the change-over from the old to the new station concludes this chapter.

COMPLETION 1911–1922

Progress so far had been slow, with each succeeding stage subject to board discussion and delay. The advent of Hugh Drummond as chairman in 1911 brought more decision, and at the general meeting on 10 February he stated that 'the company would endeavour to complete reconstruction as soon as possible.' Already the new roofing over the concourse had been extended to allow removal of the rest of the old South station roof, while on 4 August 1910 an extension of the office block had been authorised.

Reconstruction was now approaching the old Central station and the through line to the SECR was an obstacle to the provision of a continuous concourse. Use of it had declined since the SER/LCDR amalgamation, and it was agreed with the SECR managing committee that the line could be removed but the pedestrian footbridge was to remain. Abandonment was confirmed by the LSWR Act of 18 August 1911—the link was taken out of use on 26 March 1911. The same Act authorised the LSWR's acquisition of land between Waterloo station and the SECR viaduct, required for the extension of the new cab roadway past the front of the station and into York Road.

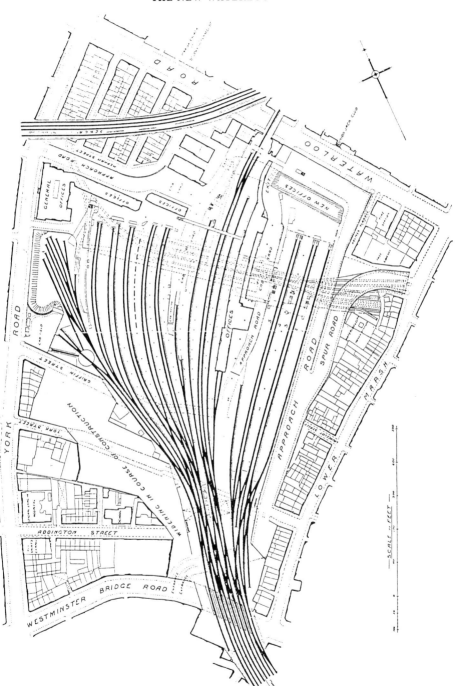

Waterloo station in 1910 after completion of the new South station

To allow the new roofing to be erected, platforms 2 and 3 were closed on 3 July 1911 and a temporary wooden gangway linked platforms 1 and 4. The Central station footbridge was removed on 7 April 1913, replaced by another temporary passage. While the new steelwork was taking shape around it, the old Central station roof was propped up; some of it was removed during 1912–1913, while the last fragments opposite new platforms 10 and 11 were taken down on 29 November 1915. Demolition of the old offices alongside platform 1 commenced in June 1912 and was completed in the summer of 1913. Their occupants moved either to the new office block in the South station, to temporary accommodation off York Road or to the former locomotive works offices at Nine Elms. The cab approaches to the main line platforms closed on 1 January 1912, superseded by the new roadways beyond the South station.

The arrival of Herbert Walker as general manager brought a further strengthening of the decision-making process. The engineering committee was able in July 1912 to set out a programme for completion of the reconstruction. The following work was included in the first stage:

1 Completion of platforms 6 – 11 and the central cab yard, cost £75,000.
2 Completion of new roofing and screen to connect with the old North station roof, cost £79,000.
3 Further office buildings (extension 2) with concourse roofing, completion of Waterloo Road cab yard and subway to concourse, cost £75,000.
4 Completion of platforms, working from the north, cost £71,000.

Section 2 above implied the preservation of the existing Windsor Line North station. The retention of its six platforms reduced the total in the new Waterloo to 21, whereas the original plans had envisaged 23 platforms in a continuous line, of which ten would have been allocated to Windsor Line traffic. Inner suburban traffic was declining, the 1885 roof was in good condition and the revised arrangement provided a more spacious Windsor Line concourse, as well as saving considerable expenditure.

Work on the first stage was approved by the board on 26 July 1912, with authority given to the general manager and chief engineer to decide the order of construction. The engineering committee also outlined the remaining stages of work on the Windsor side to achieve final completion:

(a) Completion of the main office block.
(b) Completion of the concourse roof.
(c) Roofing over the cab yard.

On 1 October 1912 the designations of South, Central and North were discontinued and the platform faces in the old station were renumbered provisionally 6 – 17 to follow on from the five platforms in the new South station. The new platforms 6 – 11 came into use during 1913. On 7 December 1913, in a further renumbering, old platforms 9 – 17 became 12 – 20. Line 18 became the milk platform and eventually platform 21. Down below, the new subway to the Waterloo & City and the Bakerloo had been extended from platform 5 on 16 December 1912; the new stairway from Waterloo Road to the concourse was opened on 13 October 1913 with a passage to the W&C following on 1 December.

When the chairman toured the station on 22 April 1913 the new steel roof was complete as far as the future platform 11. He inspected the new refreshment and dining rooms which were nearly ready to be handed over to the lessees, Spiers & Pond. Their opening on 27 June was marked by an official luncheon given by the LSWR to its guests.

Sections 1 to 3 of the July 1912 programme were now nearing completion. On 29 January 1914 the engineering committee authorised work to commence on platforms 12 to 15 and those in the North station, which comprised section 4. At the general meeting in February 1914 it was reported that construction work on extension 2 of the office block (authorised on 26 June 1913) was being held up by a builders' strike. Some of the building contracts were suspended at the outbreak of war in August 1914, due to the company's financial problems, which caused further delay.

The cab roadway along the front of the station leading to York Road was opened for traffic on 21 December 1914 and the central cab road between platforms 11 and 12 with its approach from Griffin Street followed on 24 August 1915. Meanwhile platforms 12 – 15 were taken out of use for reconstruction and realignment during 1915–17. The platforms in the North station also had to be lengthened and reconstructed in concrete, and during 1914–15 they were taken out of use in turn, rebuilding being completed in good time for the inauguration of electric services in October 1915.

Although authority had been given in June 1915 for the remaining work to complete the reconstruction of the station, under wartime conditions progress was slow and in October 1917 the engineering committee estimated that work costing some £210,000 still remained to be done. On 30 January 1914 the board had approved the construction of an escalator from the concourse between platforms 15 and 16 to the Waterloo & City. The Otis company of New York supplied the machinery, which was safely transported across the submarine-infested Atlantic at considerable cost, and the new facility came into use on 9 April 1919. The retention of the existing North station left space available between platforms 15 and 16, so it was decided in April 1918 to erect a two-storey staff block on this site. This contained the stationmaster's and lost property offices, the clerical staff dining room and accommodation for the uniformed grades. Construction was undertaken by the company itself, and the stationmaster moved in on 14 December 1919.

A new suburban booking office opposite platforms 14 and 15 opened on 22 July 1918, enabling the old Windsor Line ticket office to be demolished in November. With the return of peace, Perry & Co could proceed with the completion of the main office block to link with the existing general offices. Contracts were placed in 1919–20 for the roofing over the Windsor Line concourse and over the cab road in front of the station. A new Windsor tea room, facing the escalator, opened in July 1921, followed by a large buffet behind the suburban ticket office on 23 December, replacing a temporary refreshment room in use since July 1916.

On 20 February 1919 the engineering committee gave instructions for the archway opposite platforms 19 and 20 to be completed as the company's war memorial. This entrance was the scene of the formal opening of the new station on 21 March 1922. The ceremony should have been performed by King George V, but as the King had a cold, Queen Mary deputised for him on that chilly day. Alighting from her motor car, the Queen first inspected a guard of honour formed of 100 LSWR men who had distinguished themselves in the recent war. After the Queen had been welcomed by the chairman and deputy chairman, the survivors of a generation's work on the new station were presented to her: A. W. Szlumper, chief engineer since 1914; R. D. Hawes, new works assistant since 1909; J. R. Scott, the company's architect responsible for the whole of the building design; Dudley Bartlett, representing the main contractors Perry & Co (Bow) Ltd, whose founder Sir Herbert Bartlett had recently died; and Sir Guy Wrightson of Head Wrightson & Co, the steelwork suppliers. The construction of the station also owed much to the previous chief engineers, E. Andrews and J. W. Jacomb-Hood. Cutting a royal blue ribbon at the base of the Victory Arch the Queen declared the station open, and after studying the bronze tablets within the arch recording the LSWR's roll of honour, she made a brief tour of the concourse and buffet before driving back to Buckingham Palace through the gateway spanning the central cab road.

The Southern Railway closed the Waterloo reconstruction accounts early in 1923 at a total cost of £2,269,354, of which £567,857 had been spent on land purchase and the balance on building work. Of this

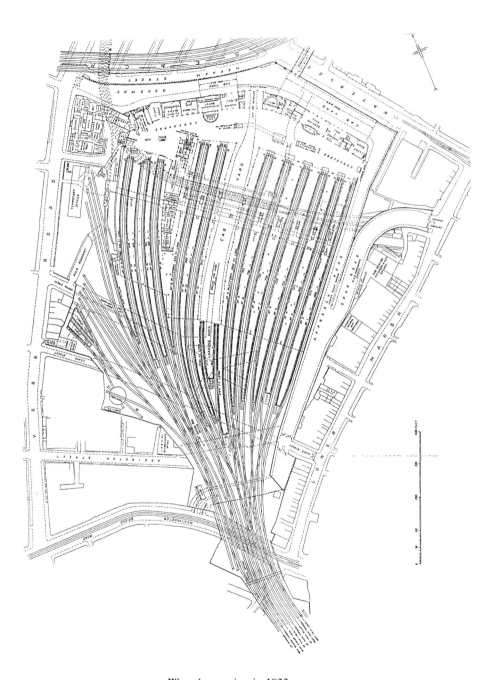

Waterloo station in 1922

total, £1,967,706 had been charged to capital and the rest to revenue, to cover the estimated value of the old station written-off and various short-term improvement works.

THE NEW STATION

We commence our tour of the station at the Victory Arch: this is surmounted by a triumphant figure of Britannia holding the torch of liberty. By the left of the archway is a group of statuary centred on Bellona, the Goddess of War, with the date 1914, matched to the right by Peace, symbolised by the figure of winged victory and the date 1918. The semicircle above the arch is decorated by panels with trophies of war and the names of the battlegrounds of 1914–18.

Passing through the arch much has changed since 1922. To the right was the main entrance to the general offices of the company and the carved stonework of the opening leading to the Bakerloo and the Waterloo & City tubes lines as well as York Road. Turning left, beyond the Windsor Line waiting rooms and toilets was the Windsor tea room, with its mirror-lined walls and elaborate cash kiosks. Adjacent was the main buffet, a large ornate room with marble walls, fluted columns and plaster ornamentation. The luggage hall and the public telegraph office preceded the central archway spanning the exit from the cab road. The arch was embellished with stained glass and stone tablets listing the counties served by the LSWR.

Beyond the arch was the refreshment accommodation opened in 1913—at concourse level a marble-lined circular buffet, on the first floor the oak-panelled 'Surrey' dining room and a ladies' tea room. The kitchens for these were situated on the fourth floor, where cooking smells would not offend the diners. The main line waiting rooms were situated between the buffet and the booking hall. When opened in 1913 it was thought undesirable that emigrants should share them with ordinary passengers, so a waiting room and lavatory were provided for them in the Waterloo & City station. The main booking hall, with access from the front roadway, dealt with the issue of long distance tickets, with suburban business being handled by the semicircular office on the concourse. The range of platform level buildings was completed by another luggage hall and the main cloak room.

Except for the restaurants and kitchens, the upper floors of the main block were occupied by offices, with the main telegraph office and telephone exchange on the top (fourth) floor. The concourse buildings were constructed in red brick with stone ornamentation; the

Waterloo platforms 1–4 with electric trains, in 1922. Note three 3-car units in platform 1. *Commercial postcard, author's collection*

Adams Class T6 4–4–0 No 686 passing Esher race platforms in 1922 with new trailer coach for the Waterloo & City Line. *L&GRP*

exterior and the staff block were faced with Portland stone. Since 1915 electric power for the station had been supplied from the company's Durnsford Road power house.

Other features in the public eye were the new mechanical departure indicators in front of platforms 6–7 and 18–19, the small enquiry office between platforms 8–9, the W. H. Smith bookstalls in the middle of both main and Windsor concourses, the clock over the central roadway installed in 1919 and the early Bodmin & Wadebridge carriage mounted in 1915 above the Waterloo Road stairway. Small hexagonal rotating departure indicators were provided over the entrances to platforms used by the electric trains (1 – 6 and 16 – 21). The platforms were guarded by iron railings and collapsible gates—platform tickets were issued from 7 May 1913.

Below platform level was a network of passages. The main passenger subway connected platforms 1 – 15 with both tube lines and the exit to York Road. It was paralleled by a luggage subway with electric lifts to the platforms, linking these to the parcels offices in the roadway below the south side of the station. This roadway also served the arches containing railway offices and stores and tenants' warehouses beneath the station.

Part of the passenger subway was used during the war as a free buffet for servicemen; in operation from 19 December 1915 until 7 April 1920, its volunteer helpers served 18 million cups of tea and their efforts were commemorated by a tablet on the subway wall. Leave trains arriving from Southampton Docks were met by the opening of kiosks for the exchange of foreign currency, much of it torn and grubby notes of low denominations from a variety of countries. The City of London Volunteer Training Corps met troops crossing London (perhaps for the first time) and escorted them through the perils and temptations of the great city. The concentration of continental traffic on the Southampton - Le Havre route led to the opening of a continental enquiry office at Waterloo on 20 November 1916.

Details of the platforms themselves are given in the summary at the end of this chapter. The introduction of regular-interval electric and steam departures had enabled platforms to be allocated to specific routes. In 1906 the old station had handled a total of 652 trains on a normal weekday. Following suburban electrification, the new station in 1922 was dealing with 1,159 trains daily; 707 electric, 326 steam and 126 empty, parcels and milk trains. Empty trips to and from Clapham Junction had been reduced by in-and-out working, but the lack of sidings near Waterloo meant that many peak hour commuter trains had to be stabled in the suburbs during the day.

The terminus was still controlled by the mechanical 'A' signalbox. Enlarged once again in 1910–11 (an engineer's suggestion of electrical signalling was not accepted), the box contained 266 levers, some double-acting—its 16 signalmen (six on each day shift) made 24,000 lever movements daily. The approaches were controlled by 'B' signalbox with 100 levers and eight men, and 'C' cabin with 30 levers and five men. Station working was now aided by track circuits on all roads and by route indicators on the 'A' box home signals.

WATERLOO STATION 1922

Main Line Station

Roof Span	Platform	Length (ft)	Traffic
1	1	696	Hampton Court electrics
	2	695	New Guildford/Leatherhead
	3	683	Shepperton electrics
2	4	685	Kingston Roundabout electrics
	5	720	Peak-hour suburban and specials
	6	720	Peak-hour suburban and specials
	7	728	Bournemouth/West of England
3	8	735	Portsmouth
	9	756	Main line semi-fast } trains reversing in station
	10	765	Main line semi-fast
	11	860	Southampton Docks/Main line fast
4	Cab roadway – at outer end		
Dock	1	160	
Dock	2	175	
5	12	843	Parcels/Main line arrivals
	13	857	Main line arrivals
	14	860	Main line arrivals
	15	635	Parcels

Windsor Line (North) Station

Platform	Length (ft)	Traffic
16	570	East Putney line electrics
17	600	Hounslow Loop via Richmond electrics
18	612	Hounslow Loop via Brentford electrics
19	605	Kingston Roundabout electrics
20	625	Windsor/Reading
21	551	Windsor/Reading

The peak-hour Shepperton via Richmond trains mostly used platform 16.

WATERLOO STATION
CHRONOLOGY OF RECONSTRUCTION

Old Station			New Station		
Platform Road	Renumbered 1/10/12,	7/12/13	Out of use	Platform	Into use
				1	24/1/09
				2	24/1/09
(South Station)				3	24/1/09
1			24/1/09	4	25/7/09
2			24/1/09	5	6/3/10
Cab road and approach				5A/6	9/3/13
Station offices				6/7	29/6/13
(Central Station)				6A/8	20/7/13
1 3	6		29/6/13	9	21/12/13
2 4			3/7/11	10	21/12/13
— 5	Middle road removed 1902				
3 { 6	(5 from 1902)		3/7/11	11	7/12/13
{ 7	7		1/10/13	Cab roadway	
4 7				Dock sidings	8/14
Dock 8	8 Siding		8/14		
(Windsor Extension)					
5 9	9	12	25/4/15	12	20/8/16
6 { 10	10	13	25/4/15	13	27/8/16
{ 11	11	14	25/4/15	14	29/10/16
7 12	12	15	25/4/15	15	30/5/17
(North Station)					
7 13	13	16	Reconstructed	16	13/6/15
8 { 14	14	17	Reconstructed	17	11/4/15
{ 15	15	18	Reconstructed	18	11/4/15
9 { 16	16	19	Reconstructed	19	14/6/14
{ 17	17	20	Reconstructed	20	14/2/15
10 18	Milk	Milk	Reconstructed	21	28/2/15

Notes: Platforms 5A, 6 and 6A were renumbered 6, 7 and 8 respectively from 1/10/13. After being taken out of public use platform lines sometimes remained as sidings, and new lines were formed as sidings while platforms were being constructed.

CHAPTER 2

THE METROPOLITAN AREA

THE WATERLOO AND CITY LINE

The LSWR advance towards London Bridge and the City had halted at Waterloo in 1848. After Waterloo Junction had been opened in 1869, City-bound commuters could cross the footbridge into the SER station and take a train to Cannon Street, but many made their way to the City by cab, bus or on foot. The success of the first deep electric tube in 1890, the City & South London Railway, offered an alternative means of linking Waterloo to the heart of the City.

When the Waterloo & City Railway was promoted, the LSWR board quickly decided on 7 January 1892 to give it financial support. The chairman, Wyndham S. Portal, recommended the scheme to LSWR shareholders, pointing out that the tube would cost only about £500,000 compared with £3 to £4 million for a surface line. Mr Portal was one of the four LSWR directors to take seats on the W&C board. Passage of the W&C Bill through Parliament was slow, Royal Assent not being obtained until 27 July 1893.

The Act authorised a line 1 mile 46 chains from the south side of Waterloo station to the Mansion House, with a capital of £540,000. The Act imposed restrictions on excavations within the City and required all antiquarian finds to be given to the Guildhall Museum. Separate running tunnels were to be built, at different levels approaching each terminus, and involving sharp curves where they were routed from Waterloo station to follow Stamford Street and where they turned to cross the River Thames.

The supervising engineers were W. R. Galbraith (the LSWR consulting engineer), R. E. Church and J. H. Greathead (inventor of the tunnelling shield), the latter being succeeded after his death in 1896 by Dr Alexander Kennedy, the electrical expert. The resident engineer was H. H. Dalrymple-Hay. The contractor for the main tunnel was John Mowlem & Co Ltd, which sank the first working shaft on 18 June 1894 in mid-river upstream of Blackfriars Bridge, evacuating spoil by barge in compliance with the City's restrictions. The first tunnelling shield began work below on 26 November 1894.

Under Waterloo station Perry & Co was the contractor. The two separate W&C platforms were at right-angles to the main line tracks 41ft above and were built within four of the supporting arches, whose foundations had to be deepened. Stairs and slopes linked the W&C to the cab yard of the South station, to platforms 3 and 4 in the Central station and to the north side of the Windsor Line station, while passages led to the streets on either side. Beyond the platforms there was a reversing siding within a combined arch, followed by the carriage sidings and the power station coal siding, partly in the open air.

The City station (Bank) was 59ft below the surface. Commuters had to trudge up a 1 in 9 inclined plane, eased to 1 in 18 by the insertion of short flights of steps in 1918. It had been the intention to provide lifts, but the cost of acquiring property for them was prohibitive. The line opened with two temporary stairway entrances, in Walbrook and at the corner of Cheapside and Queen Victoria Street, but access was improved with the completion of the public subway system beneath the Bank road junction, which provided three more entrances from 8 January 1900 and connection at that level with the Central London tube.

The W&C generated its own electricity at a power station off Lower Marsh on the south side of Waterloo. Output at 530v DC was fed to a central conductor rail. Coal wagons were lowered down the Armstrong hoist from the Windsor Line sidings, collected by a Siemens four-wheeled electric locomotive (later No 75S) and worked from the hoist siding via the up line and the departure platform to the power station. A larger Siemens Bo-Bo locomotive (No 74S) was provided as a spare.

The W&C decided to use electric motor coaches, and as British firms were unable to supply, the order went to Jackson & Sharp of Wilmington USA for 22 wooden-bodied vehicles. These were delivered to Southampton, and after completion with Siemens electrical equipment at Eastleigh works were lowered down the hoist to the W&C. Each motor coach was powered by two 60hp motors and the five trains in service were formed into four-car sets, motor, trailer, trailer, motor, seating 204 passengers on hard plywood benches. Entrance to the W&C cars was via end platforms fitted with iron gates, but sliding doors were provided at the motor end of the motor coaches and on the single cars, described later. In addition, there were two spare motor coaches. The trains were not true multiple-units and control was via the full line voltage. Originally no 'dead man' device was fitted, and two men always had to be in the driving cab. Signalling had been devised by J. P. Annett, the LSWR signal superintendent, and W. R. Sykes of the well-known manufacturers. Both stations had a semaphore starter and an electric advanced starter. If the latter was on, only the 'draw-ahead' arm was lowered on the starter, but if the line was clear to the other terminus, the main signal came off. If a signal was passed at danger, a contact arm tripped the main switch on the train. In 1901 an additional mid-way signalbox was suggested, but the Board of Trade preferred automatic signalling.

The Board of Trade inspection on 6 July 1898 imposed 15mph restrictions round the sharpest curves which upset plans for a four-minute journey time. The official opening ceremony was carried out by the 80-year-old Duke of Cambridge on 11 July 1898, half a century after the main line terminus had been opened. The royal duke made a trip to the City and back, followed by lunch in the W&C booking hall. It had been hoped to commence public service on 1 August 1898, but a fire on 19 July in adjoining arches at Waterloo caused some damage, and a strike in the engineering industry delayed the commissioning and trials of the new trains.

Eventually at 8.00am on 8 August 1898 public services started. During the peak hours all five trains were in use to provide a five-minute service and at other times four trains operated at ten-minute intervals. No trains ran on Sundays. Accommodation was one class only and fares of 2d[1p] single and 3d[2p] return remained unchanged until 1920. Ticket issue at the stations was superseded from early 1899 by the guards or travelling collectors selling Bell Punch paper tickets on the trains. There were early teething troubles with the trains and several eminent consultants submitted reports during 1899 on the electrical working.

It was soon realised that the off-peak traffic did not require four-car trains but there was a need for a more frequent service. Consequently, five double-ended single motor cars were ordered from Dick, Kerr & Co in 1899, each equipped with two 60hp motors and seating 50 passengers, enabling the off-peak interval to be reduced to five minutes. Two more trailer cars were ordered in 1903 to cover overhauls and were combined with the two spare motor coaches to form a sixth train for rush-hour use. The W&C carriage sidings were enlarged to accommodate this extra rolling stock as part of the reconstruction of the main line station.

Passenger numbers grew from 3,485,556 in 1899 to 4,546,535 in 1902, with corresponding receipts from £26,029 to £34,296; in addition the line carried many through season ticket holders from the

LSWR. After 1902 traffic remained static, but the use of single cars and other economies reduced operating costs. Services were closely tailored to the traffic flow, with a maximum three-minute frequency operating between 9.20am and 9.56am when the bankers and stock-brokers arrived for the day's work.

According to the working agreement concluded with the LSWR on 8 March 1894, the South Western was to work the W&C for 55 per cent of the gross receipts (reduced to 45 per cent from 1 July 1905). If the balance was insufficient to pay three per cent debenture interest and three per cent dividend on the ordinary stock, the LSWR would make up the shortfall; if there was a surplus the W&C was to receive two-thirds after repaying any previous LSWR subsidies.

From 1901 onwards the W&C earnings were sufficient to pay the guaranteed dividends without LSWR help, and in subsequent years the W&C dividend slightly exceeded the three per cent figure. However, growing competition from the Underground, trams and buses with their lower fares made it probable that the LSWR would have to match these, and the W&C would have to share in the reduction. Its profit margin was so small that any loss of revenue would end all hopes of raising W&C dividends, and there was a real (but unspoken) danger that the LSWR might again be called upon to make good any shortfall in earnings. Therefore, proposals for amalgamation were offered to the W&C proprietors and were confirmed by the LSWR Act of 20 July 1906 to take effect from 1 January 1907. The £66,000 W&C debentures were already owned by the LSWR and holders of the £540,000 ordinary stock were offered a choice of exchange per £100 stock—either £67 LSWR ordinary shares, £105 of 3½ per cent prefer-ence stock, or £110 of three per cent debentures.

At City station a low-level footway to the Central London Railway had been proposed in 1899, but the partly constructed tunnel was used instead for one of the two lay-by sidings there. The suggestion was raised again in 1909 and Dalrymple-Hay was asked to report, but a year later it was decided to defer construction until the Central London Railway Liverpool Street extension was nearing completion. The Metropolitan District offered in 1912 to facilitate a W&C station at Blackfriars, to be constructed at LSWR expense.

Following the construction of the LSWR's Durnsford Road power station traction current for the W&C was supplied from there, and at the end of 1915 the Waterloo generating station was relegated to stand-by, being dismantled in 1917.

During the early post-war years rush-hour overcrowding on the W&C was acute—a shareholder complained in February 1920 of having to wait for four or five trains before being able to join one. The general manager proposed to the board committees on 19 February 1920 that the six four-car trains be increased to five-car by the addition of an all-steel trailer, while electrical equipment on the trains was to be replaced to provide better acceleration on the inclines. At a cost of £75,000 this would enable 24 trains per hour to be run instead of 20, providing 102 seats per minute in lieu of 68.

However, on 17 March 1921 this decision was altered for Eastleigh to build four more of the existing type trailer coaches, which were delivered during 1922. Apparently the other two trains were not lengthened and instead of equipping the trains for better acceleration, a Ministry of Transport inspecting officer's report in November 1921 indicated that the lower uphill speed of the five-car trains would allow a reduction of signal overlap distances. The scaling-down of the 1920 plans for the improvement of the W&C may have been due to the fresh ideas the company was now considering for its access to the City.

BAKERLOO AND OTHER TUBE LINES

Better access from Waterloo to the West End was also desirable, and the LSWR supported the promotion of the Baker Street & Waterloo Railway, which was authorised on 28 March 1893. Its directors included three members of the LSWR and W&C boards, but the original promoters failed to raise sufficient capital and relinquished their powers in 1897 to Whitaker Wright's London & Globe syndicate.

The Baker Street & Waterloo Railway was planned originally to terminate on the south side of Waterloo station, but this site was required for the W&C carriage sidings. In 1899 a deviation was authorised along the north side of the terminus with a station in York Street and a depot and power house in Addington Street, mainly on land leased from the LSWR. A further change of plan took place in 1900 with the Bakerloo's decision to extend to Elephant & Castle. This included an intermediate station in Westminster Bridge Road on the frontage of the LSWR's Maudslay housing site. Powers for the surface buildings were obtained on 11 August 1903, after arbitration had settled the price of the land.

Meanwhile the London & Globe syndicate had become insolvent in December 1900. The LSWR declined to subscribe to the Bakerloo's capital and construction work ceased until, in March 1902, Charles Tyson Yerkes and the Metropolitan District Electric Traction Co secured control. Work then resumed, the Bakerloo tube opening through Waterloo to Kennington Road on 10 March 1906, with

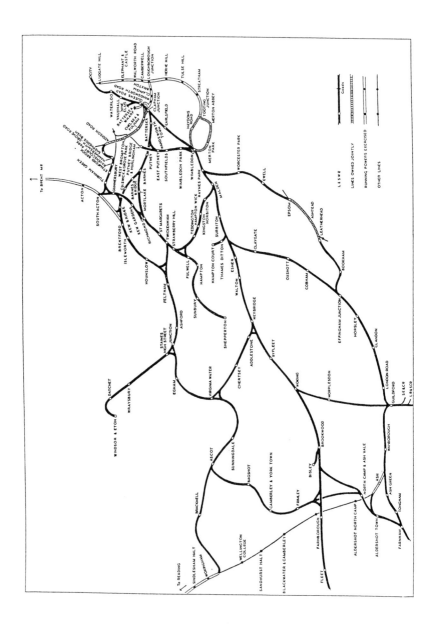

The LSWR London suburban area

completion to Elephant & Castle on 5 August 1906. At Waterloo the Bakerloo booking hall and lifts were situated on the north side of the station, adjacent to York Road.

With its contract on the Bakerloo approaching completion, H. H. Bartlett of Perry & Co approached the LSWR in July 1904 with proposals for a single line tube between Waterloo and Ludgate Circus, sharing sidings and access at Waterloo with the W&C. The cost was estimated at £253,000. The LSWR was well disposed to its regular London contractor and offered a working agreement, but would not provide any financial guarantees, so the project went no further.

In the 1905 session the Great Northern Piccadilly & Brompton Railway unsuccessfully proposed to extend its Holborn to Strand branch by a single line under the river to a station which would have shared the Bakerloo surface accommodation at Waterloo.

Following its takeover of the Great Northern & City Railway the Metropolitan Railway's 1913 Bill sought to extend that line from Moorgate to connect physically with the W&C at the Bank, with the eventual possibility of enlarging the W&C tunnels and making a connection with the LSWR surface lines. Due to opposition from property interests, Parliament refused these powers and those in the ensuing session for an extension to an exchange station beneath the W&C.

Many of the lines projected during the 'tube mania' of the early 1900s had the City as their objective, so the LSWR's Parliamentary lawyers were kept busy ensuring that the W&C was protected from interference. There were also a number of abortive underground schemes in the suburbs which would have affected the LSWR at Vauxhall, Clapham Junction or Wimbledon.

DISTRICT ELECTRICS TO WIMBLEDON
—AND BEYOND

The Metropolitan District Railway obtained powers on 9 August 1901 to electrify its system, also agreeing to provide any traction equipment for the maintenance of existing LSWR running powers over the District. A further MDR Act of 8 August 1902 authorised electrification of the LSWR line to Wimbledon, although a separate LSWR Act was necessary to confirm powers over the section of the former Kingston & London Railway between Putney Bridge and East Putney.

An agreement in February 1902 established the principle (applicable to other companies as well) that the District would pay four per cent interest on the LSWR's outlay on electrification, plus the extra cost of maintenance due to electric traction. A detailed agreement between the MDR and the LSWR was concluded on 4 December 1903. The LSWR was to lay and maintain conductor rails etc, from Putney Bridge to Wimbledon (North) station and to erect, equip and staff a sub-station at Wimbledon Park. This would receive 11kV from the District's Lots Road power station and supply the section beyond Southfields at the traction voltage of 600 through positive and negative conductor rails. All construction by the LSWR was to be to MDR standards, but in practice the track work was carried out by the London Underground Electric Company on a cost-plus basis. District electric trains to Wimbledon commenced on 27 August 1905, using the northern platform in the North station.

Local promoters had secured powers on 26 July 1910 for the Wimbledon & Sutton Railway, a 5½ mile line commencing from an end-on junction with the MDR at Wimbledon, also connecting with the LSWR main line west of the station. These junctions could only be made with LSWR agreement, and it was to be compensated for any loss of MDR terminal receipts at Wimbledon. By this Act the MDR had been granted running powers over the W&S, and in October 1911 agreed to build the line itself (the LSWR was not interested in taking part). From 5 December 1912 the W&S was effectively taken-over by the Underground group.

The new railway would have brought additional traffic to the District's Wimbledon branch, and the MDR began to plan the widening of both its own section and that of the LSWR south of East Putney. A letter from the MDR managing director, Albert Stanley, on 12 October 1911 stated that the proposed widening from East Putney to Wimbledon was due to congestion of traffic. If the LSWR would allow the MDR to obtain powers for this, the District did not intend to promote or assist in the extension of railways into LSWR territory without consent.

An agreement between the LSWR and the MDR was concluded on 17 May 1912 and was incorporated into the MDR's Act of 7 August 1912. The section between East Putney and Wimbledon was to be quadrupled by the LSWR at a cost of £170,000, widening to take place on both sides of the existing line, and District trains were to have exclusive use of the electrified western pair of lines. These were to be signalled and equipped to MDR standards, but the LSWR was to continue to staff the stations. No work had commenced when the LSWR engineering committee minuted on 23 January 1913 that lineside gardens at Southfields were not to be acquired 'due to other proposed arrangements.' On 3 April 1913 it was confirmed that the widening was not to proceed, and that the two companies would share the legal and Parliamentary costs. The proposed arrangements were the provision of two additional signalboxes at Cromer Road and Revelstoke Road at a cost of £1,800 to improve the capacity of the existing double line. This handled 14 District and three LSWR trains westbound between 5.00pm and 7.00pm, while the prospect of LSWR electrification removed the chances of delay from its steam trains.

It would have been necessary to adapt Wimbledon station for through running to Sutton, and the first stage was the conversion in 1913–14 of the northern terminal platform into an island, which would serve the through lines when extension took place. Plans were meanwhile approved on 24 July 1913 for a major reconstruction of the station, with the cost being shared between the LSWR, MDR, W&S and the London United Tramways (for road widening). The North station was the scene of a serious buffer stop collision on 14 October 1920. The 10.05am District train from Whitechapel approached No 2 platform too fast, and the stops designed for side buffer trains failed to retard the centre coupled and buffered electric train. This mounted the concourse and demolished part of the roof, killing one and injuring six of the waiting passengers, as well as injuring three people in the train.

Cheap government finance after World War I encouraged the revival of the W&S project, and in its 1923 Bill the Underground group proposed to link it near Morden with the extension of the City & South London tube. This met with strong opposition from the Southern Railway. To save the CSLR scheme in Parliament, the Underground group agreed to transfer its W&S powers to the SR, which obtained authority in 1924 for a connection to its Central Section lines at Wimbledon, nevertheless still offering running powers to the District.

ELECTRIC TRACTION TO RICHMOND

The LSWR's 1869 line from Kensington (Addison Road) to Richmond had been used beyond Studland Road Junction by Metropolitan District trains since 1 June 1877, and by Hammersmith & City (Metropolitan & Great Western) trains via Grove Road Junction from 1 October 1877. The line to Richmond was included in the MDR's electrification plans of 1901. Powers were obtained on 8 August 1902 for the section beyond Turnham Green and on 21 July 1903 for the stretch between Studland Road Junction and Turnham Green.

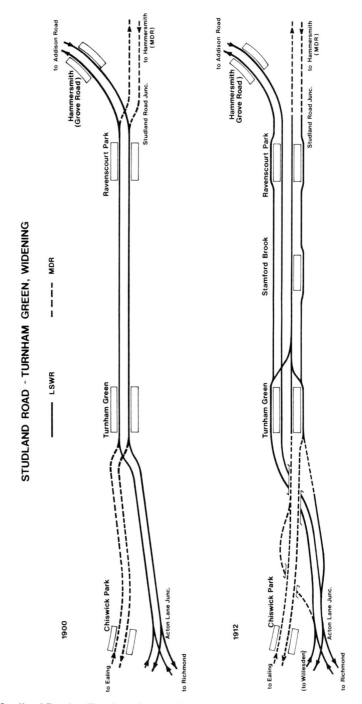

Studland Road to Turnham Green widening: track layouts in 1900 and 1912

Though the Metropolitan Railway obtained authority on 31 July 1902 to electrify the Hammersmith & City line, it did not then seek powers for the link to Studland Road Junction.

In 1901 the common section of 70 chains between Studland Road Junction and Turnham Green saw eighteen westbound steam trains between 5.00pm and 7.00pm—three LSWR, two Metropolitan and thirteen District, of which four ran to Richmond. With the prospect of electrification bringing a considerable increase in traffic, the MDR approached the LSWR in 1900 to build a third line, then in October and November 1902 for either the purchase or lease of this section, but all these proposals were rejected. The MDR then began to prepare a Bill for the 1903 Parliamentary session to authorise a duplicate line of its own and this persuaded the LSWR to enter negotiations, enabling the MDR to withdraw its proposals in return for a new and favourable rental agreement with the LSWR.

By this agreement, concluded on 23 July 1903, the MDR rent for the next ten years was to be based on the average of the previous five years, despite the expected increase in traffic. The MDR could run as many trains as it liked so long as they did not interfere with LSWR or Met & GW traffic, and could fix its fares without LSWR restriction. Finally, it did not lose the right to widen the line itself, still retaining its running powers over the existing line. According to the MDR chairman, R. W. Perks, the agreement saved the MDR spending over £500,000 on the proposed widening.

Electrification to Richmond was covered by the LSWR/MDR agreement of 4 December 1903, with the LSWR building a sub-station at Kew Gardens. The LSWR was to provide signalling to permit trains to run at the shortest possible intervals; this was still to be the well-tried Sykes Lock and Block system, with train stops provided at the home signals protecting the approach from the MDR's own lines. Electric traction between Studland Road and Turnham Green commenced with the District's Ealing service on 1 July 1905 and on the Richmond line exactly a month later. Now the two hours of the evening peak saw 30 westbound passenger trains— four LSWR, four GWR (replacing the Met) and 22 District (but still only four of these to Richmond).

As this was nearing the limit for double-track working, the MDR on 5 November 1909 asked the LSWR for permission to include in its 1910 Bill powers to widen the line from Studland Road to Turnham Green. The Bill set out a complicated sequence of ten separate lines, four under MDR and six under LSWR ownership, which the LSWR was to construct. This would result in the provision of a new northern pair of non-electrified lines for LSWR use, leaving the existing southern pair of lines for almost exclusive use by District electrics. Studland Road Junction would be abolished, and conflict at Turnham Green would be avoided by diverting the Ealing extension lines to cross the LSWR Richmond lines by a flyover, and constructing a new eastbound line for District trains from Richmond to join the Ealing line at Fishers Lane Junction, 13 chains west of Turnham Green.

Met & GW traffic was to use the LSWR northern lines, while Midland goods trains to Kensington would continue to take the existing LSWR line into Turnham Green to avoid the 1 in 50 gradient of the new MDR spur, but would cross to the southern (MDR) lines by a crossover east of the station. A new station was to be constructed on the southern lines at Goldhawk Road for District use—this was opened as Stamford Brook on 1 February 1912. If requested, a second platform would be provided for the Met & GW.

The LSWR/MDR agreement of 11 April 1910 setting out these details was included in the MDR Act of 3 August 1910, and the LSWR was to be reimbursed on the usual four per cent basis. Work commenced on 1 September 1910 (under the supervision of H. H. Dalrymple-Hay) and the widening, partly on viaduct and partly embankment, came into use on 3 December 1911. Its total cost was £186,990.

At Ravenscourt Park and Turnham Green the platform staffs were separate, but booking offices were combined. The LSWR maintained both sets of lines, but charged the MDR for the southern pair. Signalling on these was to MDR standards, fully track-circuited with automatic signals and train stops. Turnham Green signalbox had two frames: electro-pneumatic to control the MDR junctions, and mechanical for the Sykes Lock & Block still used on the LSWR lines. A new LSWR signalbox at Ravenscourt Park replaced Studland Road Junction, although the only traffic remaining on the northern lines comprised the LSWR trains to Richmond, at intervals of 30 minutes or more.

The slow and infrequent LSWR steam services were causing local authorities and property owners in the Thames Valley to consider the attractions of Underground extensions. The Central London Railway approached the LSWR in September 1912 regarding its proposed tube from Shepherds Bush via Goldhawk Road, emerging at the LSWR's Gunnersbury station, whence running powers were sought to Richmond and Twickenham. The Bill for the extension to Gunnersbury received the Royal Assent on 15 August 1913, but meanwhile the CLR had been absorbed by the Underground group from 1 January 1913 and its plans for expansion into the Thames Valley were shelved.

The second contender was the Piccadilly tube, with a connection from its existing terminus at Hammersmith to join the LSWR at Studland Road Junction, thence using LSWR tracks to Richmond and Twickenham. The London Electric Railway Bill for this link also received Royal Assent on 15 August 1913.

The Metropolitan Railway was the outsider. Before electrification of the Hammersmith & City it had operated a steam service from Aldgate to Richmond. This had been replaced by a GWR railmotor service from Notting Hill & Ladbroke Grove from 1 January 1907 until 1 January 1911. The Metropolitan wished to restore the through service and held discussions with the LSWR during 1911–13. It would be necessary to electrify the 2 miles 10 chains from Grove Road Junction to Acton Lane Junction (the MDR supplying the current), also to improve the signalling on the Richmond line. Detailed planning started and a draft agreement was drawn up in November 1913, but was never ratified. Instead, the LER informed the Met on 29 June 1914 that the LER powers of 15 August 1913 to extend the Piccadilly tube required the use of the LSWR tracks beyond Studland Road Junction for its trains. The two companies agreed on 22 July 1914 for the Met to withdraw its proposals (with suitable compensation), and on 10 September 1914 the LSWR was told that the Met would no longer exercise its running powers over the junction at Hammersmith.

Surprisingly, another CLR attempt was made to reach Richmond after World War I. By the Central London & Metropolitan District Railway Companies Works Act of 4 August 1920 a junction was authorised with the disused LSWR Kensington—Richmond line 300yd west of Shepherds Bush LSWR station, with separate up and down line tubes joining the CLR just west of its own station. While this would have been less costly than a tube all the way to Gunnersbury, the problem remained of the incompatibility of the CLR central conductor rail with the four-rail system used on the District line.

Whichever Underground line was to extend to Twickenham, widening of the Windsor Line between Richmond and Twickenham was necessary to keep the tube trains clear of LSWR traffic. The LSWR therefore obtained powers in its Act of 15 August 1913 to provide four tracks on this 2 mile 5 chain section, including reconstruction of Richmond and Twickenham stations. In conjunction with the local authority, Twickenham station was to be moved to its present site east of the London Road bridge and the bridge itself was to be widened. Some land was acquired in 1914–15, but otherwise nothing was done to carry out this scheme. In the 1920s Underground ambitions turned away from the Thames Valley.

In 1911 the LNWR announced plans for electrification of its London suburban lines, including those of the North London Railway under its management, and its 1912 Bill included proposals to electrify the NLR routes to Richmond and Kew Bridge. Agreement between the LSWR and the LNWR on 29 October 1915 provided for the latter to equip the LSWR lines from South Acton to Brentford Road Junction, Gunnersbury, and from Kew East Junction to Kew Bridge station. The LNWR would bear the cost and maintenance and pay an easement rent to the LSWR. The LNWR would contribute interest towards the capital cost of the existing electrification between Gunnersbury and Richmond. The LER was to supply current for the LNWR trains to Richmond, and with wartime inflation a fact, the charge was to be indexed to the price of coal.

Public electric services on both lines commenced on 1 October 1916. To supply the extra power the LSWR had to instal an additional rotary converter in Kew Gardens sub-station, while the length and weight of the LNWR electric trains required the bridge over the River Thames to be strengthened in 1922. To save manpower during the war the LSWR and NLR station staffs at Richmond, Kew Gardens, Gunnersbury and Kew Bridge were amalgamated from mid-1918.

THE SUBURBAN BACKWATERS

Some of the lines built hopefully by the LSWR in the 1860s were now losing their traffic to more direct routes and other means of transport. As already described, the District had become the main user of the LSWR 1869 route from Addison Road to Richmond. In 1900–1 this line was served by eleven trains daily from Waterloo via the West London Junction spur, plus nine weekday trains from Ludgate Hill (Sunday services had recently been withdrawn). Connecting trains ran from Gunnersbury to Hounslow via the Chiswick curve.

Services were improved in 1902–3 in a vain attempt to combat tramway competition. Fifteen trains from Waterloo, ten from Ludgate Hill and 16 from Clapham Junction gave a combined half-hourly frequency on weekdays between Battersea and Gunnersbury. Most of the Clapham Junction trains continued via the Chiswick curve to Hounslow and Twickenham. Sunday trains from Waterloo to Richmond mostly continued to Kingston, with frequent connections from Gunnersbury to Twickenham.

With the advent of District electric trains in 1905 the steam services became less attractive. Mansion House to Kew Gardens by District took 37 minutes, while by LSWR from Ludgate Hill it occupied 55 minutes and from Waterloo about 45 minutes, plus the W&C journey of 10 minutes or so. Thus 1909 saw the Clapham Junction—Twickenham service curtailed to a local working from Gunnersbury, operated by steam railmotors from 1 March 1910. The Waterloo—Richmond service via the West London Junction spur ceased from 13 March 1912 (due to the coal strike) and was replaced by an hourly train from Clapham Junction. The Ludgate Hill service had steadily shrunk and by June 1914 only two through trains remained, although others started from Loughborough Junction due to lack of accommodation in the SECR Holborn Low Level sidings.

The line was now caught in the vicious circle of worsening service and declining traffic. After a collision at Addison Road on 26 September 1914 it was reported that there were no passengers in the LSWR train. From 1 October 1914 only one railmotor was left in service between Gunnersbury and Twickenham, reducing the service to two-hourly, followed by the withdrawal of weekday trains from 28 December 1914. Sunday trains ran for the last time on 21 February 1915, which was also the final day for Sunday trains between Kensington and Richmond. As an operating economy the Clapham Junction—Richmond services were worked by two-coach push-and-pull trains from 6 December 1915. Ludgate Hill trains ceased in late 1915. Finally, the Kensington—Richmond trains were withdrawn from 5 June 1916, contributing an Adams 0-4-4T, two bogie carriages and 15 staff to the war effort and saving £1,962 a year for the profit and loss account.

The junction with the H&C at Grove Road Junction was severed by the Metropolitan on 24 October 1914, and removal of the LSWR connection was carried out on 7 May 1916. Signalling at Ravenscourt Park was dismantled in November 1918. Eventually the SR traffic committee authorised on 7 October 1926 the recovery of permanent way and signals from the section between Addison Road and Studland Road Junction.

The War Office is reputed to have asked for this line to be retained for emergency use. It was convenient for troops entraining at Addison Road after some public event and for the despatch of London Territorial Army units to their annual camp. These troop trains usually took the Chiswick curve on to the Hounslow Loop en route for Aldershot or Salisbury Plain.

After passenger services were withdrawn, the Chiswick curve remained in active use throughout the 1914–18 war for freight traffic, mostly in the down direction, and was traversed on weekdays by the Marylebone to Southampton Docks forces mail train. Usage declined after the opening of Feltham yard improved freight movement, but passenger services were revived on Bank Holidays during the 1920s with trains running to Staines and Windsor. The curve was taken out of use on 24 July 1932, following the transfer of the former LSWR tracks between Studland Road Junction and Turnham Green to the Underground group for the Piccadilly line extension.

The LSWR shared in the working of the Clapham Junction—Addison Road service over the WLER. On Sundays there was the confusing arrangement whereby the LBSCR and the LSWR operated the service from their respective platforms at Clapham Junction on alternate weeks. During the war LSWR participation decreased and the Sunday services were withdrawn in May 1918.

Ludgate Hill to Wimbledon via Tulse Hill was an LSWR service operated entirely over jointly-owned lines or by courtesy of running powers. When inaugurated in 1869, the service ran to Kingston (High Level) over the new direct line from Malden. Some late evening and Sunday trains still ran through to Kingston in 1913, but were not usually advertised as such because of the long delay at Wimbledon shunting from the joint line platform to the main line. The LSWR ran eleven weekday and five Sunday trains between Ludgate Hill and Wimbledon, but it was a service vulnerable to tramway competition.

Wartime difficulties caused Sunday and midday trains to be withdrawn from 28 February 1915, followed by complete closure from 1 January 1917, including the LBSCR local trains from Wimbledon to Streatham. The companies were in no hurry to restore the service after the war, until the threat of the CSLR extension made the SR reopen the line from 27 August 1923.

KINGSTON ROUNDABOUT AND THAMES VALLEY

The 2½ miles from Barnes to Richmond is notorious for level crossings, with only one overbridge (now carrying the South Circular Road) built by the LSWR in 1905 as a condition of the sale by Captain Fitzgerald of a strip of land for a contemplated widening of the line between Mortlake and Richmond. Barnes UDC petitioned against the LSWR's 1913 Bill, fearing that electrification would worsen delays at the three level crossings between Barnes and Mortlake. The company agreed in July 1914 to replace the crossings by bridges if this happened, but despite more frequent trains it was found in 1916 that interference to road traffic had not increased. Although the LSWR's undertaking had not become operative, the company offered to share with the council the cost of providing bridges at Sheen Lane and White Hart Lane and of widening the bridge at Barnes station. This proposal and a similar one to Richmond Council in 1901 for the replacement of Manor Road level crossing met with no response.

The Roundabout line crossed the Thames at Richmond and Kingston on similar arched iron bridges. On 18 October 1905 the engineering committee heard of permanent way damage on Kingston bridge due to the running of a new heavy locomotive (was this one of Drummond's new 4-6-0s on a trial trip?). This may have prompted closer examination of the bridges, as on 13 December 1905 it was reported that both required reconstruction. Meanwhile, they were to be supported by timber staging erected in the river bed, with trains subject to a 10mph limit. The external design for the permanent reconstruction of Richmond bridge had to be approved by the town council and the Office of Woods and Forests, which wished the new bridge to replicate the old one. Each track was dealt with in turn under single-line working controlled by a temporary signalbox—normal operation was restored on 29 May 1908. Meanwhile, Kingston bridge was dealt with similarly and was completed later in 1908.

An additional up line had been provided between Twickenham and St Margaret's on 26 November 1899, converting the up platform at St Margaret's into an island. A football platform on this line at Twickenham was authorised on 24 February 1921, involving the removal of sidings installed in 1899, The inspecting officer on 20 February 1922 described this sleeper platform as temporary, pending construction of the LER extension.

A new suburban locomotive depot had been opened at Fulwell on 1 May 1897, replacing small engine sheds at Twickenham and Kingston (the latter was converted to a goods shed in 1898). Fulwell shed was extended in 1907–8 to house 30 locomotives. In 1910 there was a regular morning exodus of 16 locomotives (some coupled in threes) to pick up suburban trains stabled at Kingston, Teddington, Norbiton and Wimbledon. The name Strawberry Hill for the depot seems to have come into general use with the arrival of electric trains in 1916 and its remaining steam locomotives were transferred to Feltham in 1923.

Carriage sidings were provided in 1899 on the down side of the line near Fairfax Road level crossing, Teddington, where a new signalbox was opened on 24 September 1916 to replace Hampton Wick as a block post. Kingston station displayed from 1917 the second of the preserved Bodmin & Wadebridge coaches.

The opening of the Shacklegate Junction—Fulwell Junction curve on 1 July 1894 provided the Thames Valley line to Shepperton with a second route from Waterloo, but advertised passenger traffic did not commence until 1 June 1901 with merely one evening train from

Waterloo on Mondays to Fridays. With the new electric services via Kingston making regular use of this curve, Fulwell Junction signal-box came into full-time operation and Fulwell Station box was abolished in July 1917. Traffic to the racecourse station at Kempton Park (heaviest on Easter Monday) required the provision of three temporary block posts on the branch. After unloading their passengers at Kempton Park, the race specials often berthed nose to tail on the up line between Sunbury and Shepperton, while traffic was worked over the down line under single line regulations. Requests from local people for an extension from Shepperton to Chertsey were again declined in 1903 and 1907. After electrification in 1916, the up platform at Shepperton was worked as a carriage siding.

THE WINDSOR LINES

The Hounslow Loop forms an alternative route to the line via Richmond. The only new station built for the LSWR electrification was opened here on 12 March 1916 at Barnes Bridge, close to the south bank of the Thames. The footpath crossing the river alongside the railway afforded an excellent view of the Oxford and Cambridge Boat Race and the company obtained some revenue from the sale of tickets to spectators. The LSWR Act of 23 June 1902 authorised the purchase of land for additional sidings at Brentford yard. These were approved in May 1906 as a matter of urgency, but the LSWR's problems with freight in the London area were only solved by the construction of Feltham yard. Added complication would have arisen if any of the three pre-1914 schemes for orbital freight routes starting from the LSWR in the Brentford—Feltham area had been authorised. Weekday steam passenger services on the Hounslow Loop ran from Waterloo to Feltham or Staines. With the introduction in March 1916 of the electric circular service, the link between Hounslow and Feltham was maintained by an hourly push-and-pull train, until withdrawn from 30 April 1917 due to lack of traffic.

Improvements at Staines were approved in January 1901; these included horse and carriage loading docks, a new goods yard and up and down goods loops. The new facilities were inspected by Major Pringle on 20 March 1904. Pneumatic signalling for Staines was approved in December 1902 and came into use on 24 April 1904. This comprised a 26-lever East box controlling the new sidings, and a 36-lever West box, situated in the middle of the triangle, working all three junctions. The west side of the triangle was used by the Windsor—Woking service; when this was withdrawn as a wartime measure on 31 January 1916, Staines High Street station, not served by Water-

Gunnersbury station with Adams 4–4–2T on Clapham Junction –
Twickenham train *circa* 1906. *Commercial postcard, courtesy G. Gundry*

Erecting the girder spans of Hampton Court Junction flyover, 1914. *British
Rail*

loo to Windsor trains, was closed and later demolished in 1919. Isolated passenger services over the west curve remained, including a regular Windsor—Chertsey—Waterloo train from 10 July 1921 until electrification in 1930.

A major reconstruction of Windsor station was carried out in 1900–1. According to Major Pringle's report of 8 October 1901, the three 700ft platforms were spanned by an overall roof, new refreshment rooms, cloak room and offices had been built and a new goods yard and shed provided; the improved layout was controlled from the enlarged 44-lever signalbox.

At Virginia Water an additional crossover and a siding loop for the Chertsey branch train were authorised in July 1901, following the Board of Trade report on the collision between the branch train and a horsebox special which occurred on 1 October 1900. From the end of 1915 the branch service was operated by push-and-pull trains. After the Windsor—Woking service was withdrawn on 31 January 1916, some of these units based on Guildford still provided an occasional passenger train over the Addlestone Junction—Byfleet Junction curve. The west curve at Virginia Water, mainly used for Ascot race traffic, was doubled on 10 December 1898.

The June Royal Ascot race meeting was a high point in the LSWR's year. In 1905 the company arranged to erect a cover over the footpath from the station to the racecourse. On 12 May 1910 it was agreed to provide an additional platform for the despatch of passengers from the Royal Enclosure. The grandstand authorities were to construct a footpath through the woods to this open wooden platform alongside the up line to the west of Ascot station. Improvements had been made in 1899 to the unsheltered platforms at Ascot West, which handled traffic from the Reading direction.

In fulfilment of an undertaking given to local residents, which had secured the curtailment of the GWR-backed Windsor & Ascot Railway, the LSWR obtained powers in 1899 for a new road from Ascot station to South Ascot, which it completed in 1901. The Ascot to Camberley line was associated with another abortive scheme. The Woking & Bagshot Light Railway was an electric tramway, commencing from a junction with the LSWR 200yd north of Bagshot signalbox, thence across country via Chobham and Knaphill to Woking. A branch would have terminated in the LSWR up sidings west of Woking station. A Light Railway Order was obtained on 18 May 1906, but no construction took place.

The Ascot to Frimley line had been doubled since 11 June 1893 and an additional siding, crossover and shunting neck were provided at Frimley in 1901 for military traffic. At Frimley Junction most trains from Ascot turned east to Sturt Lane Junction and ran to Woking, with some through workings to and from Waterloo. Others took the single line to Ash Vale Junction and ran to Aldershot and Farnham. The west curve to Farnborough Junction was only traversed (from 1 June 1901) by a Waterloo—Ascot—Basingstoke train; reduced to Saturdays only in October 1908, this train ran for the last time on 26 December 1914. This was another curve which saw considerable use during Ascot race week.

HAMPTON COURT, NEW GUILDFORD AND EPSOM

The railway carried large crowds to Hampton Court at weekends and on Bank Holidays, bound for the palace, the river, or Hurst Park racecourse about a mile from the station. Extension to the course had been considered in 1896–8, but the cost of £78,000 was prohibitive. Improvements at Hampton Court station were authorised in February 1897 and the completed works were inspected by Sir Francis Marindin on 28 November 1899. The old platforms had been lengthened and a new platform with verandah provided—all were now signalled for both arrivals and departures. The altered layout was controlled by a new 43-lever signalbox, which on Bank Holidays would handle 40–50 special trains. An obstacle to handling the crowds was the narrow drawbridge over the River Mole, restricting vehicles and pedestrians to single file—this was relieved in 1905 by an additional lifting bridge for pedestrians. Two more sidings for race trains were added alongside the station in 1908.

The New Guildford line had been opened in 1885 equipped as a rural branch, but its use by fast Portsmouth trains necessitated providing refuge sidings at Claygate and Horsley in 1897 and at Clandon and London Road in 1898, while footbridges were added at Oxshott in 1900 and Horsley in 1903. In 1913 five down Portsmouth trains ran via the 'New' line and three up trains. It was on one of the latter that Adams 0-4-2 No 627 was derailed between Claygate and Hampton Court Junction on 25 August 1902.

On the Epsom and Leatherhead line, a goods yard for Raynes Park was provided in the angle between the up and down branch lines, being connected to them at Raynes Crossing signalbox. The yard came into use on 22 July 1910, but was soon enlarged to cater for coal traffic. Construction of the LCC's complex of mental hospitals near Ewell required a light railway for building materials, linked to the LSWR at exchange sidings on the up side of the line 80yd south of the station, first used on 20 April 1905. During the building period some 900 workmen travelled daily to and from Ewell station.

IMPROVING THE MAIN LINE

WATERLOO TO VAUXHALL

The original four tracks into Waterloo had been increased to six in 1891 by additional up main and down Windsor lines. At Vauxhall the Station had been rebuilt with three island platforms and seven tracks (there was an up Windsor loop but no platform on the down Windsor through line). This widening was soon inadequate and on 20 January 1898 the board expressed 'the desirability of expediting the Waterloo – Clapham Junction widening (to eight tracks) due to the growing demands of traffic and the question of punctuality.' By the Act of 25 July 1898 powers were obtained for one additional track, while the second line was authorised by the Act of 30 July 1900.

The widening which was carried out on the south (down) side of the viaduct involved the demolition of many labouring class dwellings, whose inhabitants were rehoused in four tenement blocks in South Lambeth Road, appropriately named Coronation Buildings in May 1902 and completed in October 1903. It was possible to commence work between Vauxhall and Wandsworth Road (Nine Elms) under the 1898 powers and by July 1900 Perry & Co had started. Given priority, the new 36 chain down local line between Vauxhall West and Wandsworth Road signalbox came into came into use on 5 July 1903, leading into the existing widening beyond.

An additional down track as far as Waterloo 'B' box had been brought into use on 4 July 1900. Onwards to Vauxhall, extensive clearance was necessary, and it was August 1902 before Perry & Co was authorised to start work on widening the viaduct. Along the 75$\frac{1}{2}$ chains between 'B' box and Vauxhall West (South Lambeth Road) two down lines were laid on the new viaduct. At Vauxhall a 750ft platform was provided on the down local line, but there was no platform on the down through. The new down lines came into service on 1 April 1906 and enabled a series of track rearrangements to take place at Vauxhall as lines were shifted towards the down side, completed on 17 March 1907. The up main lines then occupied the first island platform, the down Windsor lines the next (the old down Windsor through non-platform line being removed on 3 March 1907), while the northernmost island continued to handle up Windsor Line trains.

Between Waterloo 'B' and Vauxhall a space had been left between the two new lines and the existing tracks; this was occupied from 24 January 1909 by a new up main relief line to carry trains bound for the new South station, opened at the same time. The layout may have been provisional, as plans submitted to the Board of Trade in 1913 showed the ultimate arrangement as four main and four Windsor lines.

The problem was raised at an officers' conference on 4 June 1913 of the increased number of up suburban trains after electrification having to cross the through lines outside Waterloo to reach the South station. In February 1914 the engineers proposed the solution of concentrating the electric suburban services on the north side of Waterloo. The down main local line would have left the terminus between the up main local and down Windsor local lines, and between 'C' and 'D' boxes would have crossed the main lines by a flyover to resume its old position before reaching Vauxhall. The estimated cost being a modest £40,000, the plan was approved on 26 February.

This plan would have been appropriate for the originally intended 23-platform terminus, but as it had already been decided to retain the existing six platform Windsor Line station, this could not have handled the whole of the suburban electric services as well as the Windsor and Reading steam trains and the milk traffic. Short electric trains would have had to use the long main line arrival platforms 13–15, with long-distance services using the suburban platforms 1–4. On 1 October 1914 the project was cancelled as 'by rearrangement of plans the necessity for the proposed flyover can be avoided for some time to come.' The 1909 layout was therefore retained but the problem remained—it was left to the Southern Railway to solve it in 1936 with the flyover just east of Wimbledon station.

Vauxhall station was a centre for London's milk supply. In 1913 it handled 1,500 full churns daily and returned 1,900 empty ones to the West Country in four special trains. The station's other task was ticket collection; in 1912–13 twenty-two collectors were employed, taking some 15,000 tickets a day and securing around £3,250 a year in excess fares. Beside the many ticketless travellers, there was the legalistic individual in 1909 who refused to give up his ticket at Vauxhall as he would then have no evidence for a compensation claim if an accident took place on the way into Waterloo. Ticket collection at Vauxhall was abolished gradually, first on the West of England corridor trains, then

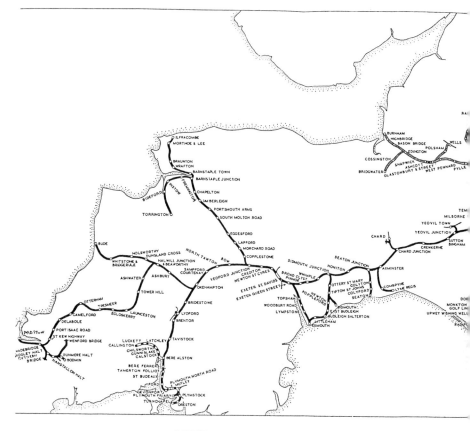

LSWR general system map

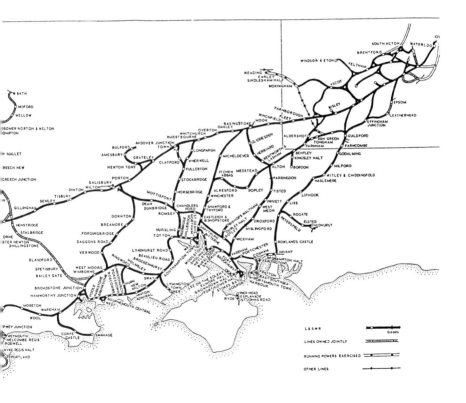

from early 1912 on morning peak-hour trains into the new South station (which had ticket barriers), followed by Windsor Line trains in October 1912. With the completion of the new platforms at Waterloo, collection at Vauxhall had ceased by 1916.

The convergence of the two up Windsor lines beyond Vauxhall was the scene of a minor collision on 20 November 1920, when the driver of the 7.42am steam train from Ascot passed his signal at danger and struck the 8.11am electric from Hounslow.

THE NINE ELMS AREA

At the turn of the century the Metropolitan Extension viaduct past Nine Elms still carried only the original four tracks of 1848. Powers had been obtained in 1898 for an additional down line and work was in hand on widening the viaduct and embankment on the down side. The new down local line came into use on 27 October 1901 as part of a 1 mile 29 chain widening from Wandsworth Road to West London Junction; in addition new sidings gave access to and from Nine Elms locomotive depot. The provision of a corresponding second up line had to await the widening and rearrangement of tracks through Vauxhall. During the winter of 1906–7 the tracks on the Nine Elms viaduct were moved, and in the space created a new up main through line 700yd long was laid from Nine Elms Loco Junction to Wandsworth Road, coming into use from 11 August 1907.

There were still only two Windsor lines here, and associated with the approval given for electrification on 6 December 1912, was the quadrupling of this section. Although the additional tracks were required on the Windsor side, the widening was carried out on the south (main line) side, where the removal of Nine Elms locomotive works had left room for extension of the viaduct. This was widened, partly by extending the existing brick arches and partly on girders spanning the low-level goods lines from Loco Junction to Nine Elms South Viaduct signalbox. When the widened viaduct was ready, the two down main lines were transferred on to it and after the usual process of slewing tracks, an additional down Windsor through line was opened on 16 January 1916, followed a week later by the up Windsor through. At a cost of £130,561 all was now ready for the delayed start of full electric services.

As part of the improvements here a new 80-lever Loco Junction signalbox was built in late 1917 on a bridge above the lines. Wandsworth Road signalbox (which had already been moved in 1915 from the down to the up side) was now abolished. Loco Junction was a busy box; in 1913 before electrification there were 314 daily locomotive movements in and out of the depot, in addition to the passing main line traffic. Following the transfer of the locomotive works from Nine Elms to Eastleigh in 1910 the running shed was enlarged and modernised. The shed building was extended to house another 60 locomotives, together with new offices, stores, repair shops and a larger turntable. Nine Elms' complement of 200 locomotives and 900 staff in 1902 had shrunk to 162 locomotives at Grouping, following suburban electrification.

Nine Elms was the focus of the LSWR's London freight traffic. A major extension to the up side yard had been made in 1898–9, providing a new shed with five platforms and nine tracks. Extra accommodation was added on the down side in 1900 for American Line traffic from Southampton. Following the removal of the locomotive works new low-level goods lines were provided in May 1914, while on the site of the old roundhouse a new mileage yard was laid out. The old erecting shop was converted into a three-road returned empties shed, while the former locomotive department offices above now accommodated the goods accounts clerks.

In 1913 Nine Elms despatched 8,249 trains carrying 900,032 tons and received 9,005 trains with 402,735 tons. Traffic had declined by 1921: 4,269 trains left with 666,626 tons and 4,446 arrived with 300,990 tons. The LSWR used Nine Elms for traffic to and from the London docks, goods being transhipped to barges at the nearby wharves. Shunting movements within the yard were guided by an elaborate system of hand signals, signs and gestures, which might have inspired the creation of a ballet.

NINE ELMS TO CLAPHAM JUNCTION

In 1900 this section had only two tracks on the main line side, but four on the Windsor Line as goods lines built in 1875–8 on the north side of the Windsor Line had been up-graded to passenger use in 1896–7. Although entitled the Windsor local lines, they had no platforms at Queen's Road, Battersea. The widening of the down main line authorised in 1898 was continued beyond Queen's Road, using a strip of land acquired from the LBSCR under powers obtained in 1899. Widening as far as West London Junction was completed on 27 October 1901, but beyond there LBSCR tracks ran close to the LSWR line and further widening had to be done on the north (Windsor Line) side.

Plans for the widening were approved in December 1900, but the work obtained low priority and progress was slow. On 11 March 1906

West London Junction signalbox was moved bodily northwards to allow for additional tracks. The Windsor lines between Queen's Road East and Ludgate Junction (Clapham Junction) retained the alternate arrangement of tracks from the original freight and passenger usage, but on 13 October 1907 this was changed to the present parallel layout. However, the down Windsor local line through Queen's Road station reverted to being a goods exit line from Nine Elms yard, and the second down Windsor line was thus curtailed to commence beyond Queen's Road West box.

An additional up local line platform at Queen's Road came into service on 1 October 1909, including a red brick booking office building in Queen's Road (now Queenstown Road), with the station name in glazed tiles on the fascia (revealed again by recent renovation). The 650ft platform was reduced by 115ft after electrification.

These changes on the Windsor Line were accompanied by alterations to the sidings between the main and Windsor lines beyond West London Junction. As space became available additional main line tracks came into use—the down through line from West London Junction to Clapham Junction East on 9 June 1907 and the corresponding up through on 4 October 1908. The continuation of this line from West London Junction to Loco Junction was achieved by acquiring more land on the down side and by converting a siding at Queen's Road to become the down local line, thus providing room for the additional up line opened on 20 December 1908, which completed quadruple track throughout the 50 miles from Waterloo to Worting Junction.

The other declared objective of the LSWR was the provision of eight running lines between Waterloo and Clapham Junction. As users of the Windsor Line are well aware, this aim has not been achieved, as there is only one down Windsor line through Queenstown Road station. If plans submitted to the Board of Trade in 1915 had been carried out, this would have been remedied. The exit from Nine Elms yard and the connections with the main line would have been situated at Queen's Road East, the goods line through the station would have become the up Windsor through (without a platform), while the island platform would have been served by two down Windsor lines. The crossovers and signalbox at Queen's Road West would have been abolished. Descriptions of the new Loco Junction box in 1918 stated that track alterations were being carried out in stages, but the only part of this scheme to be achieved was the completion of the up Windsor local line from Queen's Road East to Loco Junction on 1 December 1918.

CLAPHAM JUNCTION

Clapham Junction station was a bottleneck; the four Windsor Line tracks from Queen's Road to Barnes merged into two through the station, while on the main line quadrupling only commenced at the West box beyond the station. However, the up local line was continued as a loop platform behind the main station building. LSWR shareholders were told in February 1900 that the fast trains were continually being delayed at Clapham Junction by stopping trains.

The new carriage sidings at Wimbledon Park were a preliminary to reconstruction at Clapham Junction, where the existing sidings also were extended westward alongside the Windsor Line. Plans for the £121,000 enlargement of the station were approved in November 1899. Under the company's 1897 Act, land had been purchased for reconstructing St John's Hill bridge (at the west end of the main line platforms) to take two more tracks, and work commenced in October 1900.

The first stage was the re-siting of the up local line along the outer face of a new 700ft island platform 4, enabling the site of the original loop to be used for two new up lines. The approach from St John's Hill to the main booking office on the up (No 5) platform was severed and a temporary office at street level was used during 1903–5. The two new up lines were ready early in 1903; the local was served by the inner face of platform 4 and the through by platform 5, enlarged to 900ft by 60ft, but still retaining some of the original station buildings. With the transfer of up through traffic to the other side of platform 5, its southern face became the new down through platform on 26 April 1903. The outer face of platform 4 was now used mainly by milk and parcels trains, although available again for passenger use from 4 October 1908. Beyond were some dock roads for milk traffic, linked by lift to St John's Hill.

Following a fatal accident in 1900 on the Brighton side, South Western porters at Clapham Junction had petitioned the Board of Trade regarding their danger in having to transfer over 100 loaded milk churns daily across five sets of rails with poor visibility of approaching trains. The Board ensured that the LSWR's plans for the new station included a dual footbridge with luggage lifts to the platforms and a covered way to the parcel office in St John's Hill. Passengers also followed this gangway to a high-level booking office above platform 5, which came into use early in 1905. The new footbridge leading to all LSWR platforms and to the LBSCR station was completed to the new Windsor Line platforms in 1907.

On the Windsor side, powers had been obtained by the Act of 6

August 1897 for the widening and deviation of the West London Extension Railway adjacent to Falcon Road bridge. Work started in May 1901 on the northward extension of the station. Retaining walls and ironwork supported a viaduct carrying a new 700ft platform (No 1), which was brought into use on 24 June 1906 for the WLER Kensington service. The site of the old Kensington platform became the new platform 2 (another 700ft island) for up Windsor Line trains, ready on 4 November 1906. The old up Windsor platform (No 3) was then demolished to build the new platform 3 for down Windsor traffic; the inner face came into use on 24 March 1907 and the outer side on 13 October 1907, completing the quadrupling through the station.

The important connections at the east end of the station were controlled by the East signalbox, and as this was in the way of the Windsor Line widening a temporary overhead box was brought into service on 24 June 1906. Already in June 1905 plans had been approved for installing pneumatic signalling throughout the Clapham Junction area, enabling Ludgate Junction signalbox to be abolished. The two smaller boxes at Clapham Junction South (main line) and West (Windsor line) were commissioned on 21 May and 28 May 1911 respectively. The large overhead cabin at Clapham Junction East was brought into use on 28 January 1912 for its main line frame (39 levers) and on 4 February for the 44-lever Windsor side frame; the similar 37-lever box at West London Junction followed on 11 February. Original estimates for a saving through pneumatic operation were not realised and the total cost exceeded £41,000.

CLAPHAM JUNCTION TO HAMPTON COURT JUNCTION

This section had been quadrupled in the 1880s, but some major improvements still had to be made. At Earlsfield an island platform on the through lines was added on 1 May 1897. Approaching Wimbledon, 22 acres of land on the north side of the line were purchased in 1896 for carriage sidings. Access was off the East Putney line at Wimbledon Park and exit to the main line was at Merton Road box (later Durnsford Road). Work started early in 1898 and included the reconstruction of Gap Road bridge with a single girder span across the East Putney and main lines, enabling the headshunt for the yard to extend nearly to Wimbledon Station. Facilities in the yard included cleaning stages, water tanks and a gas plant beyond Merton Road bridge for carriage lighting. Wimbledon Park sidings (originally known as Merton Road) housed mostly suburban stock, leaving Clapham Yard to handle main line traffic.

The original connection between the East Putney and the main line at Wimbledon East was by a series of slip points. A new double junction came into use at the end of 1900, controlled from the new 110-lever East signalbox, which replaced the previous separate North and East boxes. The long siding on the down side of the main line, serving Wimbledon Corporation power station, was converted into a down goods loop in 1917 to cater for increased wartime traffic. Another down relief goods line between Wimbledon West and Raynes Park was added on 11 July 1900. The road bridge over Wimbledon station was reconstructed and widened during 1899–1901. Additional sidings were laid in Wimbledon West yard in 1900 and on the down side at Surbiton in 1898.

The Act of 20 July 1906 authorised major improvements at Hampton Court Junction, comprising a dive-under for the up New Guildford line and a flyover for the down Hampton Court branch. On 8 August 1907 the board approved the start of work on the former at a cost of £12,611, but the flyover (estimated to cost £47,440) was deferred except for the purchase of land. The dive-under was a 70-chain single line, which joined the up local line opposite the existing junction. The Act compelled the company to erect a screen where the line emerged alongside the Portsmouth Road—lest the sudden appearance of trains might frighten the horses? The line was constructed by company staff and came into use on 21 October 1908.

Powers for the flyover were renewed in the company's 1911 and 1913 Acts; its construction became a necessity with the decision in December 1912 to electrify the line to Hampton Court. The new 1 mile 36 chain down branch line commenced immediately west of Surbiton station and rose on embankment and brick viaduct to cross the main line tracks by a 159ft lattice girder skew span. This was erected by J. Westwood of Millwall, using temporary timber staging, but most of the work was done by the LSWR engineers department. The flyover came into use on 4 July 1915 and cost £50,753.

HAMPTON COURT JUNCTION TO WOKING JUNCTION

Here a third line for up traffic had been constructed during 1886–90; powers to complete the quadrupling were now granted by the Act of 30 July 1900. This Act also authorised a dive-under at Byfleet Junction for the down line from Addlestone Junction. The widening of the

75 chains on embankment between Hampton Court Junction and Esher started in March 1901 and the new down local line was ready on 27 April 1902. Four tracks had been provided through Esher station when the second up line was opened on 1 April 1888. New buildings on both local line platforms included royal waiting rooms for the use of the widow of Queen Victoria's youngest son Prince Leopold (the Duchess of Albany) who resided at Claremont. On the up side of the line, platforms and sidings had been provided during the 1880s for Sandown Park race traffic, with direct access from the course, and a second signalbox at Esher East opened on race days.

The Esher–Walton widening of 2 miles 30 chains was made on the south side of the line, in extension of the down local line through Esher station. The intermediate Mole signalbox was enlarged, and Walton East box which had controlled entry to the former down loop was abolished. This widening was brought into service on 19 April 1903. Four tracks had been in existence through Walton & Hersham station since 25 April 1893, when a new up through line was laid at the rear of the original up platform, making it an island. The existing up through and down tracks became the two down lines. New buildings served the up local line platform opened on 1 April 1888, but little was done to improve the old structure on the down local platform.

In March 1898 additional up sidings for goods and race traffic were authorised. These and the Sandown Park sidings at Esher could be used as a refuge for belated up freight trains which approached the suburban area during the morning rush hour, and to store excursion stock. An intermediate signalbox at Oatlands had been provided in 1894, which was the termination of the first 52 chains of the new down local line from Walton, opened on 19 April 1903. Widening the Walton to Weybridge cutting involved the reconstruction of two overbridges with long girder spans.

Widening at Weybridge presented difficulty; when the additional up line was provided in July 1890 it took over the existing down line through the station, the down platform was converted to an island and a new down line laid beyond it. The old station could not be adapted for further widening, and as more land was required to enlarge the cutting the whole of the Fir Grove property on the down side had to be purchased in July 1900 (the LSWR managed to sell the surplus land for building). Plans were approved in August 1902 for the reconstruction of the station with a new cab yard and booking office on the up side, linked by a footbridge to a new platform on the additional down local line and to the existing but improved up platform; a refreshment room was proposed, but the justices refused to grant a licence. No platforms were provided on the two through lines. After completion of the new station in 1904, the 1838 booking office on the road bridge was let to the Post Office. The new down line of 1 mile 29 chains from Oatlands to Weybridge Junction came into use on 5 June 1904, completing the quadrupling between Hampton Court Junction and Woking.

When the proposal for a motor racing track at Brooklands was made in 1906, the LSWR refused the request for a halt, but supplied 5,000 tons of chalk and built a temporary siding for construction materials. The section of the widening between Weybridge Junction and Byfleet (now West Byfleet) station included the construction of the burrowing line at Byfleet Junction for the down spur from Addlestone Junction, opened on 19 February 1903. The Weybridge end of the 2 mile 32 chain widening was made on the up side; a new up local line was laid on it and the existing tracks rearranged to provide the additional down local line. From 22 chains east of Byfleet station the widening for the new line was made directly on the down side and the down platform at Byfleet was converted into an island; widening here was completed on 19 April 1903. The estimated cost of the Hampton Court Junction to Byfleet widening was £128,000.

Byfleet to Woking was the first stage of the quadrupling to be completed, work on the down side of the line having started in March 1900 under previous powers. It was necessary to rebuild the Sheerwater Road bridge at Byfleet with a girder span. When the new down local line came into use on 15 September 1901, this bridge was not finished and the two down lines were interlaced for 250 yd. This 2 mile 27 chain section included an intermediate signalbox at Maybury, installed in 1894.

Woking station had gained an additional non-platform up through line in 1879 and a down local line and bay platform in July 1884. A marshalling yard on the up side had been built in August 1893, together with a new 81-lever Woking Junction signalbox. To avoid luggage transfer via the narrow subway, an elaborate overhead cableway was erected between the platforms in 1902. Woking had a small locomotive shed on the down side, but motive power was now concentrated at Guildford depot, with 23 light engines leaving for Woking every morning in 1910. It was proposed to build a new locomotive depot at Woking in the angle of the main and Guildford lines, probably incorporating a burrowing junction for the up Portsmouth line. The purchase of seven acres of land here in April 1910 was confirmed by the company's 1911 Act. However, it had already been decided that any new locomotive depot should be situated near the marshalling yard planned for the Feltham–Hounslow area. Thus an opportunity was lost of removing the busy flat crossing at Woking.

WOKING JUNCTION TO WORTING JUNCTION

Powers for the quadrupling of most of this section were granted by the Act of 6 August 1897, but as two additional tracks had to be constructed here, completion overlapped that of the Hampton Court Junction to Woking stretch authorised three years later. This Act also authorised a flyover at Pirbright to carry the up Aldershot line over the main line. Most of the widening was done on the down (south) side of the line. As soon as the earthworks were ready a new down local line was laid. This started a lengthy process of rearrangement and resignalling of tracks, and sometimes the demolition of station buildings, which led to the opening of the second new down line and finally to the conversion of the original down line into the second up (through) line.

Westward from Woking Junction, the first section of the widening was the 1 mile 20 chains as far as Goldsworth Cutting signalbox. J. Aird, who was the contractor for most of the Woking–Basingstoke widening, started work at the end of 1899 and the new down local line came into service on 18 May 1902. This widening was extended for a further 1 mile 65 chains to Brookwood East on 18 January 1903, and onward through Brookwood station for another 1 mile 70 chains to Pirbright Junction on 15 November 1903. At Brookwood a new 576ft down platform was built alongside the local line, connected by subway to new buildings behind the existing up platform. The old down platform and footbridge were then removed to make room for the second new down line and the connections to the Necropolis and Bisley branches altered. The 50 chain deviation of the up Aldershot line over the Pirbright Junction flyover was inaugurated on 30 June 1901, together with a new 19-lever signalbox. The final stage in the Woking to Pirbright Junction widening (which cost £90,000) was the completion of the new up through line throughout the section on 18 December 1904.

Beyond Pirbright Junction, the line enters the deep Frimley cutting, with the Basingstoke Canal crossing by an aqueduct at Deepcut, near the western end. By the Act of 1897 the LSWR had to maintain the level and safety of the canal and its water supply. As the bed of the canal was only inches above the roof of the existing tunnels, it was impossible to bore parallel tunnels for the two new tracks. Eventually it was agreed in May 1902 to close the canal for five months (maintaining the water supply through a temporary conduit) on payment of £5,000 compensation to the canal company; this was a windfall, as the canal was already in the hands of a receiver. The two new tunnels for the down lines could thus be built by cut-and-cover methods. Work was completed and the canal re-opened on 1 December 1902, a fortnight within the five months allowed. The 2½ miles of new down line from Pirbright Junction came into use on 26 June 1904. At Sturt Lane Junction the line led into the first section of the widening to be built, a 1 mile 3 chain loop terminating at Farnborough East, opened on 4 June 1899.

The next section of widening extended from Farnborough East to Elvetham signalbox, between Fleet and Winchfield, a distance of 3 miles 34 chains. Alterations at Farnborough approved in August 1900 sadly involved the demolition of one of Sir William Tite's original London & Southampton stations, a classic building with massive Corinthian columns, which *The South Western Gazette* dismissed as 'unsuitable and inconvenient.' In its place a substantial new brick building was erected on the down local platform, with a similar but smaller structure on the up platform, replacing a draughty little wooden shelter. No platforms were provided on the through lines, but a grassy mound between the tracks left room for their addition. On the down side was a 900ft long military platform, high and wide for easy loading of vehicles.

Fleet station was re-sited some 200yd eastward, by the historical Fleet Ponds. The local lines were served by two 650ft platforms with timber buildings, an exception to the red brick construction elsewhere on the widening. The new down local line was ready on 26 June 1904, followed by the down through on 11 December 1904. The old down main line was then converted on 5 March 1905 into the additional up through line for the whole distance from Elvetham box to Pirbright Junction, completing the quadrupling between Woking and Basingstoke. Between Farnborough and Fleet a halt for the Bramshot Golf Club opened on 10 May 1913; two 500ft platforms were provided on the local lines and were served when required by a morning down train and a late afternoon up service.

The Elvetham to Old Basing section of the widening was the second contract to be placed, in November 1898. This included the deep cutting at Winchfield, where the tunnel had to be opened out, and another at Newnham, from which 20,000 tons of chalk had to be excavated. Several overbridges had to be rebuilt; the demolition of the old arches was usually carried out during the Sunday afternoon interval in the train service. Landslips in Winchfield cutting during 1900 caused trouble for the contractor, J. Aird, who was granted an additional price allowance and an extra payment of £20,000 towards his increased costs.

Winchfield station already had a down loop which was incorporated in the new down through line and a new platform was built alongside the new down local line. Hook station was similar, with a new plat-

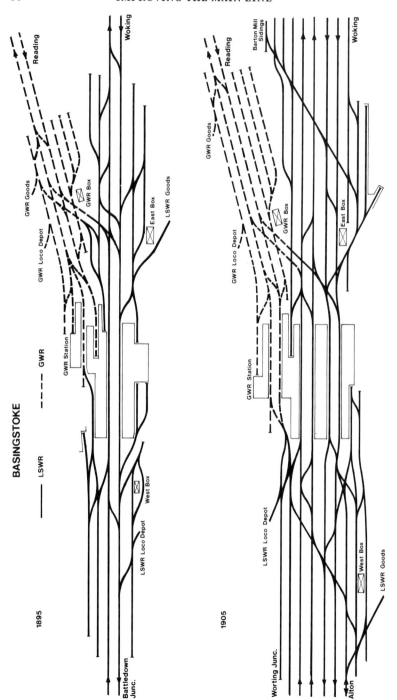

Basingstoke station reconstruction: track layouts in 1895 and 1905

form on the down local and the existing up side buildings being retained. The two new down lines over the 8 miles 70 chains between Elvetham and Old Basing signalboxes came into use on 25 May 1902 and at the same time the new down through line was extended from Old Basing to Barton Mill signalbox. The down local line over this section had already been brought into use on 21 April 1901. The parallel second up track between Barton Mill signalbox (just east of Basingstoke) and Elvetham was then formed from the old down line, probably coming into service in June 1902, as Major Pringle had inspected these works on 22 May.

At the turn of the century, Basingstoke station was a two platform bottleneck, with an awkward junction to the Great Western Railway. Enlargement could only be on the south side because of the GWR station and church ruins to the north. Plans for the £117,800 project were approved in August 1900 and J. T. Firbank was appointed as main contractor. Preliminary stages involved the construction of a new goods yard on five acres of land on the down side west of the station, and the removal of the locomotive shed to a new site on the up side. Some 130,000cu yd of infill was required for the goods yard and the station enlargement.

Work started in April 1903 on a range of new station buildings on the down side, whose 80yd frontage contained the usual offices as well as a three-storey section housing the dining and refreshment rooms with living accommodation for their staffs. These buildings stood on the new down local platform, which had a bay at the west end for the Alton service. The old station could then be demolished to convert the former down platform into an island, serving the two through lines. A new subway linked the station entrance to all the LSWR platforms, while the original one now led directly to the GWR station. As the latter company was not prepared to rebuild its station, only minor improvements could be made to the adjacent LSWR up local platform—however, the junction with the GWR at the east end of the station was remodelled. Quadrupling was completed on 18 December 1904.

Four tracks beyond Basingstoke had existed since 30 May 1897, when the flyover at Battledown carrying the up Bournemouth line over the Exeter lines was brought into use. The Act of 6 July 1895 authorising this also provided for a two track widening on the north side of the line between the new Worting Junction and Basingstoke 'C' signalbox. The existing tracks then became the down lines and an intermediate box was provided at Winklebury. A signalbox was retained at the original junction site at Battledown, principally to control a second connection (mainly for goods traffic) from the down

Exeter to the down Bournemouth line. The Park Prewett Mental Hospital branch was on the up side near Basingstoke. Authorised on 31 October 1912 its opening was delayed until August 1917 when the Canadian army took over the new hospital. Freight traffic was propelled up the steep and curved branch by a shunting engine.

The quadruple tracks finish at Worting Junction, 50 miles 30 chains from Waterloo, though the Bournemouth and Exeter lines do not part company until the site of the original junction at Battledown. The widening of the main line occupied over a quarter of a century; to assist the reader a summary follows this chapter, which sets out the dates on which as far as can be ascertained the additional tracks came into service.

In June 1897 the traffic committee had recommended the provision of six additional permanent and eleven occasional block sections between Woking and Winchester, including the small 8 to 10-lever boxes at Hermitage, Cove and Elvetham, installed in 1898 between Woking and Basingstoke. When the board was considering in December 1901 the adoption of pneumatic signalling here, the veteran Archibald Scott advocated automatic working to eliminate these intermediate boxes. A £70,000 contract with the British Pneumatic Railway Signal Co was approved on 7 August 1902. New boxes were built at each station, and power for the pneumatic operation (at a pressure of 15lb/sq in) came from a generating station at Fleet.

The first section to come into operation was Barton Mill to Winchfield, inspected by Major Pringle on 10 June 1904, prior to inauguration on 28 September. This comprised new boxes at Barton Mill (21 working levers), Hook (28) and Winchfield (24). Pneumatic operation was next extended on 25 May 1905 from Winchfield to Farnborough, with boxes at Fleet (27) and Farnborough (31). Between these boxes the automatic signalling divided the line into sections of approximately 1,600yd. The Basingstoke station installation came into use on 27 May 1906, with new East (45) and West (55) boxes. Farnborough—Sturt Lane Junction—Brookwood—Woking was inspected on 26 October 1906, but was not brought into use until June-July 1907. This section included boxes at Sturt Lane (20), Pirbright Junction (12) and Brookwood (35). For the next 60 years the lines between Woking and Basingstoke were straddled by massive lattice girder gantries with pairs of lower-quadrant home and distant signals above each track. A summary of the transition from mechanical to pneumatic signalling concludes this chapter.

The rebuilt Basingstoke station, 1909. *British Rail*

Low-pressure pneumatic automatic signals just west of Farnborough station. *British Rail*

QUADRUPLING THE MAIN LINE—SUMMARY

1. DOWN LINE WATERLOO-WORTING JUNCTION

Waterloo Station—Waterloo 'B' signal box	4 July 1900
Waterloo 'B' signalbox—Vauxhall West	1 April 1906
Vauxhall West—Wandsworth Road	5 July 1903
Wandsworth Road—West London Junction	27 October 1901
West London Junction—Clapham Junction East	9 June 1907
Clapham Junction East—West (station)	26 April 1903
Clapham Junction West—Wimbledon East	2 March 1884
Wimbledon East—Malden & Coombe	1 April 1884
(re-arrangement of Wimbledon-Kingston independent line opened	
	1 January 1869)
Malden—Surbiton Cutting signalbox	11 September 1882
Surbiton Cutting—Hampton Court Junction	29 July 1883
Hampton Court Junction—Esher East	27 April 1902
Esher East—Esher West (station)	1 April 1888
Esher West—Walton East	19 April 1903
Walton East—Walton West (station)	25 April 1893
Walton West—Oatlands signalbox	19 April 1903
Oatlands signalbox—Weybridge Junction	5 June 1904
Weybridge Junction—Byfleet (West Byfleet)	19 April 1903
Byfleet—Woking East	15 September 1901
Woking East—Woking Junction (station)	27 July 1884
Woking Junction—Goldsworth signalbox	18 May 1902
Goldsworth signalbox—Brookwood East	18 January 1903
Brookwood East—Pirbright Junction	15 November 1903
Pirbright Junction—Sturt Lane Junction	26 June 1904
Sturt Lane Junction—Farnborough East	4 June 1899
Farnborough East—Elvetham signalbox	26 June 1904
Elvetham signalbox—Old Basing signalbox	25 May 1902
Old Basing signalbox—Basingstoke 'A' signalbox	21 April 1901
Basingstoke 'A' signalbox—	
'C' signalbox (station)	18 December 1904
Basingstoke 'C' signalbox—Worting Junction	30 May 1897

2. UP LINE WORTING JUNCTION—WATERLOO

Worting Junction—Basingstoke 'C' signalbox	30 May 1897
Basingstoke 'C' signalbox—Barton Mill signalbox (station)	
	18 December 1904
Barton Mill signalbox—Elvetham signalbox	June 1902
Elvetham signalbox—Pirbright Junction	5 March 1905

Pirbright Junction—Woking Junction   18 December 1904
Woking Junction—Woking East (station)   1879
Woking East—Byfleet Junction   15 August 1886
Byfleet Junction—Weybridge East   6 July 1890
Weybridge East—Hampton Court Junction   1 April 1888
Hampton Court Junction—Surbiton East   14 October 1883
Surbiton East—Surbiton Cutting signalbox   29 July 1883
Surbiton Cutting signalbox—Malden & Coombe 1 December 1882
Malden—Wimbledon East (re-arrangement)   1 April 1884
Wimbledon East—Clapham Junction West   30 March 1883
Clapham Junction West—East (station)   5 October 1885
(Additional Up Loop platform—passenger use   4 October 1908)
Clapham Junction East—Queen's Road West   4 October 1908
Queen's Road West—Nine Elms Loco Junction 20 December 1908
Loco Junction—Wandsworth Road   11 August 1907
Wandsworth Road—Waterloo   8 June 1891
(additional Up Main Relief line 'C' signalbox—Waterloo
                                              24 January 1909)

WIDENING THE WINDSOR LINE—SUMMARY

1. DOWN LINE WATERLOO—CLAPHAM JUNCTION

Waterloo—Wandsworth Road   26 April 1891
Wandsworth Road—Nine Elms Loco Junction   16 January 1916
Queen's Road East—West London Junction   30 May 1897
(Goods line opened 18 January 1875 upgraded to passenger
    use, Queen's Road East to West reverted to goods use
                                              13 October 1907)
West London Junction—Ludgate Junction   12 June 1896
(Goods line of 1878 upgraded to passenger use)
(Queen's Road West—Clapham Junction East—tracks
    re-arranged for parallel working 13 October 1907)
Clapham Junction station   13 October 1907

2. UP LINE CLAPHAM JUNCTION—WATERLOO

Clapham Junction station   4 November 1906
Clapham Junction (Ludgate Junction)—
West London Junction (upgraded)   12 June 1896
West London Junction—Queen's Road East (upgraded)30 May 1897
(Clapham Junction East—Queen's Road West—tracks
    re-arranged for parallel working 13 October 1907)
Queen's Road East—Loco Junction   1 December 1918

Loco Junction—Wandsworth Road   23 January 1916
Wandsworth Road—Vauxhall East   8 June 1891

WOKING TO BASINGSTOKE
CONVERSION TO PNEUMATIC SIGNALLING

Manual signalboxes	Side	Pneumatic boxes (Side)	Automatic sections Down (Numbers)	Up
Woking Junction	Down	Mechanical box retained		
Goldsworth Cutting	Down	Abolished 7 July 1907	1	12
Hermitage	Up	Abolished 7 July 1907	2	11
Brookwood East	Down	New Box (Down)		
Bisley	Up	Temporary box 1902		
Pirbright Junction	Up	1901 box adapted		
Frimley Cutting	Up	Abolished 23 June 1907	3	10
Sturt Lane Junction	Up	New box (Down)		
Farnborough Junction	Down	⎰ Removed to Up side 1899 ⎱ Abolished 1907		
Farnborough	Down	New box (Down)		
Cove	Up	Abolished 25 May 1905	4	9
Bramshot	Down	Temporary box 1902	5	8
Fleet	Up	New box (Down)		
Elvetham	Down	Abolished 25 May 1905	6	7
Winchfield	Down	New box (Middle)	7	6
Holt	Up	Temporary box 1902	8	5
Hook	Down	New box (Middle)		
Newnham Cutting	Up	Abolished 28 Sept 1904	9	4
Newnham Siding	Down	Ground frame 1904	10	3
Old Basing	Down	Abolished 28 Sept 1904	11	2
Barton Mill	Up	New box (Up)	12	1
Basingstoke 'A'	Down	New box—East (Down)		
Basingstoke 'B'	Down	New box—West (Down)		

The temporary signalboxes were provided for
the Coronation Naval Review traffic in 1902

CHAPTER 4

HAMPSHIRE AND DORSET

PORTSMOUTH—DIRECT AND JOINT

The Portsmouth Direct line was not a high priority for LSWR investment. Improvements at Petersfield in 1901–3 included additional sidings and the conversion of the up platform to an island; similar work had been done at Haslemere in 1898–9. The route joined the LSWR and LBSCR joint lines at Portcreek Junction. Here the line crossed Hilsea Creek by a swing bridge, subject to a severe speed restriction. As the defence departments still required the water barrier to be spanned by an opening bridge, the LSWR designed a pair of independent swing bridges pivoted on the north bank; completion was reported in January 1911.

Powers for the enlargement of Portsmouth Town Low Level station had been granted by the LBSCR Act of 20 July 1896, but it was only after repeated civic pressure that the joint committee approved plans for the work in January 1904. The LBSCR's contractor rebuilt the station offices on the extended boundary of the property to provide room for an additional 520ft island platform and widening of the three existing platforms. Track re-arrangements included four lines between Fratton and Portsmouth Town. The completed work was inspected by Colonel Von Donop on 8 January 1906.

The enlargement of Portsmouth Harbour station was an LSWR project, authorised by its Act of 6 August 1897. Land at the Gun Wharf on the down side of the station was acquired in January 1900, on which J. Aird erected an extension of the steel viaduct carrying the station above the foreshore. An additional 720ft island platform and a siding alongside came into use on 13 July 1903, with final Board of Trade inspection on 4 February 1904. Simultaneously, a 55ft turntable and locomotive yard were provided at Burnaby Road, between the Town and Harbour stations.

EAST SOUTHSEA

This 1 mile 19 chain branch occupies a place in railway history as the birthplace of the steam railmotor. To combat tramway competition, the LSWR obtained in October 1902 the Board of Trade's agreement in principle to operation by a combined locomotive and carriage. Nine Elms built two small vertical-boiler tank engines to be linked to 56ft saloons constructed at Eastleigh. Joint status of the branch was shown by the use of both LSWR and LBSCR liveries on the railcars.

Cost reduction was also achieved by operating the branch from 1 June 1903 as a single line with one car (or locomotive) in steam. The down line only was used, the up track being converted to a siding; all points and signals were taken out of use. Among criticisms made by Major Pringle during his inspection on 27 June 1903 was the permanent presence of the driver on the locomotive footplate, leaving the guard on the return journey from East Southsea to keep a lookout from the balcony at his end of the car and to be ready to apply the handbrake. He accepted this working provisionally, but the Board of Trade ruled on 23 January 1904 that a trained driver should always be present in the leading cab.

The locomotives proved to be under-powered and were rebuilt with larger horizontal boilers in 1903–4. On 1 July 1904, intermediate halts (72ft long) were opened at Jessie Road Bridge and Albert Road Bridge, while at East Southsea a 265yd deviation was made to a new station adjacent to Granada Road. One local resident wrote to the Board of Trade complaining that the new station had no lavatories. The LSWR replied 'that it was not a station, but only a shelter for railmotor passengers comparable to a tram stop, and full facilities were available at Fratton.' The old station building at East Southsea proved an embarrassment; various optimistic but unsuccessful entrepreneurs tried to lease it and eventually it was requisitioned by the Admiralty in 1918.

The railmotors operated a 20-minute service, which attracted back some of the lost passengers as well as saving expense, and the 1902 loss of £1,862 had been reduced to £225 in 1905. However, the outbreak of World War I brought suspension of services from 6 August 1914, as the line was to be used for berthing rolling stock for military requirements. Some movement on the branch may have taken place, as a temporary crossover was installed in July 1915, to be removed if railmotor services were resumed. Nevertheless, the joint committee gave instructions on 9 October 1917 for the removal of redundant track, wires and poles. Powers for formal abandonment were obtained in the SR Act of 31 July 1923.

Portsmouth Town Low Level station concourse 1909 – the King's victory in the Derby and naval construction plans compete for newspaper readers' attention. *Commercial postcard, courtesy G. Gundry*

LSWR Farnham – Haslemere motor bus at Hindhead. *Commercial postcard, authors' collection*

MAINLY MID-HANTS

Considerable improvements at Aldershot Government Siding were made in 1912–13, at the request and cost of the War Office. The troop platform was extended to 850ft, new sidings were added, and a double line junction made at Aldershot Military Siding signalbox with the line from Pirbright Junction to Aldershot.

Farnham station was the starting point of the LSWR motor bus route to Haslemere. Operated experimentally by Thornycroft in 1904, that company ran the service on a 10d [4p] per mile contract for a year from 16 September 1905. The LSWR then took over the service and bought the bus, replacing it with new Thornycroft vehicles in 1907. These were said to provide a reliable service, even in snow and ice, and the route made a profit during the summer. However, the LSWR's failure to obtain motor vehicle powers in 1913 led to the sale of the two buses and the transfer of the route to the Aldershot & District Traction Co on 12 June 1913.

The doubling of the line between Farnham and Alton resulted from the two branches planned at Alton. Powers were obtained on 3 June 1897 for the 8 mile 16 chain widening on the north side to form the new up line. Commenced in the autumn of 1898, part of the widening at the Farnham end was available in 1900 for stabling troop trains from Aldershot. The double line came into service on 2 June 1901. New signalboxes were built at both ends of Farnham station, a new (but short-lived) cabin was provided at Bentley, while at Alton the existing box was lengthened.

Further changes at Alton followed the opening of the Meon Valley line in June 1903. The down platform was then converted into an island and the old down line became an up loop; the enlarged layout was controlled from a new 32-lever signalbox. 1 mile 3 chains west of Alton was Butts Junction, where the new branches to Basingstoke and the Meon Valley diverged. This section was doubled as part of the Meon Valley project, but came into use on 1 June 1901 for the opening of the Basingstoke & Alton light railway. A new 39-lever signalbox was built at the junction, controlling also a contractor's temporary line to the Meon Valley, until that opened to public traffic on 1 June 1903.

At Medstead there were two runaways during 1900; on 1 May the rear 20 vehicles of an up freight ran back as far as Alresford, while on 27 December a horsebox which had been detached from the 2.45pm from Waterloo was not secured and followed its train down the bank, colliding with it at Ropley. As recommended in the Board of Trade reports, the passing loop was lengthened and catch points provided.

BENTLEY & BORDON LIGHT RAILWAY

The War Office asked the LSWR in 1901 to build a light railway to serve a new camp in Woolmer Forest, and the company obtained a Light Railway Order on 6 October 1902 for a branch from Bentley to Bordon. Financial terms were agreed with the War Office on 13 July 1903. The LSWR was to be paid interest at $3^{1}/_{2}$ per cent on its capital outlay and was to charge the WD at 3s 0d [15p] per train mile for working expenses, but any net profit made on this was to be deducted from interest due to the company; the agreement was for 30 years or until the line earned four per cent for ten consecutive years.

Construction was in the hands of the LSWR engineers department which started work early in 1904 using two former Southampton Dock Co locomotives to haul ballast trains. The 4 mile 42 chain line was inspected on 25 November 1905 and public services commenced on 11 December. At Bentley a new 27-lever signalbox was built at the junction (replacing the 1901 cabin) and a bay platform was added on the down side for the branch train. The branch was single, but land had been taken for double track. Bordon was equipped with two 585ft platforms, a locomotive shed, a goods shed and loading facilities for military vehicles. The total cost of the branch was £46,220, with the War Office paying interest on £40,000.

An intermediate halt at Kingsley was opened on 7 March 1906, when railmotor operation commenced (it ceased by 1 October 1909). Some of the railmotors ran through to Farnham or Aldershot, in conjunction with workings to and from their base at Guildford. At weekends there were through trains for the troops to and from Waterloo, while the opening of the Longmoor Military Railway to Bordon in 1907 brought increased traffic to the branch.

BASINGSTOKE & ALTON LIGHT RAILWAY

During 1895–6 a £2 million scheme for a Portsmouth, Basingstoke & Godalming Railway had been projected, with its main line running from Basingstoke through Alton and down the Meon Valley. Its Bill was rejected in May 1896, but the LSWR undertook to seek powers for new lines in Hampshire to meet the need for a north–south link. The thinly populated country between Basingstoke and Alton 'with not enough people along the route to pay for grease for the engines' in one resident's opinion was a doubtful prospect for a railway. The LSWR therefore took advantage of the newly-passed Light Railways Act of 1896 to make the first application under its less stringent rules for construction and operation. After due consideration of the precedents it would set, the Board of Trade confirmed the Light Railway Order on 9 December 1897.

As this was the pioneer line to be built under the 1896 Act, the President of the Board of Trade, C. T. Ritchie, cut the first sod near Basingstoke on 29 July 1898. The main construction contract was awarded to J. T. Firbank, who was paid £53,104. At Basingstoke a private siding was provided for the Thornycroft works, which was in use by March 1900. Track laying was nearly complete by that summer and the line was being used for the transport of chalk from a quarry at Viables crossing to the Basingstoke station enlargement; however, this work delayed the completion and opening of the branch.

Following Board of Trade inspection on 22 May 1901, the line was opened without ceremony on 1 June. The steeply-graded 12 mile 35 chain single line had intermediate stations at Cliddesden, Herriard and Bentworth & Lasham, of which Herriard only had a passing loop. Services increased from an initial three mixed trains daily to six per day. Railmotors were tried unsuccessfully between July and October 1904. Close to Butts Junction, Alton, points had been laid in 1901 for a siding to serve a military hospital, built under the auspices of the 'Absent-minded Beggar Fund.' Not being required then, the connection was removed until a similar siding was provided on 5 April 1910 for the Lord Mayor Treloar's Cripples Home, together with a 200ft passenger platform on the branch itself, used on request to set down parties of children.

Traffic on the line was always light, which made it an appropriate choice for the twelve miles of track required from the LSWR for military railways in France, for which the company received £23,911 from the government. Closure from 1 January 1917 was authorised, but Herriard and Cliddesden stations remained open for milk and parcels traffic conveyed to and from Basingstoke by an LSWR Karrier bus converted to a lorry—this traffic ceased in May 1922. The line was now curtailed to the two sidings at each end—to Lord Mayor Treloar's Home at Alton and to the Thornycroft works, where a stub end also remained to serve a WD hay dump.

The LSWR board considered on 13 October 1921 an accountants' report on the re-opening of the line. At 1913 prices, it was estimated that the company would save £4,200 a year by keeping the line closed and the board agreed with this course. The outstanding capital investment of some £80,000 was to be written-off at the rate of £4,000 per annum. As the LSWR had no Bill before Parliament in 1922, it was left to the Southern Railway to secure powers for formal abandonment in its 1923 Bill. Unexpectedly, the House of Lords rejected this

Opening day of the Basingstoke & Alton Light Railway at Cliddesden – the windmill powered the pump for the station water supply. *L&GRP*

Bournemouth Central station with steam railmotor car. *Commercial postcard, authors' collection*

clause and the SR had to relay the line, reopening it on 18 August 1924.

THE MEON VALLEY RAILWAY

This line fulfilled the rest of the LSWR's promises to build new railways in East and South Hampshire. In contrast to the light railway construction between Basingstoke and Alton, the Meon Valley line was built to main line standards. The new route would provide an additional link between Aldershot and Portsmouth, and while it had undoubted strategic value, there is no evidence of War Office financial assistance.

Railway No 2, authorised by the LSWR Act of 3 June 1897, was a 22 mile 24 chain line from Butts Junction to join the Eastleigh to Gosport line at Knowle, some 2¹/₂ miles from Fareham. The contract was awarded in November 1898 to R. T. Relf of Plymouth. The undulating country between the Wey and Meon valleys required some extensive engineering works, notably the 1,056yd tunnel at Privett (the second longest on the LSWR) and a troublesome viaduct at West Meon. Labour shortages (common to the LSWR's other Hampshire contractors, Aird and Firbank) and earth slips delayed the work, increasing the cost. A year's extension of time was obtained and the LSWR provided financial support for Relf, whose eventual bill for £377,709 was some £54,000 more than the contract price.

Eventually the line was ready for inspection by Major Pringle on 2 and 3 April 1903. Though single, land had been purchased for double track and all overbridges and tunnels had been constructed for this. Stations at Tisted, Privett, West Meon, Droxford and Wickham were all equipped with passing loops, signalboxes, 600ft platforms and substantial buildings. Faringdon and Mislingford had sidings in lieu of the stations requested. At Knowle a new junction signalbox controlled the connection with the Eastleigh line.

The new line opened without ceremony on 1 June 1903, with a service of six stopping trains each way on weekdays and two on Sundays. Some of the weekday trains ran through to Waterloo and others continued from Fareham to Gosport. However, traffic never reached LSWR expectations—Privett was abolished as a crossing place on 20 June 1922 and the footbridges were removed from the stations.

KNOWLE TO FAREHAM DEVIATION

Railway No 1 authorised by the Act of 3 June 1897 was a 2 mile 7 chain line from Knowle Junction to Fareham to provide a deviation for

Fareham tunnel, where the unstable terrain had caused trouble ever since opening in 1841. Land was taken for a double line, but financial constraints caused several changes of policy and work commenced in the summer of 1901 on a single track. Construction was delayed by earth slips and Relf withdrew from the contract in March 1904, leaving the LSWR engineers department to complete the work. The single line for up trains came into use on 2 October 1904, replacing the original up line through the tunnel. Meanwhile, approval had been given in December 1902 for a second track on the deviation, but construction was again hampered by slippage; it was September 1906 before it could be brought into service as the down line, enabling the tunnel route to be closed for reconstruction.

This was re-opened on 2 June 1907 as a single line for Meon Valley traffic and included a 1,100yd widening to provide a third track from Knowle Junction, where the link between the Meon Valley and Eastleigh lines was severed. At Knowle a 100ft open platform was provided for County Asylum staff, served by two Meon Valley trains in each direction. The connection at Knowle was restored on 24 June 1921, but in the opposite direction to the 1903 junction, enabling freight trains to and from Eastleigh to avoid the gradients on the deviation.

These works involved various alterations at the east end of Fareham station, including a bay platform for Meon Valley trains and an enlarged East signalbox.

BISHOP'S WALTHAM

Three light railways in this area were proposed in 1899, but the only one to obtain an Order (on 26 October 1900) was the Bishop's Waltham Light Railway, from that town to Droxford to connect with the Meon Valley line. No construction took place on this 4 mile 28 chain line and the powers lapsed.

The LSWR's 3³/₄ mile branch from Botley to Bishop's Waltham was chosen for railmotor operation, commencing on 10 October 1904. A 120ft platform (Durley Halt) was added at Durley Mill level crossing on 23 December 1909. Railmotors ceased from 31 August 1914 to enable one locomotive to work both passenger and goods traffic.

GOSPORT AND STOKES BAY

During Queen Victoria's lifetime the Royal Clarence Yard at Gosport was the starting point for the royal train on her journeys from Osborne

House to Windsor or Balmoral. Her funeral train in February 1901 was hauled from Gosport to Fareham by Adams 0-4-2 No 555, before being handed over to the LBSCR for the journey to Victoria. Osborne then ceased to be a royal residence and Gosport became a quiet branch, operated by push-and-pull trains from December 1915.

On the Stokes Bay branch the viaducts over Haslar Creek and Workhouse Lake were partially replaced by embankments. Ballast for the Meon Valley line came from a new siding near Anglesea Road level crossing. After final withdrawal of steamer services from Stokes Bay at the end of the 1913 season, local trains continued to serve the branch (some direct, but usually via Gosport) until 1 November 1915, when the Admiralty requisitioned the pier and station. The Royal Navy remained in occupation after the war and in 1922 purchased for £25,000 the pier and the railway as far as Gosport Road station. The triangular junction outside Gosport remained for turning locomotives, and the line as far as Gosport Road was used for carriage storage.

Another Admiralty development on the Gosport branch was a siding at Bedenham, installed in 1911 to serve an ammunition depot. At Fort Brockhurst, nearer Gosport, a siding and a platform were provided for the War Department in 1899. At this barracks, men who had completed their service were discharged from the Army; on those occasions a special train ran to Waterloo, with through carriages for the north via Clapham Junction. Latterly, this train provided the unique instance of a scheduled express over the Meon Valley line.

LEE-ON-THE-SOLENT

The Lee-on-the-Solent Light Railway had been authorised on 5 July 1890 by Board of Trade certificate, under the Regulation of Railways Act 1868. Land for its 3 mile 9 chain line from Fort Brockhurst was leased from the War Department for 99 years. To add to the company's difficulties—shortage of capital and trouble with its contractor—it was at odds with the Board of Trade. The promoters wanted to build a light railway with unmanned level crossings and rail-level halts, but this was before the passing of the 1896 Act and the Board's officials insisted on all the features of a normal railway being provided.

Eventually, the line opened on 12 May 1894 with request halts at Privett and Browndown and a station with a loop and a siding at Lee-on-the-Solent. The light railway had its own rolling stock, but the LSWR supplied an elderly tank engine as motive power. Understandably, the LSWR board declined to purchase the line in March

1896, but in 1903 Sir Charles Owens offered assistance with publicity and recommended the use of railmotors.

With working expenses exceeding receipts, the local company requested the LSWR to lease and work the line. Their agreement of 10 March 1909 was confirmed by the LSWR Act of 16 August 1909. The LSWR was to retain gross receipts up to £1,400 per annum, any excess being divided 75 per cent to the Lee company and 25 per cent to the LSWR. The LSWR would also retain four per cent on the cost of any additional works and overall it was guaranteed 60 per cent of gross receipts.

LSWR operation started with the introduction by October 1909 of a more frequent railmotor service. Elmore Halt was added on 11 April 1910 (its provision had been abandoned in 1894) and Privett Halt was renamed Fort Gomer to avoid confusion with the Meon Valley station. The 1914–18 war brought increased traffic from the construction of a naval seaplane base at Lee-on-the-Solent. The LSWR eventually obtained Light Railways Act powers for the line on 11 November 1921—level crossing gates and their keepers were abolished on 8 May 1922. Under the Railways Act 1921, the LSWR had to absorb the Lee-on-the-Solent company. As its revenue had never reached the £1,400 a year specified in the lease and it had few assets and no freehold tenure of its track bed, the South Western viewed this obligation with reluctance.

THE NETLEY LINE

The opening of the section between Fareham and Netley on 2 September 1889 had completed the direct link between Portsmouth and Southampton. The route from Fareham to St Denys was single track throughout, but earthworks had been provided for a double line. Some improvement came from the addition of a crossing loop at Woolston in January 1901.

The Royal Victoria Military Hospital, Netley, treated many of the casualties of the Boer War, and at the suggestion of Queen Victoria a branch line was built from Netley station to the hospital. Authorised in January 1900 at a cost of £4,090 to the War Department, it came into use on 18 April 1900. The 48 chain branch terminated in a loop with a 196ft platform adjacent to the hospital. The first of many casualties from World War I arrived on 24 August 1914; later the discharge of convalescent patients required a regular through train to Southampton West on Tuesdays and Fridays.

Doubling of the Netley line was decided and on 4 November 1909 the board authorised the section from St Denys to Netley. The 43 chains from Adelaide Crossing, St Denys, to Bitterne station came into use on 27 February 1910. Continuing the down side widening, the 1 mile 53 chains to Woolston followed on 10 April 1910 and was completed through to Netley in June, including the reconstruction of Sholing station for double track.

Approval was given in June 1910 for the continuation of the doubling from Netley to Fareham, a proposed station at Titchfield having been abandoned. Here the doubling took place on the up (south) side of the line. The second track on the 3 miles 58 chains from Fareham to Swanwick came into service on 18 December 1910. Double line working through to Netley was completed on 9 April 1911; Bursledon station had to be rebuilt with two 550ft platforms and an additional signalbox.

WORTING JUNCTION TO SOUTHAMPTON TOWN

Additional block sections and refuge loops were required on the double track Southampton line beyond Worting Junction. The widenings were authorised by the Act of 30 July 1900. The board approved in August 1900 passenger loops through the station at Micheldever, but after some preliminary work had been done further progress was deferred in October 1901. When work resumed at the end of 1903, initial plans for a pneumatic signalbox were replaced by a less costly mechanical cabin. The new down platform came into use on 26 March 1904, the full quadrupling being completed on 26 March 1905.

The two new tracks were constructed on the down side, with a platform on the down loop only; the existing double lines became the two up lines and the old down platform went into disuse for the next 60 years. Fortunately, this left intact the original London & Southampton station building on the up (now loop) platform. In May 1907, sidings within the quarry area for storage of excursion stock were authorised; these became the resting place for carriages awaiting repair or scrapping at Eastleigh Works.

The next widening was over the 1 mile 38 chains between Weston and Wallers Ash East signal boxes, where up and down loops were built mainly for freight trains, providing a welcome respite on the up line from the 1 in 252 climb to Litchfield tunnel. J. T. Firbank was given the contract in June 1901 and the loops were ready for through running by freight traffic on 4 June 1902 and for passenger trains on 24 July.

Approaching Eastleigh, a new signalbox was provided at Allbrook Junction in December 1898 to control the entrance to up and down goods loops. These were upgraded to passenger lines on 3 December 1905 and the up local line was extended from Eastleigh station to join the up loop on 10 March 1907. These changes necessitated the new 122-lever East signalbox on the down side of the line. On 1 January 1903 the new Eastleigh locomotive depot opened within the area between the main and Portsmouth lines which had been selected as the site for the future locomotive works. Eastleigh became the second largest shed on the LSWR, with 108 locomotives stationed there in 1922.

The third widening authorised by the 1900 Act covered the 3½ miles between Eastleigh and St Denys. This Act also included a 1½ mile diversion of the Portsmouth line to run along the southern boundary of the works site, and for the up Portsmouth line to cross the main line by a flyover. The original course of the Portsmouth branch would then become part of the works yard. Plans for the widening and for purchase of land were approved in May 1901, but the whole project was postponed in October 1901 because of the company's financial problems, and was thereafter regarded as being in abeyance.

St Denys station had been rebuilt in 1899 with separate platforms for the Netley line; the new junction was inspected by Sir Francis Marindin on 15 August 1899. Additional down and up running lines between St Denys and Northam Junction were brought into use on 4 May 1902. At Bevois Park, on the up side of the line, a marshalling yard came into use on 16 September 1901 and was extended in 1907. On the down side, the removal of Northam locomotive shed in 1903 following the transfer of its allocation to Eastleigh, enabled the site to be used for sidings, but the re-arrangement as a down marshalling yard was not authorised until June 1922 and completed by the SR in 1923.

By agreement with Southampton Corporation, the level crossing at Dukes Road, St Denys, was replaced by an overbridge in 1903 and the existing road bridge at Northam Junction was rebuilt with a girder span, being completed on 12 April 1908.

SOUTHAMPTON, WINCHESTER & GREAT WESTERN JUNCTION RAILWAY

The LSWR monopoly at Southampton had been threatened during the 1880s by the proposed Didcot, Newbury & Southampton Railway line from Winchester to a station near the Royal Pier. Authorised by the DNSR Act of 10 August 1882, construction had ceased through lack of funds, and the DNSR link to Southampton was eventually made by the connection to the LSWR at Shawford Junction. In 1901 a Bill was submitted to Parliament for a similar line, under the title of the Southampton, Winchester & Great Western Junction Railway; its promoters included three directors of the DNSR as well as other prominent local figures.

The Bill was supported by the Mayor of Southampton and the chamber of commerce, attracted by the new company's promise of shore reclamation. Despite the LSWR witnesses' recital of the benefits the company had brought to the town and docks, and its plans for the future, Parliament decided to pass the Bill. Traffic to Southampton Docks during the South African War had caused some congestion on the LSWR and there was a feeling that such an important strategic port deserved alternative rail access. The Bill obtained Royal Assent on 17 August 1901, but construction required the financial support of a major railway company. The GWR found itself unable to assist and its working agreement with the DNSR prevented any other company intervening. The project was formally abandoned by an Act of 30 June 1905.

SOUTHAMPTON–BOURNEMOUTH–WEYMOUTH

Southampton West was becoming the town's principal station and the down platform was improved in 1905 and 1910. Most of the old Blechynden station was demolished in 1906. The Central district superintendent, controlling the lines from Basingstoke and Portsmouth westwards, moved from Eastleigh to new offices at the West station in 1913.

The LSWR Act of 20 July 1906 authorised a 21 chain curve from the Andover line at Redbridge Causeway level crossing to join the Bournemouth line, seven chains west of the viaduct over the River Test. This would have enabled Waterloo–Bournemouth fast trains to avoid the congested Eastleigh—Southampton area, by taking a longer 112½ mile route via Hurstbourne, Fullerton Junction and Romsey. The LSWR sought unsuccessfully in its 1909 Bill to alter this curve to 45 chains—instead, extensions of time for the original curve were obtained in 1911 and 1913, but the board decided in June 1917 to let the powers lapse.

Lyndhurst Road station is over 2½ miles from the village of Lyndhurst. The Lyndhurst Electric Lighting & Traction Co obtained on 23 January 1902 a Light Railway Order for an electric tramway between these points. The LSWR refused to work or purchase the line, so construction never took place. Instead, the LSWR started on 24 October 1904 a motor bus service between station and village, using two Milnes-Daimler vehicles. These proving unreliable, the service ceased on 13 February 1905 and the buses were sold. Another bus route between Lymington, Milford-on-Sea and New Milton also met difficulties. After a brief experiment with Thornycroft vehicles in 1904, a regular service started on 19 July 1905 with two Clarkson steam buses. These heavy vehicles did such damage to the roads that the service had to be withdrawn on 15 September 1906.

Competition from the electric trams in the Bournemouth area was met by the introduction of railmotor services on 1 March 1906. These cars operated about ten irregular-interval trips daily from Bournemouth West to Christchurch, New Milton and Ringwood. A railmotor halt at Meyrick Park, between the Central and West stations, was opened at this date—it closed on 1 November 1917 and was demolished in 1919.

The LSWR proposed in 1908 to build a locomotive depot within the Branksome triangle, thus releasing the shed site at Bournemouth Central for enlargement of the station. Powers were to be sought in the company's 1909 Bill, but the proposal was withdrawn in the face of strong opposition from the town council and local residents, fearing that smoky locomotives would lower the value of their properties.

The original Southampton & Dorchester Railway branch from Hamworthy Junction to Hamworthy (closed to passenger traffic since 1 July 1896) was reduced to single track from 10 September 1905, retaining the previous down line.

WEYMOUTH AND PORTLAND JOINT LINES

The Weymouth & Portland Railway was leased jointly to the LSWR and GWR, each company operating it for alternate five-year periods. In 1901–2 negotiations for purchase of the line by the leasing companies broke down over financial terms. The GWR secured Weymouth Corporation's agreement to the replacement of the timber Backwater viaduct with an embankment by providing a new station on the branch at Melcombe Regis to avoid the time-consuming reversal in and out of Weymouth station. This opened on 30 May 1909 and was followed on 1 July by the introduction of a frequent railmotor service to Portland, with new halts at Westham and Wyke Regis. The LSWR took over the operation of this service from 1 January 1910, employing a motor tank and three trailers.

The Easton & Church Hope Railway was worked jointly by the LSWR and GWR for 2s 6d [12½p] per train mile, according to an agreement of 5 August 1897. Freight traffic to Easton commenced on 1 October 1900 and passenger services on 1 September 1902, although arrangements at Portland were temporary until the new through station was opened on 7 May 1905. The E&CH directors suggested in July 1907 that the working companies might purchase the line, which offer was quickly declined as the E&CH had been in the hands of a receiver since 1901 and an insurance company had a first charge on its revenues.

Of the 20 or more services between Melcombe Regis and Portland, only four daily continued to Easton. This section, which was vulnerable to landslips and rock falls, also passed through the naval rifle ranges. The gunner-in-charge received a copy of the working timetable and was advised of all special trains. During the 1914–18 war the Portland lines saw great activity. On the Admiralty-owned section at Portland there was a platform serving the naval hospital, while a branch entered the dockyard itself. Beyond Easton, the army laid sidings at Sheepcroft for military stores traffic. The Whitehead torpedo factory brought 1,000 workers a day to Wyke Halt.

The LSWR/GWR accord of 1910 led to the GWR abandoning its costly plans for a new harbour at Weymouth, and from 22 July 1912 the GWR-operated motor bus services in the Weymouth area were placed under joint ownership.

SOUTH WESTERN & ISLE OF WIGHT JUNCTION RAILWAY

This was the name of the company incorporated by an Act of 26 July 1901 to build the Solent Tunnel. With an authorised capital of £600,000 it proposed to build a 7 mile 60 chain line from the LSWR's Lymington branch to join the Freshwater, Yarmouth & Newport Railway between Freshwater and Yarmouth. The 2½ mile tunnel under the Solent was to be operated by electric traction. Running powers were sought over the LSWR to Brockenhurst and over the FYNR and IWCR. The driving force behind the scheme was F. G. Aman, who had obtained control of the FYNR in 1901—he was also a vocal shareholder at the LSWR's general meetings.

The scheme required the co-operation and financial support of the LSWR, but negotiations for a working agreement were conducted fruitlessly from 1901 to 1914. Meanwhile, the SW&IOWJ obtained further powers in 1903, 1909 and 1914 for additional capital and to build a branch line to a pier near Hurst Castle. This would have been used by tenders meeting ocean liners and for a ferry to Yarmouth; both would have been in competition with LSWR interests and therefore not likely to secure its goodwill for the SW&IOWJ. However, F. G. Aman always held that the LSWR should not become involved in the docks or shipping business. The powers were kept alive until 1921, but the Minister of Transport, Sir Eric Geddes, had already told a deputation that the current £2 million cost of the scheme made it viable no longer.

CHAPTER 5

THE WEST COUNTRY

WORTING JUNCTION TO SALISBURY

Two abortive schemes of the 1900s would have involved this line. The grandiose Bristol, London & Southern Counties Railway of 1903 was to have joined the LSWR near Overton, while the more modest DNSR-sponsored Bourne Valley Light Railway, authorised on 26 October 1900, would have had a connection to the LSWR at Hurstbourne. The branch from Hurstbourne to Fullerton Junction had been built in 1885 largely to block DNSR and GWR approaches to Southampton. Local traffic was light; between 1 June 1906 and February 1910 it was handled by steam railmotors (running to and from Whitchurch). Four passenger services and one goods train daily in each direction did not justify double track, so the branch was reduced from 13 July 1913 to a single line without passing loops. Track improvements at Andover Junction were made during 1903–4. A new locomotive shed on the up side replaced one destroyed by fire.

The traffic committee in July 1898 had authorised three additional block sections between Worting Junction and Salisbury. In November 1900 the engineer recommended that a trial should be made of the proposed pneumatic signalling system at Grateley, where changes were required in connection with the new branch to Amesbury, also between Andover Junction and Grateley, to provide automatic signal sections. Tenders were accepted from the British Pneumatic Railway Signal Co for the Grateley station work at £5,974 (an equivalent manual signal box would have cost £2,810), and for the automatic signals at £3,500, but eliminating Monxton signalbox.

The introduction to the United Kingdom of this new system required the presence of both Colonel Yorke and Major Pringle to carry out the Board of Trade inspection of Grateley signalbox on 30 June 1901—pneumatic operation of the station area commenced on 21 July. Major Pringle returned on 20 October to review the operation of the automatic signalling, a novelty on a main line. This divided the 6½ miles between Andover Junction and Grateley into six block sections, each protected by a post carrying a home and distant signal. Trials had commenced on 1 September 1901, but the inspecting officer required that three months' trial working must elapse before approval could be given. This was granted on 20 February 1902 and the automatic signals came into use on 20 April.

In October 1916 the replacement of the pneumatic signalling by mechanical equipment was recommended as this would save £1,000 a year on maintenance. The construction in January 1919 of the new Red Post Junction connection to the MSWJR within the automatic section also made a change necessary; in consequence the whole area reverted to mechanical signalling between 1919 and 1921.

Salisbury station was another bottleneck. There was only one through platform for each direction, staggered on either side of the Fisherton Street underbridge. The connection to the GWR was via a single line subject to a 4mph speed restriction. To provide room for the enlargement of the LSWR station, an agreement was made with the GWR on 28 January 1898 for an exchange of lands, for additional transfer sidings and for the LSWR to contribute to the cost of a new GWR locomotive shed. The LSWR's own shed had to be moved west to a new site, where a five-bay building to house 50 locomotives was completed in December 1901.

Plans for rebuilding the station were approved in October 1899 and J. T. Firbank was appointed as the main contractor. The new platforms were built opposite the existing down platform, which was lengthened and provided with a bay at its western end. The first up platform came into use on 6 April 1902 and the new double junction with the GWR on 7 June. When Major Pringle made his inspection on 8 August the station works were complete except for the east bay extending across Fisherton Street bridge. When completed, the rebuilt station had four through platforms and two bays linked by a subway and an improved footbridge. The new red brick station offices on the down side formed a westward extention of the old frontage.

In addition to the rebuilding, which cost around £106,000, it was decided to equip the new station with pneumatic signalling at a cost of £9,000. This was brought into use on 2 November 1902, with two new boxes; East (46 slide levers) and West (48 levers).

AMESBURY & MILITARY CAMPS LIGHT RAILWAY

Salisbury Plain was unpromising territory for railway promotion until the War Office purchased 60 square miles of land for army camps and exercise areas. It approached the LSWR in 1897 for a branch from the

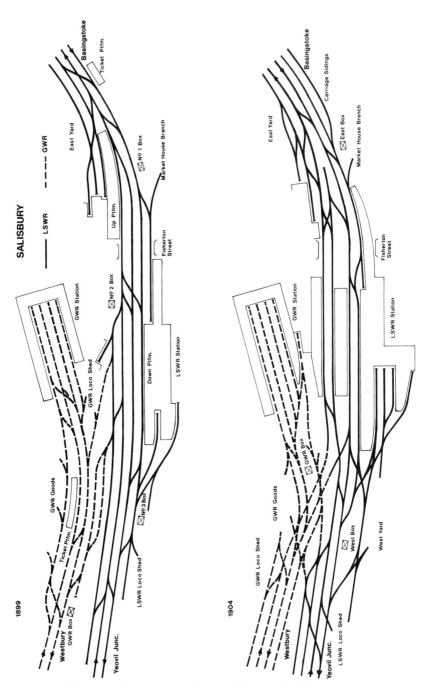

Salisbury station reconstruction: track layouts in 1899 and 1904

West of England main line towards Amesbury and Bulford, where the new camps were to be sited. A party of LSWR directors and officers went over the ground with General Sir Redvers Buller, and in the words of Sir Charles Scotter 'in deference to his opinion the route was altered to go west from Amesbury.' This took the line over the Avon valley on a viaduct, then within ³/₄mile of Stonehenge and across Durrington Down to terminate east of the village of Shrewton.

The LSWR accordingly applied in November 1897 for a Light Railway Order. With support from the military authorities this was confirmed on 24 September 1898 for a 10 mile 62 chain single-line branch, leaving the LSWR main line at the 75 milepost near Newton Tony intermediate box. The cost was estimated at £62,517 and in January 1899 J. T. Firbank was awarded the contract.

Meanwhile, the GWR had been promoting its own light railway across the Plain from Pewsey to Bemerton, near Salisbury. However, the proposed line crossed 4¹/₂ miles of War Department land, and although the GWR offered to remove all obstacles to the movement of troops, the War Office made formal objection. In consequence, the Light Railway Order granted in August 1898 allowed this section to be built only with the agreement of the military authorities (the GWR timetable map of 1902 showed the proposed line as two separate branches). The GWR agreed with the LSWR on 10 August 1899 for a connecting curve between the two companies' lines near Amesbury, and for the section on to Shrewton to be built and operated as a joint line.

The LSWR line to Shrewton was outside the boundaries of the WD land, but on 22 November 1899 the War Office asked the LSWR to divert its route as 'it was essential that no obstacle be placed in the way of manoeuvres.' Finding it impossible to vary the authorised route, the LSWR began negotiations with the War Office to abandon the line beyond Amesbury. Firbank had already started on the earthworks, so he settled for £3,500 compensation and the promise of alternative work at Basingstoke or Salisbury. The LSWR obtained an abandonment Order on 16 November 1901, reducing the line to 4 miles 78 chains. A contribution to the legal costs of this Order was the only recompense obtained from the War Office. The episode leaves the impression that the army regarded manoeuvres as a kind of parade ground exercise.

As well as the junction at Newton Tony, there was to be an independent single line from Grateley station, built on the up side of the main line and authorised by the Act of 9 August 1899. By December 1901, both camps and railway were ready. Major Pringle during his inspection on 28 February 1902 referred to the probability of

A Territorial Army regiment alighting from a double-headed troop train at Amesbury 1908. *Commercial postcard, courtesy G. Gundry*

Yeovil Junction station after rebuilding, 1909. *British Rail*

exceptional military traffic and that troop trains might have to start from any line under hand signalling. The branch may have been used for military traffic before full completion, on the evidence of photographs in *The Railway Magazine* of July 1902, but for civilian traffic freight services commenced on 29 April 1902 and passenger trains on 2 June.

Although the branch was single, land had been taken for double track and some of the embankments had been widened with chalk excavated from the abandoned section. The start of this formed the site of four long military sidings. Amesbury station also had a military platform, three loading docks and a turntable as well as two passenger platforms. The sharp ridge between Newton Tony and Amesbury, approached on each side by 1 in 50 and 1 in 60 gradients, made double heading necessary for any train exceeding eight bogies. Newton Tony station had a passing loop and small signal frame. The independent line from Grateley was completed on 24 May 1902. The initial service was six weekday trains, two running through to Andover Junction, worked by Adams 0-4-4Ts, while the freight traffic was in the charge of his 395 Class 0-6-0s, these types being within the weight limits imposed by light railway operation. However, Major Pringle described the permanent way itself as being of heavy type.

The junctions facing London met military requirements, but local inhabitants wanted to go to Salisbury and they supported the LSWR's application for a curve at Newton Tony, for which an Order was granted on 28 April 1903. This joined the main line at a new box named Amesbury Junction, with a dive-under for the 32 chain down line and a direct spur of 22 chains for the up line. Passenger services over this curve commenced on Monday 8 August 1904, with four services daily to Salisbury, while five trains continued to run to Grateley or Andover Junction.

The new cabin at Amesbury Junction replaced in May 1904 the existing box at Newton Tony Junction, where the connection between the main line and the branch was removed. The title Newton Tony Junction was then given to the small 13-lever signal box at the junction of the new curve and the line from Grateley, and the double line was extended through to Newton Tony station. Gradually train services were concentrated on the Salisbury direction; the last weekday train from Andover Junction ceased on 1 June 1919 and the Sunday night train for troops from Waterloo ran for the last time on 3 October 1920.

Before the line to Amesbury was finished, the War Office asked for an extension to Bulford, where barracks had already been built. They confirmed in May 1902 that Bulford was their objective (Durrington had also been suggested) and the LSWR obtained a Light Railway

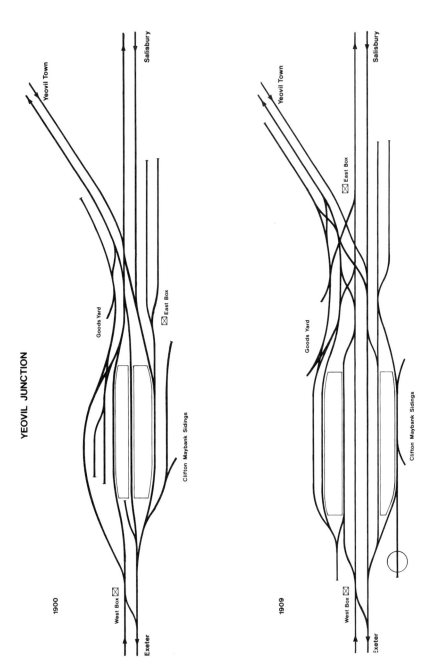

Yeovil Junction station reconstruction: track layouts in 1900 and 1909

Order on 10 January 1903, with the War Office urging early completion. Land was taken for double line, much of it WD property, for which the LSWR paid a nominal rent of £1 per annum—otherwise the financial terms were similar to those agreed for the Bordon branch. The total cost amounted to £28,370, with the government paying interest on £28,000.

Construction by the LSWR engineers department started early in 1904, using another of the former Southampton Docks locomotives on ballast trains. The total length of the single line extension was 2 miles 69 chains, but Major Pringle's inspection on 3 April 1906 covered only the 1 mile 59 chains open for public passenger traffic as far as Bulford (village) station, where a 320ft platform and loop were provided. The section beyond to Bulford Camp Platform was only to be used for military traffic. Passenger services commenced on 1 June 1906 with all nine trains daily being extended from Amesbury to Bulford.

Plans for extensive manoeuvres by the newly-formed Territorial Army on Salisbury Plain in 1909 required the doubling of the section from Newton Tony to Amesbury to handle the 42 special trains expected. Work started without any of the usual formalities and the 3 mile 33 chain doubling on the up side was ready on 23 May 1909 for a Whitsun influx of Lancashire Territorials. To divide this steeply graded section, an intermediate signalbox was provided at Allington.

SALISBURY TO EXETER

In November 1905 the engineering committee authorised expenditure of £37,030 to strengthen permanent way and bridges along this line, probably in anticipation of the arrival of the massive Drummond 4-6-0s. The board now realised that the approaching completion of the GWR cut-off routes to the west would place the LSWR in an unfavourable competitive position.

Of the three major improvement projects then authorised, only the rebuilding of Yeovil Junction station was completed. The main lines curved sharply round the two island platforms of the old station, imposing a 20mph limit on non-stop trains. Powers were obtained in the 1906 Act for additional land on the down side, and at a cost of £47,400 a completely new station emerged during 1907-9. This had two through roads for non-stop trains, two platform loops plus an up side loop for Yeovil Town branch trains and another behind the down platform. The goods yards were also remodelled and extended, a new 52-lever East box built and a new frame installed in the existing West box. The completed layout was inspected by Major Pringle on 3 March 1909.

One of the objects of the LSWR/GWR agreement of 1910 was to secure operating economies through co-operation in areas served by both companies. Little was achieved until the pressure of wartime shortages began to be felt, when a series of joint projects was undertaken in the West Country. Although each project was designed to provide manpower and material savings, financial economies were carefully costed every time. It was agreed on 27 January 1916 to combine the separate East and West signal boxes at Yeovil Town, while at Chard Town the LSWR station was to close and a joint passenger service would be provided by the GWR from Chard Junction to Chard Joint station. These two schemes gave a payout of £859 per year on a capital outlay of £2,965, and were effected from 1 January 1917. Elsewhere, signalboxes were merged during 1916–17 at Cowley Bridge Junction, Lydford and Launceston.

The Crewkerne, South Petherton & Martock Light Railway was a locally-promoted scheme which obtained an Order on 31 December 1909 for a 10¾-mile line from Crewkerne LSWR station to Martock on the GWR Yeovil to Durston branch. Neither company offered any assistance and the project lapsed through lack of capital.

A railmotor service was introduced on 26 January 1906 from Exeter to intermediate stations as far as Honiton. Three new halts were provided on the outskirts of Exeter—at Whipton Bridge, Mount Pleasant Road and Lions Holt Bridge. Another platform opened on 22 September 1906 at bridge 476, just west of Honiton. Named Roundball Halt, this served a rifle range and the railmotors stopped on request at times convenient for parties of Territorials to have an afternoon's shooting. Being little used and in need of repair, its removal was ordered in January 1921. Whipton Bridge Halt also was closed on 1 January 1923.

Some improvements to the layout at Exeter Queen Street were made during 1900–5. The Western district superintendent, controlling the LSWR lines west of Salisbury, had his office in one of the company's houses in Queen Street.

AXMINSTER & LYME REGIS LIGHT RAILWAY

Proposals for rail connection to Lyme Regis were accomplished by the Axminster & Lyme Regis Light Railway, which obtained its Order on 15 June 1899 with an authorised capital of £55,000 and loans of £12,000. The local promoters found difficulty in raising capital, so in

April 1900 the LSWR subscribed for £25,000 ordinary shares and three South Western directors joined its board. The working agreement of 4 April 1900 gave the LSWR an option to purchase the line; meanwhile it was to work it for 55 per cent of the gross receipts, plus four per cent on the cost of any works undertaken by the LSWR, and to guarantee dividends by a 10 per cent rebate on through traffic.

Construction started on 19 June 1900, but the difficult terrain and trouble with the line's major engineering feature, Cannington Viaduct, delayed completion. Eventually Major Druitt inspected the 6 mile 46 chain single line on 22 August 1903 and public traffic commenced two days later. Branch trains departed from an up side bay at Axminster, crossing the main line by a flyover, but there was also a connection from the down side goods yard which fell into disuse and was removed on 5 September 1915. Combpyne had a single platform and a siding loop (raised to the status of a passing place with tablet instruments between September 1906 and August 1921), while Lyme Regis had one 300ft platform, a run-round loop, locomotive shed and goods shed. Light permanent way, sharp curves and 1 in 40 gradients made the branch a perennial problem for the LSWR operating departments.

The delay in opening the line increased the need for capital; the LSWR in 1902 and 1904 took up £25,000 in 3½ per cent preference shares as well as more debentures in 1903. With its effective control, the LSWR decided to exercise its option to purchase the light railway, which was authorised by its Act of 20 July 1906 to become operative from 1 January 1907. LSWR 3½ per cent preference stock was exchanged for A&LR ordinary shares and the South Western already held all the preference and debenture stocks.

RAILWAYS TO EXMOUTH

The branch from Sidmouth Junction to Sidmouth had been built by the Sidmouth Railway in 1874, being leased and worked by the LSWR under an agreement of 17 March 1871. An offer of purchase by the LSWR in 1894 was refused, and the company remained nominally independent until absorption in 1922. Its station at Tipton St John's had been enlarged in 1897 to meet its new role as the junction for Budleigh Salterton.

The Budleigh Salterton Railway was authorised by an Act of 20 July 1894 to build a 6 mile 33 chain single line branch from Tipton St John's. Intermediate stations without passing loops were at East Budleigh and Newton Poppleford (opened 1 June 1899); public services commenced on 15 May 1897. The LSWR worked the line for 60 per cent of the receipts by an agreement of 9 August 1894. Perhaps the greatest asset the local company provided was its Chairman, Hugh W. Drummond, who joined the LSWR board and became the latter's final Chairman.

In November 1898 the LSWR declined an offer from Drummond and his Exeter Bank to dispose of a controlling interest in the BSR. However, in 1910 the LSWR offered to purchase the local company and the agreement was confirmed by the LSWR Act of 18 August 1911 to become effective on 1 January 1912. The BSR share capital of £60,000 was exchanged for LSWR 3 per cent debentures.

Much of the land in East Devon belonged to the trustees of the Rolle family, who in 1896 proposed the construction of a railway from Exmouth to Budleigh Salterton. Where the proposed line crossed Rolle property the land was donated free by an agreement of 24 June 1898. The wishes of the Hon Mark Rolle had to be met regarding the line's course, including the provision of a station at Littleham. His example was not followed at Exmouth, where the landowner required the railway to buy the whole of the Marpool estate for its line.

The new line was authorised by the Act of 25 July 1898 and Henry Lovatt & Sons commenced work early in 1901. The line involved heavy earthworks, 1 in 50 gradients and a viaduct outside Exmouth; total cost was £111,378. The completed railway was inspected on 22 April 1903. It was single line with room for doubling, Littleham was a passing station, while a second platform had been added at Budleigh Salterton (this station was placed in joint LSWR/BSR ownership in 1908). Public services commenced on 1 June 1903. A direct curve outside Exmouth towards Exeter was considered in 1902, but the price of the land was too high. The two branches to Budleigh Salterton were worked as one, with through coaches to Sidmouth Junction and (seasonally) to Waterloo.

The line from Exeter to Exmouth has always had a semi-suburban character, and on 20 July 1906 the LSWR obtained powers to double the whole of this single line branch. However, immediate plans only covered the 4 miles 10 chains from Exmouth Junction to Topsham. The additional track was laid on the east side of the line to carry down trains; railmotor halts were built at Polsloe Bridge and Clyst St Mary & Digby. The widening and the halts came into use on 1 June 1908. Purchase powers for the continuation of the widening beyond Topsham expired on 20 July 1909 and the company hastened to acquire land at Lympstone and Woodbury Road, but no construction ever commenced. Railmotor cars maintained a local service between Exeter and Topsham until withdrawn from 1 January 1917.

TOWARDS NORTH DEVON

LSWR trains to North Devon and Cornwall had to share the busy GWR tracks between Exeter St David's and Cowley Bridge Junction. To prevent these delays the LSWR board decided in November 1905 to build its own 2½ mile avoiding line; commencing at Queen Street it would have passed over the lines at the south end of St David's station and then followed the River Exe to rejoin the existing route 34 chains north of Cowley Bridge Junction. Publication of the LSWR Bill aroused GWR protests that this line would breach the agreements of March 1860 and October 1884. The dispute was referred to the arbitration of Lord Robertson, who ruled in April 1906 that the LSWR was prevented from building the line by the provisions of the 1884 agreement; the proposal was accordingly deleted from the LSWR Bill.

The third project to meet GWR competition was the completion of the doubling of the North Devon line over the 18 miles 72 chains from Copplestone to Umberleigh. Powers were obtained in the Act of 20 July 1906, but work did not start immediately as various station improvements were suggested which would have increased the cost. It was decided in February 1908 to keep to the original scheme; land was purchased, plans approved and Perry & Co given the contract. Then on 4 March 1910, the general manager told the board that in view of the probable agreement with the GWR provision of the second line might be dispensed with to save capital. It was decided that Perry & Co should complete its contract for earthworks and bridges, but no further work should be done; the total cost of this fruitless project was £75,640.

The Bideford, Clovelly & Hartland Light Railway obtained an Order on 24 January 1906 to build a 13½ mile line between these places and connecting with the LSWR at Bideford. Prolonged negotiations were conducted by its engineer, W. T. Foxlee, for a working agreement with the LSWR (terms depended on the line's ruling gradient). Finally, the LSWR agreed to work the line for 60 per cent of receipts and to guarantee interest and dividends by a rebate on through traffic. These terms were approved by the LSWR board on 24 July 1914, but with war only days away it was too late to start work.

DARTMOOR AND PLYMOUTH

Chagford was a market town eleven miles from Exeter on the fringes of Dartmoor which had been denied rail access; the LSWR introduced a bus service from Exeter on 1 June 1904, using two second-hand Milnes-Daimler vehicles. The service ceased after 30 September and was resumed on 3 June 1905 with Clarkson steam buses (maintained at Exmouth Junction locomotive depot). These again proved too heavy for the roads and were replaced in June 1908 by two light 30hp Thornycroft buses. By 1914 the Thornycroft buses were worn out and were succeeded by two Karrier buses from the Clayton Co. One of these was transferred to Basingstoke in 1917 to operate the parcels service to Herriard, but the Chagford route was maintained with some interruptions and in 1922 showed a profit of £92. However, in 1924 the SR discontinued this survivor of the LSWR's motor bus ventures.

Extra land was taken at Okehampton in 1909 (under 1906 Act powers) for the construction of sidings and a loading dock, intended for handling artillery arriving for practice on the Dartmoor ranges.

A railmotor service between St Budeaux and Plymouth Friary was introduced, probably from 26 September 1906, three halts being added at Weston Mill, Camel's Head and Albert Road. A frequent service was provided (17 trains on weekdays) and to cater for dockyard workers the cars carried third class passengers only. The up platform at Camel's Head Halt was resited in September 1920, while nearby Weston Mill Halt closed on 27 June 1921.

The LSWR had to pay its half-share of the enlargement in 1908 of the jointly-owned Plymouth North Road station. At its own station of Plymouth Friary, a new locomotive depot came into use in June 1908. Nearby was the start of the Turnchapel branch, on which a railmotor service was inaugurated on 10 October 1904. Lucas Terrace Halt was erected only 55 chains from Friary (opening probably on 1 June 1905).

Railmotors provided a generous 23 services daily on the branch, which was the property of the Plymouth & Dartmoor Railway and worked by the LSWR for 50 per cent of receipts, under an agreement of 10 December 1896. The LSWR also worked the Cattewater goods branch by agreement of 9 December 1897, while its Act of 16 August 1909 authorised the purchase of the Cattewater Western Extension line from the P&D for £2,000. The P&D was one of the minor companies absorbed by the LSWR in 1922.

PLYMOUTH DEVONPORT & SOUTH WESTERN JUNCTION RAILWAY

The LSWR's independent access to Plymouth had been achieved on 2 June 1890 over PD&SWJ metals from Lidford to Devonport. By an agreement of 24 October 1883 the line was leased and worked by the LSWR, which granted a rebate of £15,650 per annum. The PD&SWJ also had its own ambitions, which need only be described here in relation to the LSWR's financial involvement.

The PD&SWJ had acquired the 3ft 6in gauge East Cornwall Minerals Railway and wished to connect it to its main line at Bere Alston. The LSWR agreed on 7 December 1901 to guarantee three per cent on the new capital of £135,000, recouping any shortfall from sums due to the PD&SWJ from the main line lease, and to grant a 10 per cent rebate on through traffic from the new light railway. In fact the LSWR subscribed itself in August 1903 for the £135,000 of three per cent guaranteed stock (at a price of 90); it invested a further £10,000 in 1906 to finance the conversion of the mineral line and the new connection to standard gauge.

The 9 miles 54 chains of new and reconstructed line from Bere Alston to Callington Road opened on 2 March 1908 and was worked by the PD&SWJ itself. The company obtained powers in February 1909 for a 6 mile 71 chain extension towards Launceston, the LSWR agreeing to subscribe £10,000 towards its capital, but the PD&SWJ decided not to proceed with the scheme. Absorption of the PD&SWJ by the LSWR in 1922 was followed immediately by grouping within the SR, but its three locomotives did receive LSWR livery.

NORTH CORNWALL

The LSWR had attained its objectives in the west by the end of the 19th Century, reaching Bude on 11 August 1898 and Padstow on 27 March 1899. The line from Halwill to Padstow had been built by the North Cornwall Railway, which was leased and worked by the LSWR. Between Meldon Junction and Ashbury, an additional passing loop was provided at Maddaford Moor, approved by the Board of Trade on 21 April 1900. The signalbox was closed on 22 April 1919 and the loop removed in 1921. Another post-war economy measure was the closure from 15 June 1920 of the loop and signalbox at Tower Hill.

The North Cornwall Railway joined the Bodmin & Wadebridge line at Wadebridge Junction, about a mile outside Wadebridge. To improve track capacity and save the expense of the junction signalbox, an independent single line for North Cornwall trains was laid over the 65 chains into Wadebridge station, coming into use on 3 February 1907. Near Wadebridge Junction on the B&W line was Wadebridge Rifle Range platform erected in 1901; LSWR trains from Bodmin called on request for not less than six Volunteers.

The Wadebridge–Bodmin local trains were replaced by steam rail-motors from 1 June 1906, which were provided in 1908 with their own shed at Wadebridge. Railmotor halts, only 60ft long, were opened on 2 July 1906 at Grogley, Nanstallon and Dunmere—in 1910 they were lengthened and equipped with shelters. When the general withdrawal of the railmotors took place in October 1916, it was considered that they could still be used economically on this service, but mileage figures indicate that railcar operation ceased at the end of 1917. The return of peace made unnecessary a 1918 proposal to close the LSWR station in Bodmin and run a joint LSWR/GWR service between Wadebridge and Bodmin GWR.

At the LSWR's extremity of Padstow, the company and the govern-ment wanted to encourage the Cornish fishing industry. A scheme for the enlargement of Padstow harbour was launched in 1911, with the LSWR subscribing to its bonds and providing material assistance. Following a visit in July 1912 by the LSWR chairman and general manager, an extension of the work was recommended and the com-pany spent £10,350 on the dock wall, fish shed and sidings. The LSWR took up £30,000 of the Harbour Commissioners' bonds and gradually assumed more control over the port by carrying out dredg-ing and collecting dues. The work was largely complete by 1920.

The Padstow, Bedruthan & Mawgan was another abortive light railway project. It obtained its Order on 14 January 1903, but as its route lay within LSWR/GWR boundary territory neither company offered any assistance.

The North Cornwall Railway had advanced westwards as quickly as its finances permitted. For convenience in raising capital it had been divided into four separate undertakings, marking its four principal stages of construction, successively to Launceston, Delabole, Wade-bridge and Padstow. Each undertaking had its own capital structure and its separate working agreement with the LSWR. Herbert Walker proposed a financial rationalisation in October 1912. The existing NCR issued capital of £574,000 and debentures of £162,000 would be converted into a single NCR Leased Line stock of £825,000, on which the LSWR would pay a fixed annual rental of £25,250. Agreement was reached on 25 April 1913 and Parliamentary authority obtained in the Act of 15 August 1913.

CHAPTER 6

ELECTRIFICATION

STEAM FACES COMPETITION

Through its support of the Waterloo & City Railway the LSWR had been involved in one of the pioneer electrification schemes, but above ground it showed little enthusiasm for the new form of traction. In August 1902 its Chairman, Lieutenant Colonel H. W. Campbell, said that the company would not electrify until there were eight lines into Waterloo (progress with the reconstruction of the terminus was also needed). The LSWR co-operated with the MDR in the conversion of its branches to Wimbledon and Richmond for the District electric services, as already described. Sir Charles Scotter, the succeeding LSWR chairman, said cautiously in February 1905 'We shall watch the working of these branches very closely in order that at the proper time we may see how far it will be possible for us to adopt electrical working for our own suburban traffic.' The effect was soon apparent as commuters deserted the slow and circuitous LSWR steam trains in favour of the quick, clean and frequent District trains to the West End and City. Although not in direct competition, the overhead wires of the LBSCR's Elevated Electric appeared in 1911 alongside the LSWR tracks at Clapham Junction.

However, the most serious competition came from the electric tramways. From its termini at Shepherds Bush and Hammersmith, the London United Tramways Co (LUT) cars reached Hounslow in 1901, Twickenham in 1902 and Hampton Court in 1903; the LSWR lost 64 per cent of its receipts on the Hounslow route, despite putting on extra trains. Having secured powers in 1902 for routes to Wimbledon and Sunbury, the LUT 1904 Bill for an extension from Hounslow to Staines met with strong LSWR opposition. At a meeting on 21 April between the respective general managers, James Clifton Robinson and Sir Charles Owens, it was agreed that if the LSWR withdrew its petition against the Bill, the Staines line would not be started for three years without LSWR consent—in fact it was not built—and no further lines would be promoted in the South Western area without

99

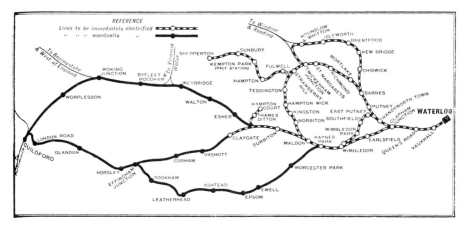

Suburban electrification scheme, showing extent of stages 1 and 2

Poster advising the public of the electric services and train headcodes

consulting that company. The two managers expressed a desire to effect a friendly alliance between their companies. The authorised LUT extensions to Kingston, Surbiton, New Malden and Wimbledon were completed in 1906–7, creating a tramway system paralleling many of the LSWR's inner suburban lines.

The London County Council (LCC) was slower in making the change to electric traction, and it was between 1906 and 1912 that its routes in the Vauxhall, Clapham Junction, Wandsworth and Putney areas were converted. The weakness of Hammersmith Bridge and environmental objections to overhead wires kept the electric tramcar out of Barnes, Kew and Richmond, but only to the benefit of the motor omnibus. From 1912 the General buses were operating in conjunction with the Underground railways. There was also the threat of tube extension into the Thames Valley.

The LSWR general meeting on 7 February 1913 was told that local traffic worth £100,000 a year had been lost and passenger numbers were falling by over a million each year. The first intimation of coming electrification had been made a year earlier when the company's new chairman, Hugh W. Drummond, admitted that 'the illness of Sir Charles Scotter and the pending retirement of Sir Charles Owens had prevented full attention being given to the question, but it was now to be taken seriously in hand.' As a defensive measure until electrification came to fruition, London area fares were reduced from 1 January 1914 at a cost of £38,500 per year.

THE ELECTRIFICATION PLAN

At the board meeting on 12 July 1912 the LSWR's new general manager, Herbert Walker, reported on electrification, and it was agreed that Sir Alexander Kennedy should act as planning consultant. The company's electrical engineer, Herbert Jones, was sent to the United States to study suburban electric railways in the New York area. Jones had joined the Waterloo & City from the City & South London Railway in 1898, and had been engineer-in-charge from 1900 until promoted to the new post of LSWR electrical engineer in 1912.

Jones' report was submitted to the board on 6 December 1912, together with comments by Herbert Walker. With speed and decision the board that day accepted the report and approved the largest electrification scheme which a British railway had yet undertaken. It was to be carried out in two stages. The first totalling 47 route and 150 track miles comprised the following lines:

1 Kingston Roundabout and East Putney

2 Hounslow Loop
3 Malden - Hampton Court
4 Strawberry Hill/Teddington - Shepperton

Work on this stage was to commence forthwith and on its completion the second stage would follow, covering the routes to the south of the main line, a further 50 route and 100 track miles, namely:

5 Hampton Court Junction - Woking - Guildford
6 Hampton Court Junction - Cobham - Guildford
7 Raynes Park - Epsom - Effingham Junction

Traction supply was to be at 600 volts DC third rail, generated in the company's own power house. Trains were to be formed of multiple-unit compartment stock with side doors. The estimated cost of stage one was £1,159,284 and of stage two £493,599. On stage one, higher annual charges of £172,252 would be offset by savings in locomotive expenses of £82,000 and increased revenue of £176,672 to provide an improvement in net earnings of £86,000 per year.

No Parliamentary authority was sought. The LSWR held that the powers granted by the London & Southampton Act of 1834 did not preclude the use of electric traction, while the Board of Trade felt unable to intervene. However, the fact that the LSWR had a Bill before Parliament in 1913 gave various interested parties the opportunity of obtaining protective clauses.

Although the Office of Works had been informed that the power station was to be situated between Earlsfield and Wimbledon, it secured clauses to prevent the erection of generating stations in the neighbourhood of Windsor Castle and the royal parks. More relevant was the concern of the National Physical Laboratory in Bushy Park over possible interference with its instruments by earth return currents. An agreement made on 30 June 1913 with the Commissioner of Works was attached to the Bill, by which the LSWR undertook not to cause electrical interference within the surrounding area. Despite insulating the return running rails around Teddington, allegations made in 1917 of disturbance to the magnetic field were proved when referred to arbitration; the company had to carry out additional insulation between Fulwell Junction and Hampton.

Kennedy & Donkin was appointed on 24 January 1913 to supervise the execution of stage one at a fee of £16,000, and to act as electrical consultant for an annual retainer of £500. Some changes were made to the original plan. The W&C generating station was not to be used as the Waterloo sub-station; instead, the tube line was to be supplied from the main power house via a sub-station on the surface. An officers' conference on 25 February 1914 decided to extend electrification from Hampton Court Junction to Claygate, which was part of stage two. The probable object was to reduce steam working within the electrified area and to provide a semi-fast service between Waterloo and Surbiton, but as this was not a convenient point for terminating trains, the short 1 mile 60 chain extension enabled the electric to steam transfer to be made clear of the main line at Claygate, where suburban development was already taking place. Consequently, the live rail was extended along the down through line from Marsh Lane signalbox (Berrylands) to Surbiton and on the up through from Hampton Court Junction. In practice, little use was made of these added facilities in LSWR days.

POWER SUPPLY

Electric power came from a 25,000kw generating station built on company-owned land at Durnsford Road, Wimbledon, alongside the main line and adjacent to the River Wandle for its water supply. Wagons of coal for the boilerhouse were propelled up a viaduct to the bunkers by the BoBo electric locomotive (No 74S), built for the W&C in 1899. Alongside stood two 230ft brick chimneys, while the 16 Babcock & Wilcox boilers provided steam for the five Dick, Kerr 5,000kw turbo-generators which produced the high tension supply at 11kv 25 cycles AC. In addition there were smaller generator sets for auxiliary power and lighting. Station operation was controlled by British Thomson Houston switchgear. Water supplies were normally drawn from the River Wandle, but outlet water could be passed through three 70ft cooling towers for re-use. J. Mowlem was the contractor for the foundations and Walter Jones & Co for the station's brick buildings.

The 11kv power supply was distributed through 77 miles of three-phase armoured cable to the nine sub-stations, which converted it to the 600volt DC traction current. These sub-stations were equipped with BTH transformers, rotary converters and switchgear. Those dealing with heavy traffic had 1,875kw converters: Waterloo (four), Clapham Junction and Twickenham (three each), Raynes Park and Barnes (two each). At Hampton Court Junction, Kingston, Sunbury and Isleworth two 1,250kw machines sufficed. The Waterloo sub-station also supplied the W&C line; it had available a spare motor generator and an emergency storage battery to enable the tube to be evacuated in the event of a power failure. With the exception of Clapham Junction, built on a restricted site at the end of platform 5, all the sub-stations were built in brick to a standard pattern. The rotary converters were shut down during the night, so the all-night service on the Kingston Roundabout remained steam-hauled.

From the sub-stations low tension cables fed the 150 miles of conductor rail, supported on ceramic insulators. Return current was via the running rails, both these and the conductor rails being bonded. The approaches to Waterloo were already track-circuited, and these had to be converted from DC to AC to protect them from the return traction current. The LSWR/MDR agreement of 4 December 1903 provided in principle for the supply of current to LSWR trains on the East Putney to Wimbledon line from the Underground group's power station at Lots Road. By an exchange of letters between Herbert Walker and Albert Stanley in November 1913, this current was supplied at Durnsford Road generating cost plus a small addition to cover Underground standing charges. It was necessary to bond the District negative rail to the running rails on this section to secure a common return with the LSWR system.

The 1912 cost estimate had been £587,500 for the power house, high tension supply and sub-stations, and £132,541 for track equipment. The costs reported at the end of 1916 were £609,594 and £193,436 respectively.

ROLLING STOCK

The electric services were to be operated by three-car multiple-unit trains, formed motor - trailer - motor, each unit weighing 94 tons and powered by two pairs of 275hp motors. The trains were to be capable of 52mph with rapid acceleration and braking characteristics being required. Collector shoes were mounted on each side of the motor bogies. Each pair of motors had it own set of switchgear, situated accessibly between the motorman's cab and the luggage compartment. The drum type controller, with its automatic 'deadman' cut-out, was designed to be simple to handle by non-technical drivers and could be used in multiple operation of up to four units. The stock was never shown to the Board of Trade inspecting officers, until in 1921 ASLEF complained of the presence in the motorman's cab of un-protected main controls and junction boxes at full voltage. Some changes were made, but Major G. L. Hall still found a number of objectionable features in the Southern Railway 1925 stock.

It had been the original intention to build new stock, but it was possible to save £56,000 by converting 63 of the wooden-framed four-coach bogie block sets used in the London area, which were less than ten years old, into 84 three-car electric sets. British Westing-

Electric train from
Waterloo to
Wimbledon via East
Putney, passing
Cromer Road signal
box in 1915. *Authors'
collection*

Female ticket
collectors at gates of
Windsor Line
platforms, Waterloo,
circa 1916. *National
Railway Museum*

house supplied the electrical equipment, and the conversion was carried out at Eastleigh Works. The bogie block sets accommodated all three classes, but the electric trains were to provide first and third class only, and because of the varying composition of the original vehicles, two main varieties of electric set appeared. Forty-two units were 157ft long with 120 third and 62 first class seats (some of these in a small saloon), while the remaining units were 2ft longer and provided 100 third and 72 first class seats (the latter split between the trailer and one of the motor coaches). The traditional LSWR salmon-and-brown livery was replaced by a plain sage green with yellow lining. The final cost of the trains at 1916 prices was £383,258.

Maintenance facilities were provided on the former gasworks site at Durnsford Road, comprising a six-track repair shop and an inspection shed with nine roads. It was decided in July 1915 to electrify some of the adjacent Wimbledon Park sidings and to erect a carriage cleaning shed, which came into use in March 1917. Berthing sidings were provided at Waterloo, Hounslow, Shepperton and Hampton Court, while there was a larger stabling facility at Strawberry Hill, which became a full electric depot after the steam shed closed in 1923.

ACHIEVEMENT

The main contracts had been placed during the summer and autumn of 1913; work had started at the power station site on 21 July 1913 and on the track at Teddington in October. Statements to the press anticipated that the East Putney and Kingston Roundabout lines would be in operation by the end of 1914, with the rest of stage one during 1915. By March 1914 30 miles of high tension cable and 25 miles of conductor rail had been laid. According to contract the first four electric units were due for completion in May 1914. The first arrived at Wimbledon in June, for trials on the East Putney line, where the necessary alterations had been made to the MDR negative return.

Reviewing the position in August 1914, construction work on the power house and sub-stations was going ahead rapidly. Conductor rails had been laid on most of the Kingston, Shepperton, Hampton Court and Hounslow lines, while cable laying and rail bonding was well advanced. However, the outbreak of war brought a financial crisis, and some of the electrification contracts were suspended until the end of October. Coupled with the increasing demands of the war effort on the engineering industry, this caused the programme to fall well behind schedule.

When the officers' conference surveyed the position on 15 July 1915, trackwork was nearly complete on the East Putney, Kingston, Shepperton and Hounslow lines, but HT cabling was still unfinished on the two latter routes: little progress had been made with the conversion of track circuits to AC between Waterloo and Barnes. Rolling stock delivery was satisfactory, with 39 units available and 25 drivers trained. The five sub-stations feeding the Kingston Roundabout were complete, but delays were affecting Durnsford Road power station, with only eight boilers installed and two main generating sets ready. It was hoped to start running the machinery before the end of July and the conference proposed to begin partial electric services via East Putney from 30 August and on the Kingston Roundabout from 12 September.

By October 1915 the Durnsford Road repair shops were nearly complete and building work at the power station was finished, but delivery of generating equipment was still slow and limited the introduction of the electric services. Eventually, after more postponements, three units began to operate an electric service between Waterloo and Wimbledon via East Putney on 25 October 1915. Conductor rails between Waterloo and Raynes Park were energised on 8 November and on the Kingston Roundabout a week later. Trial trips commenced on 21 November, with the hope of public service from 5 December. However, interference with Post Office telephone circuits caused a postponement until 30 January 1916 for the start of electric working on the Roundabout and to Shepperton. The Hounslow Loop was switched on from 15 February 1916, but public services had to be deferred from 27 February to 12 March. Traction current was extended to Hampton Court and Claygate on 12 June, but while electric trains to Hampton Court commenced on 18 June, arrangements at Claygate were not ready for their operation until 20 November 1916.

The final cost of electrification totalled £1,365,055, of which £1,186,963 was charged to capital. The increase of some £200,000 over the original estimate can be accounted for by the extension to Claygate, the Wimbledon cleaning sheds and the effects of wartime inflation. The locomotive committee resolved in January 1916 that the locomotive stock could be reduced from 946 to 890 as a result of electrification, but not until the war was over.

TRAIN SERVICES AND TRAFFIC

The electric trains operated according to Sir Herbert Walker's basic principle of frequent regular-interval services (summarised in Appendix 6). Journey times were reduced considerably; Waterloo to Wimbledon from 21 minutes to 16, Richmond from 34 minutes to 22 and Kingston from 35 minutes to 26. Train mileage increased 154 per cent from 26,428 to 67,151 miles per week. The 51 electric units in use replaced 36 steam locomotives, while the 153 coaches did the work of 362 steam-hauled vehicles. Destination boards on the trains were replaced by stencilled letter headcodes on the front of the units, which identified the different routes.

Two changes were made to the route pattern. The Hounslow Loop operated as a circular route and in consequence weekday Shepperton trains were transferred to run via Kingston. A few peak-hour services continued to run via Richmond and these were steam-worked until 30 April 1917. Hounslow also had some steam workings until 31 July 1916. Steam trains were retained between Waterloo and Guildford via Cobham during the rush hours, but during weekday off-peak periods alternate Claygate electrics connected with an hourly push-and-pull train to Guildford. Summer Sunday traffic to the riverside was catered for by extra trains from Kingston to Shepperton and by a half-hourly service on the Hounslow Loop. On the Windsor line the electric trains served the inner suburban stations, Vauxhall, Queen's Road and Wandsworth Town, by a skip-stop pattern.

Publicity for electrification was enterprising, with slogans such as 'Home and City quickest way by Electric,' posters featuring the headcode letters and interval departures, prominent signs outside stations and the showing in local cinemas of a film describing the conversion work and the new trains. There may have been teething troubles with the new equipment, as in March 1916 only 40 per cent of electric trains were on time and lateness averaged 6.13 minutes, but by the summer of 1917 services had settled down to 75 per cent punctuality and average delays of less than half a minute. Worsening wartime shortages of manpower, materials and fuel caused a reduction in electric services from 1 May 1918. Some mid-day trains were withdrawn, the East Putney service was limited to peak hours and late evening trains were halved, to save 6,482 train miles per week.

Passengers on the LSWR suburban services in 1913 had numbered 25,000,000 annually, falling to a low of 23,300,000 in 1915. Electrification produced a steady increase; 29,000,000 in 1916, 33,000,000 in 1917 (swollen by removals from districts affected by air raids to more secure places on the company's system), 40,376,000 in 1918, 47,885,000 in 1919 and reaching a peak of 52,587,000 in 1920. Overcrowding during rush hours became acute, with as many as 20 passengers packed into a compartment. From 1 June 1919 services were revised to concentrate resources on the most crowded sections: the

Claygate electrics were withdrawn, enabling the Kingston service to be increased, while the peak-hour trains via East Putney stopped only at East Putney and Clapham Junction, offering Wimbledon passengers an alternative to the crowded trains on the main line.

To provide more accommodation in the electric trains, the traffic committee on 29 May 1919 authorised the conversion of six bogie block sets into two-car trailer sets to be coupled between the three-car units during peak hours. Electrical equipment for ten sets was ordered from British Westinghouse in July 1919, but because of a strike in the foundry industry delivery of the ten converted sets did not take place until July 1920, when nine were rostered for work on the Kingston Roundabout. Eight more sets were ordered in May 1921 for the Hampton Court line, coming into use in June 1922, and finally six sets were authorised in October 1922 for the Shepperton service, which the SR introduced in July 1923.

The mileage figures reflect the service and stock changes. Initially, in 1917 3,990,049 train miles and 15,640,894 carriage miles were operated, but following the service reductions and the arrival of the first trailer sets, in 1920 3,652,949 train miles provided 17,307,241 carriage miles. (All-day services on the East Putney line had been restored on 16 November 1919, but at reduced frequency). Post-war punctuality was not good, with only half the trains on time and average lateness in June 1922 of 2.05 minutes. Shareholders were still complaining that year of delays and overcrowding.

The LSWR is open to criticism over electric stock policy. The three-car units had a large proportion of first class accommodation—with the 1914 fare reductions it was probably hoped that former second class passengers would transfer to first class after electrification abolished second. However, the success of electrification was based on winning back passengers from the egalitarian benches of LUT trams and General buses, while the social changes caused by the war made class distinctions less appropriate. The introduction of the two-car trailer sets, each providing 170 third class seats, was an ingenious method of adjusting the class division and of providing increased accommodation only where it was needed, without having to withdraw motor units for lengthening at a time of rolling stock shortage.

STAFF MATTERS

The establishment of the electrical department in 1915 was 287, including 90 motormen who were paid between 30s 0d [£1.50] and

45s 0d [£2.25] per week, according to length of service. Steam drivers retained their existing rates of pay on conversion, and footplatemen had the first opportunity for transfers to the motormen's grade. Some guards were trained to drive trains in an emergency and received an allowance of 1s 0d [5p] a week.

The introduction of the electric service was accompanied by widespread changes in other departments. Train operating staff was reduced from 218 to 141, despite the increased service, while the regularity and higher speed of the electrics enabled block posts at Norbiton and Chiswick to be abolished. Economies were made by replacing stationmasters with foremen at the quieter stations, such as Queen's Road and Southfields. On the other hand, increased passenger flow required more ticket collectors and improved barriers at busy stations like Surbiton and Wimbledon. Appropriately, electric lighting was installed at many stations, though the cost was sometimes reduced by shortening the platforms.

Seventy-eight cleaners (many of them women) were employed at Wimbledon Park and Durnsford Road depots, replacing staff at Kingston, Teddington and Twickenham. In its staffing estimates the company had not realised that the 150 per cent increase in suburban trains would require a proportionate effort by signalmen working the Sykes Lock & Block system. Following complaints of overwork, additional men were posted to the signal boxes between Waterloo, Malden and Barnes. There was one reduction in horsepower; the proximity of the live rail caused the retirement of the horse used at Surbiton to shunt in the up goods yard and nearby traders' premises.

EXTENSION PROSPECTS

Operating results from electrification had been good, and 1916 showed an immediate improvement of £30,000 in earnings. With the end of the war thoughts turned toward the completion of stage two of the 1912 scheme, but the pre-war cost of £493,599 was now estimated to be £1,300,000. Nevertheless, the LSWR board on 25 March 1920 authorised a start on the sections to Guildford via Cobham and via Epsom at a cost of around £750,000, three times the pre-war figure. Manufacturers and contractors were unwilling to guarantee prices or delivery dates, so on 24 June the board decided not to proceed with the work.

The LSWR chairman stated in March 1922 that capital expenditure on electrification would not be incurred until prices had fallen to 50 per cent above pre-war. However, in a letter written in February 1922

to Sir Philip Nash of the Ministry of Transport, Sir Herbert Walker
had outlined proposals for further electrification, once stage two was
completed. This would have covered another 67¼ route and 137½
track miles, from Hounslow and Whitton Junctions to Ascot, Staines
to Windsor, Virginia Water to Weybridge, Ascot to Ash Vale Junction, Woking Junction to Farnham and Aldershot Junction to Guildford. Electrification to Portsmouth was a more distant prospect.

Including the Waterloo and City line and those sections served only
by District and LNWR trains, the LSWR handed-over to the Southern Railway 61 miles 75 chains of route and 178 miles of track
(including sidings) equipped for electric traction. Authorised under
stage two were 45 miles 25 chains of route and 115 miles of track,
which were converted by the SR in 1925 and 1937.

CHAPTER 7

THE FIRST WORLD WAR

GOVERNMENT CONTROL OF THE RAILWAYS

In time of war the government was empowered by the Regulation of the Forces Act of 1871 to take control of the railways, and in 1912 the Railway Executive Committee was created to exercise these powers. Formed of the general managers of the principal railways, its ex-officio chairman was the President of the Board of Trade, but its meetings were invariably presided over by the acting chairman, initially Sir Frank Ree, general manager of the LNWR, with Herbert Walker of the LSWR as his deputy. The death of Sir Frank Ree in February 1914 led to Walker succeeding to the acting chairmanship from 28 April 1914.

With the outbreak of hostilities, the government took over the railways on 4 August 1914 and the Railway Executive Committee (REC) assumed its wartime role. Walker brought over from Waterloo his personal assistant, Gilbert S. Szlumper, to act as the REC secretary for the duration of the war. During the initial months the committee was in almost continuous session, but gradually routine matters were delegated and the full REC needed to meet only about once a week. For his work in ensuring the successful mobilisation and despatch of the expeditionary force to France, Herbert Walker was knighted in the 1915 New Year's honours. The LSWR having long ceased to name its locomotives, it fell to the LNWR to honour the REC chairman by christening a Claughton class 4-6-0 *Sir Herbert Walker KCB*

Under government control, the basic financial principle was the guarantee of the railways' 1913 net earnings, but the Treasury later made various concessions to the companies. For example, the cost of war bonuses was to be met by the government, interest at four per cent would be allowed on capital investment made since the end of 1912 and there would be compensation for abnormal wear and tear and for deferred renewals. Government control continued until 15 August 1921, when the new Railways Act was about to come into force.

THE FIRST WORLD WAR

MILITARY AND MUNITIONS MOVEMENTS

The LSWR had always been known as the military line and had accumulated much experience in handling troop movements. The first task at the outbreak of war was the mobilisation of reservists and the return of Territorial Army units from summer camps to their bases. Embarkation of the leading five divisions of the British Expeditionary Force (BEF) commenced on 10 August 1914: War Office sailing schedules from Southampton determined railway timings, and trains were booked to enter the docks at 12-minute intervals. To fit the times that the troops were due at the quayside, the LSWR specified either the departure from its own stations or the arrival from the GWR at Basingstoke or Salisbury. In turn the GWR would calculate timings over its system and thence back to the originating point. Between 10 and 31 August 670 trains ran to Southampton Docks, with the build-up continuing into September, when in one day, 100 trains arrived bringing a total of 31,192 men. There were some temporary reductions in normal train and steamer services between 5 and 24 August, but the despatch of the BEF was achieved with little disturbance and with excellent punctuality.

The flow of reinforcements overseas continued throughout the war, together with a movement in the opposite direction of Dominion and United States forces arriving in the UK. In October 1914 the landing of Canadian troops at Plymouth required 92 special trains to take them to their camps on Salisbury Plain. After the entry of the USA into the war in 1917 the LSWR handled 1,695 troop specials for their forces, conveying 868,577 men. On 10 July 1918 the arrival of an American troop convoy in the western ports brought 53 trains to the Winchester area within 24 hours.

The traditional military centres of Aldershot and Salisbury Plain were vastly expanded, with 176 camps established there and elsewhere on the LSWR system. Besides organised troop movements, these camps created considerable leave traffic at weekends and public holidays—Christmas 1914 saw the LSWR providing 237 special trains for 164,780 men. Despite efforts by the REC and the War Office to reduce journeys on leave, the troops were eager to spend their weekends among the pleasures of London. On Sunday evenings in 1916 Waterloo despatched four special trains to Bordon and to Liphook, two each to Bulford, Dinton and Shawford and one each to Tidworth, Eastleigh, Farnborough and Aldershot.

The resources of the LSWR were stretched to handle all this additional traffic. An observer at Swaythling in April 1915 noted within a few minutes two complete GER trains, a GWR 4-4-0 on an

LNWR train and L class 4-4-0 No 772 on a SECR special. The direct route from Aldershot to Southampton was via the steeply-graded Mid-Hants single line, and it seems that much use was made of an alternative route by going up to Frimley, reversing there and taking the west curve onto the main line at Sturt Lane Junction. Regular passenger services were consequently withdrawn between North Camp (Ash Vale Junction) and Frimley from the autumn of 1914 until 19 November 1916. The Amesbury and Military Camps light railway also caused problems. The line's steep gradients and its weight restrictions required almost all troop and many freight trains to be double-headed, although the Board of Trade eventually granted some relaxation on the classes of locomotive which could be used.

The heavy casualties suffered in the 1914–18 war involved the LSWR in running 10,332 ambulance trains carrying 1,848,623 wounded men. Of the 196 stations receiving patients, 40 were situated on the company's system; Southampton Docks was the base for fourteen ambulance trains. To sum up the military activity of four years of war: the LSWR ran 58,859 special troop trains conveying 20,223,954 men, 1,477,148 horses, 11,208 guns, 2,166 tanks and 114,278 vehicles.

The rapid expansion of the army required the construction of numerous camps; between January and July 1915 the LSWR conveyed 83,929 wagonloads of building materials to 14 of its stations. The cessation of timber imports led to a large increase in the use of home-grown woodland; timber traffic on the LSWR swelled from 11,025 tons in 1913 to 223,690 tons in 1917. The navy was still mainly dependent on coal, so that there was heavy traffic from South Wales to Southampton (283,353 tons) and to Gosport (213,224 tons). Between Salisbury and Eastleigh these 60 wagon coal trains were to be worked by the Drummond 4-6-0s of the 330 and 453 Classes.

Ammunition for the fleet was worked daily from the explosives factories on the lower Thames via Redhill and Guildford to Portsmouth, Portland and Devonport. Mail for the forces overseas was handled at Southampton, with special trains daily from Waterloo or Nine Elms; by 1918 Marylebone was being used to relieve Waterloo. In peacetime the LSWR did not deal with a large volume of freight, but the conflict brought onto its system traffic for military camps, aerodromes, storage depots, ammunition dumps and all kinds of factories engaged in the war effort. The change caused considerable congestion of freight traffic on the LSWR during early 1915 and passenger services had to be reduced. The situation improved through the gradual adoption of the common use of wagons, which

Adams 4–4–0 and six-wheeled stock on British Expeditionary Force troop train entering Southampton Docks. Note the detail variations of the two B4 0–4–0 Dock Tanks in the background. *Imperial War Museum*

Troops embarking for France from berth 42 Southampton Docks. The LSWR steamer *Lydia* is on the left next to Cold Storage Co building. *Imperial War Museum*

relieved the LSWR from having to send empties back to the owning companies.

MILITARY RAILWAYS

The extent of some of the military establishments served by the LSWR required their own internal railways. The first to be built was the Larkhill Military Railway on Salisbury Plain, which left the Amesbury–Bulford line at Ratfyn Junction, where a signalbox was opened on 22 October 1914. When completed, it ran for some nine miles via Durrington, Larkhill and Rollestone, serving camps and barracks, Army Service Corps depots, a military hospital and a balloon flying shed. Its course was parallel and to the north of the line authorised in 1898 and abandoned in 1901. In 1918 six goods trips per day were scheduled from Amesbury to the exchange sidings at Ratfyn Junction, where WD locomotives took over. Traffic soon declined with the return of peace, and Ratfyn Junction box was reduced to a ground frame on 6 November 1919. The military railway was finally closed in 1929.

During 1915 an Australian Army camp was built at Fovant, linked to the Salisbury–Exeter main line at Dinton by a military branch 2 miles 30 chains long, mostly on a 1 in 35 gradient. This was opened on 17 October 1915, worked by WD personnel and motive power, although during 1916–17 this was ex-LSWR Adams radial tank No 424. Regular military passenger services began in 1918, but the railway saw its peak of activity after the Armistice, when Fovant Camp became the demobilisation centre for South West England, handling 2,000 to 3,000 men per day, with three LSWR clerks manning the booking office at the camp station. Demobilisation ceased on 16 January 1920 and the branch was handed over on 26 April to the LSWR, which worked a twice-weekly freight train (limited to ten wagons) until the camp closed on 23 November 1920. The line was re-opened from 3 March 1921 until 23 August 1922 as a private WD siding for the disposal of roadstone.

The Brookwood to Bisley branch was extended by the army in 1917 to serve camps at Pirbright, Deepcut and Blackdown. The Officer Commanding, Longmoor, was in charge. It was agreed that from 1 March 1917 the Bisley branch should be brought under military operation, although the LSWR would continue to maintain it. The line as far as Deepcut was opened on 25 July 1917, and had the honour of conveying King George V and Queen Mary the following day, with regular military passenger services commencing on 1 August. Deepcut station was remarkable in being built by Canadian Army engineers in Rocky Mountain log cabin style. The line was completed to Blackdown in December 1917.

The War Office requested the LSWR to take over working the line from 8 August 1918. The WD locomotive—radial tank No 424 again—and the passenger stock of South Western origin, were to be retained by the LSWR, but wagon stock was returned to its owners. The military operating staff were to be transferred to the army reserve and engaged by the LSWR—this at a time when the army was scraping the barrel for manpower! Under LSWR operation, derailments at unsecured hand-worked points were reported on 19 and 22 October 1918. The Armistice was soon followed by the cessation of passenger services on 22 December 1918, but the line re-opened on 21 July 1919 with a thrice-weekly LSWR freight train as far as Deepcut, continuing to Blackdown when required. Closure of the WD extension line took place on 16 January 1922.

The Bovingdon Camp railway was planned late in the war to serve the depot of the newly-formed Tank Corps. It was opened on 9 August 1919, and extended 2 miles 15 chains from Wool station on the Weymouth line to the camp, climbing most of the way at 1 in 60. The line was used only for freight and the daily train was limited to 15 wagons, or four military tanks, plus brake van. Locomotives permitted on the branch were the O2 Class 0-4-4Ts, with a selection of Beattie and Adams veterans from the duplicate list. The branch was closed on 4 November 1928.

SIDINGS AND SUCHLIKE

World War 1 transformed life at many LSWR country stations. The establishment of military camps nearby would be accompanied by the arrival of wagonloads of building materials, followed by the coming and going of troop trains, while at weekends crowds of servicemen would throng the platforms, seeking relaxation in London or some other large town. To accommodate all this extra traffic, numerous stations were provided with additional sidings, loading docks and roadways, sometimes even with larger passenger facilities.

It is possible to mention only some of the more important works. At Farnborough a connection was made to the Royal Aircraft Factory light railway, built by Royal Engineers from Longmoor. Aviation also brought sidings at Ascot West for the Royal Flying Corps, and west of Feltham station for the Aeroplane Acceptance Park. This had its naval equivalent at Hamble, whose construction drew in 300 workmen daily from Southampton to Netley by special train; on completion a siding served the airfield.

The Portsmouth area contained many military and naval establishments and among the facilities they required were extensive new sidings at Fratton, which the SR purchased in 1923. On the Netley line the Ministry of Munitions requested the provision of a halt near Bursledon brickworks. Named Crow Park Halt, its two platforms came into use on 20 June and 27 July 1918 respectively; the inspecting officer observed that they were built of planks laid on empty ammunition boxes filled with clay. The halt's use was probably brief, as it never appeared in the working timetable. Another ammunition depot was served by the brickworks siding between Oxshott and Cobham on the New Guildford line.

Along the Bournemouth main line there was a succession of wartime developments. At Micheldever additional sidings built for the War Department were used after the war to relieve Eastleigh yard, and were purchased by the LSWR in 1922. Eastleigh itself was given three miles of sidings in a new down marshalling yard, also bought by the LSWR in 1922 for £11,000. Just north of Winchester a platform and siding were built by US Army engineers in November 1918 to serve their large camp on Winnall Down.

Beyond Southampton, extra sidings were laid at Millbrook in 1917, also included in the LSWR's post-war purchases. Timber traffic from the New Forest required new sidings at Lyndhurst Road, Woodfidley and Brockenhurst, which also gained a siding for military hospital movements.

West of Bournemouth were other important works. The construction and operation of the Gardiner Shipbuilding & Engineering Co yard brought workmen's trains back to the old Hamworthy branch from 22 June 1918, when Lake Halt opened 73 chains from Hamworthy Junction. The 500ft long platform was served by a daily train from Christchurch until 4 October 1920.

Between Hamworthy Junction and Wareham the Admiralty started to erect the Royal Navy Cordite Factory in March 1915, and Holton signalbox was provided on 10 May 1915 to control its sidings. A halt with a platform on the up line only was built for construction workers, being served initially by some of the last duties of the Drummond motor tanks and trailers. Further west a permanent station, Holton Heath, was opened on 3 April 1916. Day shift workers were brought from Christchurch, Bournemouth West and Poole each morning by three special trains, formed mainly of vintage six-wheel stock. The factory continued operating after the war; Holton Heath station gained public status on 14 July 1924.

At Wareham sidings were constructed on the up side of the station in 1915 to serve an ordnance depot, while in 1918 a connection was provided on the down side into Worgret Camp, controlled by a small signalbox situated 550 yd east of Worgret Junction. Both sidings were removed soon after Grouping.

To serve a Royal Naval airship station, Woodsford siding between Moreton and Dorchester was built in May 1918; a nearby halt at Woodsford Crossing with two 500ft platforms had an unadvertised weekday stop for workmen from 3 May 1919 until 20 September 1926.

The intense military activity on Salisbury Plain required increased rail facilities. Congestion on the MSWJR line was to be relieved by a new connection to the LSWR main line at Red Post Junction west of Andover, although not opened until 5 January 1919. The building of the airfield at Boscombe Down in 1918 was supplied via a branch from the Amesbury & Military Camps light railway, controlled by a new Boscombe Down signalbox between Allington and Amesbury. Additional sidings were provided at Amesbury in 1914, and on the Bulford extension at Bulford station, Bulford Camp and Sling Camp in 1915. On the main line, the Experimental Trench Warfare Establishment was set up on Porton Down in 1916, linked to Porton station by a WD 2ft 0in gauge light railway, on which 300 to 400 workmen rode daily to and from the camp.

In the West Country, sidings holding 180 wagons were built at Yeoford Junction to relieve Exeter of pitwood traffic, some of which originated from a new siding between Halwill and Ashwater, constructed for the Monmouthshire and South Wales colliery owners. On the Torrington line, a siding was added near Barnstaple Junction in 1918 for the shipyard of the British Construction Co. Another siding was provided in 1915 at Bideford for the explosives firm of Kynoch Ltd. which had also built a wood distillate plant at Longparish on the Hurstbourne to Fullerton Junction line.

ROLLING STOCK AND MUNITIONS—THE LSWR CONTRIBUTION

At the outbreak of World War 1 the railways were called upon to provide ambulance trains for service within the United Kingdom to supplement the handful of WD ambulance coaches based at Netley which sufficed for peacetime needs. The LSWR supplied a nine-coach train in November 1914 and a ten-coach train a year later. These were converted from gangwayed vans and former emigrant coaches, and fitted with dual brakes, gas and electric lighting.

It also became necessary for the British army to provide stock for its ambulance trains in France. In December 1917 the LSWR formed Overseas Ambulance Train No 35 of thirteen corridor vehicles, accommodating 380 casualties. The LSWR bought this train back from the WD in December 1920 and re-converted it for passenger service. The arrival of the American Army on the Western Front required more ambulance trains, and the LSWR converted Train No 62 for their use. This was formed of fourteen 56ft corridor coaches and two vans, holding 418 stretcher cases or 680 troops if walking wounded were aboard. The vehicles were sold to the War Office in 1917 for £22,233, despatched to France by the Southampton train ferry in May 1918, and re-purchased by the LSWR in July 1919 for £12,800.

A variety of other vehicles was disposed of for military use; in 1918 twenty-five vans were fitted with end doors to convey aeroplane fuselages around the country. Military traffic on the French railways required 50 former banana vans in 1915 to carry the armies' meat rations, 40 old passenger brake vans in 1918 for use as goods brakes, and 20 others were converted in 1917 into mobile workshops. Some old passenger stock was sold to the Admiralty for use in workmen's trains at Invergordon and Bedenham.

No sooner had the locomotive committee congratulated itself that electrification had saved 56 locomotives than the War Office demanded 50 of the Adams 395 class 0-6-0s for service overseas. Thirty-six of them went to Palestine, nine to Mesopotamia and five to Salonica; none ever returned to Britain. There were also sales and loans of locomotives within the UK. The Adams radial tanks surplus from electrification were available; four were loaned to the Highland Railway in 1918 and two to the MSWJR, while two were sold to the WD. Advantage was taken of the Ministry of Munitions' and the Admiralty's need for small shunting engines to dispose of nine of the feeble Drummond 2-2-0T and 0-4-0T motor tanks.

With the loss of 50 of its limited stock of 0-6-0s the LSWR needed to borrow similar locomotives from other companies; five C Class from the SECR in 1916, three Midland Class 2s and seven Great Northern J4s during 1917–20.

At the end of 1916 the government demanded that the railways supply 200 miles of permanent way material to strengthen the lines of communication in France. The South Western share was 12 miles, which was met by lifting the Basingstoke & Alton line, as described in Chapter 4.

As a modern well equipped engineering works, Eastleigh played its part in munitions production. Within its normal field the works built fifty 20-ton covered wagons for use in France; less familiar was the construction of narrow gauge railway track for the armies' lines behind the front. Under general engineering products came fittings for gun carriages, parts for shells, stretchers, army general service wagons and bodies for lorries.

TRAIN SERVICES

After the restrictions imposed during the mobilisation period in August 1914 it was business as usual for a time. The winter timetable of 1 October 1914 brought the customary seasonal reductions, plus the withdrawal of the Bournemouth two-hour expresses. The freight traffic congestion of early 1915 may have been responsible for a drastic reduction of Sunday services in the London area from 28 February 1915, and some were never restored. The main difference between 1915 and a peacetime summer was the absence of the various duplications of the 11.00am Waterloo–West of England service: in fact the 11.00am continued to run to its pre-war schedule until the last year of the war. As the war intensified in 1916, the attempt to maintain normal timings led to punctuality reaching its nadir in December, with only 29 per cent of trains on time and average lateness of 12 minutes.

Further service reductions and decelerations which took place from 1 January 1917 helped to improve performance by the remaining trains. The Portsmouth line suffered worst from these cuts—of the not over-generous pre-war fast service only one semi-fast survived in 1918, other services calling at all stations beyond Guildford. The five principal trains to the West of England continued to run, although connections to North Devon and North Cornwall were curtailed in May 1918. On the Bournemouth line the five daytime through trains from Waterloo, plus the two mail trains, provided an adequate though slow service. Cuts made on 1 May 1918 to save coal included the Sunday services on many branch lines, and the withdrawal of the service from the Havant-Cosham direct line.

The best journey times from Waterloo to the principal LSWR destinations during the 1914–18 war are included in Appendix 5.

The need to reduce unnecessary haulage at last persuaded the company to abolish second class from 22 July 1918, thereby saving 33,252 carriage miles per week. The LSWR did not go as far as some other companies in withdrawing restaurant cars, and it was still possible in 1918 to eat on twelve of its West of England and Bournemouth trains.

Many of the more powerful locomotives were being used on military and freight traffic. Some West of England trains were double-headed between Salisbury and Exeter by older 4-4-0s, while the decelerated Portsmouth services could be handled by the small Drummond mixed-traffic 4-4-0s. Soon after their introduction, the massive Urie H15 Class 4-6-0s in September 1914 were saving 1,115 freight train miles per week and two locomotive duties, while the fuel shortage of 1918 found them working combined trains of 65 wagons between Nine Elms and Salisbury.

INCIDENTS AND ACCIDENTS

In November 1914 a notice appeared in LSWR trains 'In view of possible attacks by hostile aircraft it is necessary that blinds in the carriages of all railway trains should be kept down after daylight.' Guards of up trains were instructed to extinguish corridor and van lights at Woking or Guildford. At Waterloo normal lighting was replaced by low-power lamps during air raids, while the arches under the station were used as shelters by many local inhabitants.

In fact, the LSWR suffered little damage from enemy air attacks. On 13 October 1915 a Zeppelin airship dropped a bomb between the tunnels at Guildford doing minor damage to track and signalling, but not interrupting traffic. Two bombs were dropped by German aircraft at Waterloo on 29 September 1917. One fell on the North sidings, doing £175 damage to twelve coaches and nine wagons. The other landed on the Down Main line near 'A' box, breaking windows and causing enough harm to the permanent way to interrupt traffic for 16 hours. Kew Bridge station building and the adjacent main road bridge were damaged by a cluster of bombs on 29 January 1918, and the 10.52pm Waterloo-Hounslow electric ran into debris washed onto the line by broken water mains.

Vulnerable points on the railway were guarded by troops, and railwaymen were warned to answer promptly challenges by sentries. On 13 October 1914 a GWR light engine collided with a trolley taking food to troops guarding Fox Hills tunnel between North Camp and Pirbright Junction. Guard duty on the busy approaches to Waterloo could be as dangerous as the trenches; two private soldiers of the Hampshire Regiment were killed at Loco Junction and West London Junction in October 1915.

Another tragedy, which was probably caused by unfamiliarity with conditions on British railways, occurred on 24 September 1917. A contingent of New Zealand troops had arrived at Plymouth Millbay docks and had boarded a special train for Bulford. The men had been told that a meal would be provided at the first stop, and when the train

Urie H15 Class 4–6–0 No 486 passing Raynes Park during indicating trials in 1914 – note conductor rails laid on local lines. *Courtesy G. Gundry*

Bisley to Blackdown military railway; the station for Deepcut camp built by the Canadian army. *Commercial postcard, courtesy G. Gundry*

halted for signals at Bere Ferrers, many of them jumped out and ten were run down and killed by the 2.12pm Exeter-Plymouth.

In spite of the increased volume of traffic being handled by a depleted staff with reduced lighting at night, the LSWR had few major accidents attributable to war conditions. The worst was at Wilton on 7 August 1915. The goods yard which could accommodate 242 wagons had 239 on hand, and shunting could only be carried out by using the down line between trains. During one of these shunts three wagons became detached and were not noticed by the shunter or the signalman, who cleared his signals for the 8.50am from Waterloo, which collided with the wagons at nearly 50mph; fortunately only five passengers were injured. Colonel Druitt, the inspecting officer, recommended the provision of track circuits at Wilton, but the capacity problem had also to be relieved by additional sidings.

Troop trains were often formed of an assemblage of passenger coaches, horse boxes, cattle wagons and carriage trucks, sometimes numbering 30 or more vehicles. On two occasions in 1915 such empty trains returning from Southampton Docks to the Aldershot area via the Mid-Hants line, having stopped at Medstead & Four Marks to detach the pilot engine (often a Drummond C8 Class 4-4-0), the unbraked tail rolled back and became derailed at the catch points. The remedy was to take the pilot through to Alton.

An insight into the heavy freight traffic being handled and its effect on key junctions such as Woking is given by reports to the traffic officers' conference. On 2 February 1916 an incident concerned a convoy of seven locomotives running light from Woking to Guildford shed, while at 9.00am on 23 September 1916 there was a collision between two freight trains waiting on the Up Local line to enter the yard, one of which had left Dorchester 12 hours earlier.

MEN, MONEY AND MEMORIALS

The LSWR pre-war staff totalled 24,170, of whom 6,621 men (27.3 per cent) joined the Colours and 585 lost their lives. For service on the railways and docks in France, the company in 1917 raised No 6 Platelaying Company of the Railway Operating Division from among its own permanent way employees. Women took the place of men, not only in offices and at ticket barriers, but cleaning locomotives and carriages (the ladies of Durnsford Road enjoyed much publicity), and even carting heavy loads in good depots. Beside losing men, the company saw 260 of its London carthorses requisitioned by the army at the outbreak of war.

The war soon brought a rise in prices; from February 1915 compensatory pay increases began to be made through the institution of War Bonuses. At first confined to the lower-paid conciliation staff, the system spread to all weekly-paid and most clerical grades. Even senior officers received salary increases to match the growing inflation. From 1 August 1917 the War Bonus was re-styled as the War Wage and counted for the calculation of overtime rates. By the end of the war, even the lowest paid men were receiving 33s 0d [£1.65] per week above their basic wage.

There was a month's strike in October and November 1917 by craftsmen at Eastleigh works and at many locomotive depots, because pay rates in the LSWR workshops had not kept pace with wages paid in munition factories at Southampton and elsewhere. The dispute went to arbitration, and a twelve per cent increase was awarded in April 1918. There was often dissatisfaction at the increments made to the War Wage and there was a partial locomen's strike in September 1918 over a 5s 0d [25p] increase. This was ended by a legal injunction prohibiting strike pay and by the threat to withdraw the men's exemption from call-up.

The LSWR played its part in patriotic activities by investing its surplus funds in War Loan and by promoting the cultivation of food crops. Money was given towards prizes and lectures for its six thousand allotment holders, while seed potatoes were sold to them at cost price. Potato crops were consequently grown in such unfertile surroundings as the old locomotive works site in Nine Elms yard.

Staff instructions for the European war were contained in a substantial booklet outlining procedures for such matters as the documents needed for travel to France, the return home of recruits' civilian clothing after enlistment, what to do about Belgian refugees who had lost their luggage, the free conveyance of gift parcels to the forces, and the use of brake vans for servicemen escorting army horses or dangerous goods.

Beside the company's official war memorial in the Victory Arch at Waterloo, there was a desire by some of the staff to commemorate their own comrades who had given their lives. Among these local memorials that at Strawberry Hill depot should be mentioned. The depot had a fine war record, 142 men had joined the forces and 19 had been killed. The roll of honour unveiled on Armistice Day 1921 was flanked by a soldier and a sailor, a Urie G16 hump shunting tank and a bull-nose electric unit, reflecting the depot's mixed traction status.

At the first post-war general meeting on 21 February 1919 the LSWR chairman told proprietors that 'by your holding in this company you did your bit and helped to win the war.' Shareholders' rewards were patriotic rather than pecuniary.

CHAPTER EIGHT

POST-WAR AND GROUPING

LABOUR TROUBLES

The pre-war master and servant relationship on the LSWR had now given way to government interference and trade union militancy. Under its powers of control the government granted the eight-hour day to railwaymen from 1 February 1919, meeting a demand long made by the unions, but involving the companies in employing 76,000 extra staff. Sir Herbert Walker remained unreconciled, speaking in 1921 he described this as 'perhaps the most wicked thing that had been perpetuated on a community.'

Introduced in haste, there were disputes over the operation of the eight-hour day. The question of meal breaks brought Underground motormen out on strike, and they were joined by some LSWR footplate staff and motormen on 6 and 7 February 1919. The militant reputation of locomen in the South Western's London area was also shown by a three-day strike in August 1919 as a mark of sympathy with London policemen dismissed after their strike.

These disputes were only a prelude to a more serious clash between government and unions. By 1919 the accumulated War Wage for the lower grades of the uniform staff considerably exceeded their basic rates of pay. Government proposals to end the War Wage system and to double pre-war wages would have penalised these men. With the failure of negotiations, the NUR called an official strike from 27 September 1919; settlement was reached on 5 October with the government conceding the continuance of existing pay rates until the cost of living fell.

The majority of LSWR staff joined the strike, but 1,182 trains were run during its nine days by the efforts of non-strikers, management and volunteers. A regular half-hourly service of electric trains to Hampton Court, Kingston and Barnes was soon organised, with some connecting steam trains to the Leatherhead and Guildford lines. A chain of 14 control sections was established between Waterloo and Southampton in lieu of normal block signalling—that at Woking was guarded by army barbed wire and machine guns. A skeleton service of one or two trains daily was operated on all main lines, while trains ran on many branches. Efforts were made to keep milk and perishable foodstuffs moving into London (Sunday was devoted to this traffic) and the government loaned the company twenty military lorries for this purpose. Navy volunteers helped out at Nine Elms locomotive depot.

The post-war higher rates of pay and the shorter working hours combined to increase the LSWR's wage bill from £2,065,000 in 1913 to £6,265,000 in 1921, while staff numbers rose from 24,091 to 31,247.

Labour unrest was not confined to the railways; the coal industry had a brief strike in November 1920 followed by a bitter three months' struggle between April and June 1921. There were reductions of train services during both disputes. The 1921 strike brought drastic cuts, with the few remaining main line trains stopping at all stations. Even the electric services had their hours of operation curtailed. Some improvement took place from June with the use of imported coal and the conversion of three 4-6-0s and four 4-4-0s to oil-burning.

FELTHAM MARSHALLING YARD

The LSWR's freight operation in the London area was unsatisfactory. Traffic, mostly coal, from the LNWR at Willesden Junction, the MR at Brent, the GCR at Neasden and the GNR via the Widened Lines could not be combined due to the lack of a suitable marshalling yard. The company's own London traffic to and from Nine Elms formed another separate flow. There was a small shunting yard at Brentford which had been enlarged in 1906, but this was incapable of further expansion. In 1913 this received daily all six freight trains off the GNR and a similar number of trip workings from Willesden Junction, Brent and Neasden. In turn Brentford despatched services to Eastleigh, Reading, Woking and Richmond.

The main movement of transfer freight traffic was direct from the northern companies' yards to LSWR destinations. In effect, primary marshalling for the LSWR was done on other companies' premises, and the South Western maintained a staff of shunters at Brent to handle its traffic. In consequence services were duplicated—Woking had through trains from Brent, Willesden and Neasden, and the yard would then have to undertake the secondary sorting of these wagons. Even a branch like Shepperton had separate departures for Nine Elms and for Willesden.

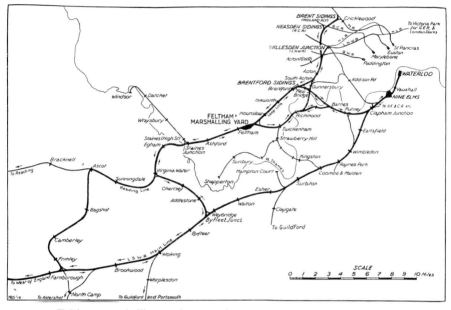

Feltham marshalling yard approach routes

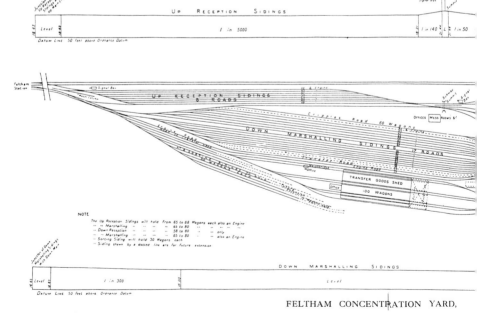

FELTHAM CONCENTRATION YARD,

Feltham marshalling yard plan 1922

The search for a marshalling yard site started in 1900, when 30 acres of land at Sheerwater (near Byfleet) were considered, but this site would have been too far from the exchange points with the other companies. Next, some 17½ acres of land at Feltham Junction were offered to the LSWR in 1901, but a price could not be agreed. Eventually on 28 April 1910 negotiations commenced for the purchase of 41½ acres to the south of the Windsor Line between Feltham Junction and Feltham station. Agreement was reached in July and the purchase was confirmed by the LSWR Act of 18 August 1911; additional land was acquired in 1915–16.

LSWR officers visited a large number of marshalling yards before deciding on the layout at Feltham, but no construction started. On 30 March 1916 plans for the yard were approved, and authorisation was given to start preparing the site; this involved the diversion or culverting of three watercourses and the excavation and removal of 120,000cu yd of material. The bridge at the west end of the site (now Harlington Road) had to be lengthened to a 70ft span. Orders were given on 22 February 1917 for the construction forthwith of eight sidings to relieve congestion at Brent; all work was done by company staff with the doubtful assistance of 200 German prisoners of war.

On 9 December 1917 these sidings were opened. Marshalling of

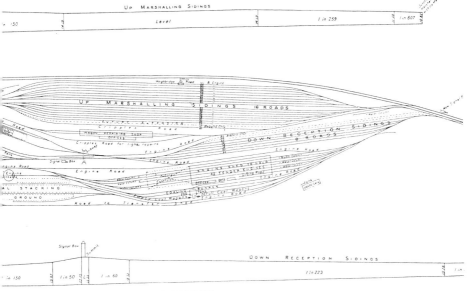

LONDON & SOUTH WESTERN RAILWAY.

LSWR traffic at Brent ceased, and its staff there were transferred to Feltham. The eight sidings, 1,162ft to 1,636ft long, handled down traffic. The March 1919 working timetable listed twelve daily arrivals from Brent, nine departures and two trains calling en route. Authority was given on 25 July 1918 for nine more sidings and a shunting neck, which was the first stage in the construction of the 16 down sorting sidings which came into use from 3 October 1920. These sidings held 1,138 wagons; with 23 arrivals and 19 departures, Feltham yard now handled all down traffic. On 1 May 1921 six down reception sidings were opened at the east end of the yard. These were 1,056 ft to 1,211ft long and were linked to the existing down marshalling yard over Feltham's first hump, worked temporarily by ground frames until the electric hump cabin came into use on 2 April 1922. The down marshalling yard now consisted of 17 double-ended sidings, 1,435ft to 1,639ft long.

Until now the only up traffic handled by the yard had been some local trips to Windsor Line stations, but from May 1921 it became possible to despatch nine trains daily to Willesden. The final stage in construction was the completion of the up yard, which came into full use on 2 October 1921. This comprised the eight reception roads of the 1917 yard, now 1,288ft to 1,477ft long, leading via the up hump to 12 (later 14) marshalling sidings 1,331ft to 1,662ft in length. New signalboxes at Feltham Junction and Feltham East controlled respectively the eastern and western access to the yard. The floodlit humps were each provided with an electrically-operated cabin. It was claimed that a 70-wagon train could be sorted in 12 minutes. As well as the main hump yards there were eight flat secondary sorting sidings at the west end of the yard. Altogether, there were some 30 miles of track within the yard. Upon completion Feltham Yard was handling 2,500 wagons per day, brought in by 50 down and 26 up arrivals, then despatched by 18 down and 46 up departures.

Facilities within the yard included office buildings, cattle pens and a wagon repair shop. However, locomotives were still based at Strawberry Hill, including the four 4-8-0Ts Urie had designed for hump shunting and the five 4-6-2Ts for local transfer workings (these replaced ROD 2-8-0s on loan to the LSWR since 1919). Plans for a locomotive depot at Feltham were approved in November 1921, and this was ready in March 1923.

It was realised that large numbers of staff would need to live near the yard, and originally 11 acres of land were acquired in 1918 near Hounslow Junction for housing. Instead, in January 1922 land was obtained off Bedfont Lane for the staff village of 80 houses and 48 flats, costing £77,830 to build. Work did not start until late 1922, so completion of the estate was left to the SR, which named its principal thoroughfare Southern Avenue. The whole area has now been re-developed. The estimated cost of Feltham yard was £250,000, but the actual cost, including locomotive depot and housing exceeded £550,000, which was provided out of the company's existing financial resources without any increase of capital.

TOTTON, HYTHE AND FAWLEY LIGHT RAILWAY

The idea of a railway along the west bank of Southampton Water had originally been promoted by the Swindon, Marlborough & Andover Railway, which obtained an Act on 10 August 1882. LSWR co-operation did not extend to providing capital, nor could the SMAR raise funds for construction on its own.

The project was revived by local interests in 1898 for a light railway under the 1896 Act to run from Totton to Stone Point, where a pier would have been only a short crossing away from the Isle of Wight. Unable to finance the work themselves the promoters approached the LSWR in 1902, and after a visit by the general manager and other officers the South Western board decided on 26 October 1902 to apply for a Light Railway Order. At the hearing before the Light Railway Commissioners on 27 March 1903, opposition from local landowners caused the line to be shortened from 10 miles 68 chains to 8 miles 53 chains, now terminating near Fawley, and the Order for this was confirmed on 10 November 1903. No start was made, and the LSWR directors decided on 3 May 1906 to take no action to prevent the powers lapsing in November.

Perhaps as a recompense to local inhabitants, the LSWR inaugurated on 13 August 1906 a thrice-daily omnibus service between Totton and Hythe, operated by a Thornycroft 24hp motor bus. The service was not successful and was withdrawn from 14 November 1908.

The light railway proposal was raised again in 1921 with the backing of the Agwi Petroleum Co (an associate of the Atlantic Gulf Oil Corporation) and local landowners. The Agwi company planned to erect a small oil refinery at Fawley and expected to despatch by rail 150,000 tons of petroleum products per annum. Sir Joseph Davies, MP, chairman of Agwi, was also chairman of the light railway company, with the two principal landowners as fellow directors. Of the £120,000 equity capital and £80,000 debentures, the LSWR was to take up £20,000 of preference stock and all the debentures. It was to have a seat on the board, have power to lease or purchase the line, to construct, maintain and operate it.

The proposed light railway, 9 miles 1 chain in length, followed the 1903 route for four miles, then diverged to the east; its estimated cost was £252,327. At the enquiry on 11 May 1921 the scheme was supported by the Admiralty and Air Ministry, the Light Railway Order being confirmed on 21 December 1921.

It was soon realised that a 58 chain extension at Totton to Eling Crossing would save a separate signalbox at the junction with the main line, while a 1 mile 48 chain deviation near Hythe would save £15,000 on earthworks and bring the line nearer the village. The light railway company in August 1922 sought an amending Order for these changes, also to transfer its powers to the LSWR. The deviation at Hythe brought the line between the shore and Longdown House, the residence of Sir Robert Hobart, and protracted negotiations followed in an effort to preserve his view without incurring additional construction costs. Thus it was the Southern Railway which obtained an Order on 27 February 1923 for the transfer of powers and for the altered route. Construction by Sir Robert McAlpine & Sons Ltd of the 9 mile 31 chain single line (costing £219,000) was completed for inspection by Major Hall on 8 July 1925, with public opening on 20 July.

NORTH DEVON & CORNWALL JUNCTION LIGHT RAILWAY

An abortive scheme for a Torrington and Okehampton railway had finally been abandoned in 1907. In its place came a proposal for a light railway from Torrington to Halwill, to link North Devon with the LSWR's North Cornwall line and to serve the clay pits around Meeth en route. In November 1909 application was made for a Light Railway Order for a 19 mile 70 chain line, of which some 5½ miles would be a reconstruction of the 3ft 0in gauge Torrington to Marland mineral line. The key figure behind the scheme was Colonel H. F. Stephens as engineer and agent, with financial support from the neighbourhood, the City and the local authorities. Share capital was £140,000 and the cost of the line was estimated at £133,053.

The working agreement offered by the LSWR to Colonel Stephens on 25 June 1913 was based on its taking 60 per cent of the gross receipts and guaranteeing four per cent interest on the debentures and 4½ per cent on the preference stock. The Light Railway Order was not confirmed by the Board of Trade until 28 August 1914, when war prevented work starting.

The post-war coalition government wanted to encourage light railways in rural areas. A joint inter-departmental development committee in 1919–20 carried out a survey of the Torrington-Halwill scheme, ranking it second in priority among projects under consideration for a Treasury grant. Construction costs were now estimated at between £220,000 and £327,000, while the LSWR felt that it would need to have all the receipts to cover its operating costs.

The Ministry of Transport applied to the Treasury in June 1920 for a grant, but no decision was made until February 1921; by then financial stringency compelled its refusal. The end of the post-war boom also meant rising unemployment, even in Devon. The Ministry of Transport sought the support of the Ministry of Labour for its renewed application to the Treasury in October 1921, pointing out that the construction of the line would employ 1,250 men for eighteen months, also that half of the building cost of £235,000 would be spent on wages.

Formal agreement was reached on 7 April 1922. The Treasury was to provide £125,000, half of the capital, split between ordinary shares and debentures. The balance was to come from the local authorities, and by payments to landowners, contractors and the Meeth Clay Co in shares rather than cash. The LSWR was to work the line for 75 per cent of receipts and guarantee five per cent on the debentures. Both the LSWR and the Treasury were to have a director on the light railway board.

Unskilled labour for construction was to be supplied through the Ministry of Labour from the unemployed in the dockyard towns of the Plymouth area, and Colonel Stephens was to erect hutments for their accommodation. In the event, these men proved to be a very unsatisfactory labour force. The main construction contract was awarded to P. W. Anderson Ltd for £197,000 and the first sod was cut ceremonially on 30 June 1922. The completed 20 mile 40 chain single line was inspected by Major Hall on 10 and 11 July 1925. Operation by the SR commenced on 27 July 1925.

ABSORPTION AND AMALGAMATION

Following the end of the war, the Ministry of Transport was created in 1919 to re-organise the transport industry, with the option of nationalising the railways. In 1920 the ministry issued a White Paper on the Future of the Railways, which included such novel suggestions as worker directors and the co-option of managers to sit on railway boards. The Railway Companies Association, concerned at these proposals and at details of the scheme for grouping the railways, appointed in July 1920 a committee of seven general managers to negotiate with the ministry. Sir Herbert Walker was chosen as the spokesman to present the companies' case, in view of 'his intimate knowledge of the matter.' The LSWR board relieved Sir Herbert of routine managerial duties to enable him to concentrate on these negotiations.

Most of the controversial features were absent from the draft Bill placed before Parliament in 1921; there was general agreement that the railways in the South of England should form a Southern Group, and the LSWR board accepted this on 28 April 1921. The constituent companies of the Southern Railway would be the LSWR, LBSCR, SER, LCDR and the SECR Managing Committee. The minor and leased lines within the area would be absorbed by one of the constituent companies, the LSWR being responsible for the Plymouth Devonport & South Western Junction, Plymouth & Dartmoor, North Cornwall, Sidmouth, Bridgwater, Isle of Wight, Isle of Wight Central, Freshwater Yarmouth & Newport and Lee-on-the-Solent railways.

Pending completion of purchase, the LSWR arranged to pay its leased and worked companies a fixed annual rent in lieu of the customary percentage of receipts. Negotiations continued throughout most of 1921 and 1922 and terms were agreed with the majority of companies. Usually their shareholders were offered exchange into similar categories of LSWR stock, but fortunes of these companies varied and all that holders of £100 of IWCR ordinary stock received was £3 in cash.

Agreement could not be reached with two companies in the LSWR sector; the FYN was in the hands of its joint receivers and managers, Sir Sam Fay, General Manager of the GCR, and F. G. Aman, promoter of the Solent Tunnel scheme. The FYN refused to accept the LSWR's terms on the grounds that they did not take into account its potential earnings if the tunnel were built; the dispute went to the Railway Amalgamation Tribunal which fixed terms on 30 July 1923 for the company's belated absorption by the SR. The Lee-on-the-Solent was an impecunious concern (see Chapter 4). The LSWR and subsequently the SR were reluctant to take-over its £14,600 liabilities without any equivalent asset, but after taking the case to the High Court, the SR had to comply with the Amalgamation Tribunal ruling made on 31 July 1923 and absorb the company, debts and all.

Terms were agreed with the minor companies for compensation to be paid for loss of office and, for example, the name of W. T. Foxlee appears again, to be paid £1,800 as former engineer to the PD&SWJ.

The Lynton & Barnstaple Railway was not included in the Railways Act, but as it was starting to lose money its chairman asked the LSWR in November 1921 to purchase the line. The terms agreed on 23 June 1922 required the LSWR to pay £20,000 in cash and to cancel its holding of £20,000 first debentures (acquired in October 1905) to make up the £39,267 purchase price. It was necessary to await the SR Act of 31 July 1923 to obtain Parliamentary powers, the purchase becoming effective from 1 July.

As soon as the Railways Act had become law on 19 August 1921 the constituent companies began to negotiate their terms of amalgamation, with Cosmo Bonsor, chairman of the SECR managing committee, taking the lead in preparing draft schemes. In reply, the LSWR board on 15 December 1921 set out five points for agreement. Four of these were designed to ensure that government compensation money should be spent either on arrears of maintenance or should go into the funds of the amalgamated company, and not be paid out as increased dividends. The fifth point required that no electrification work involving large expenditure should be undertaken by any company without the consent of the others; this point was not acceptable to the LBSCR and SECR.

Cosmo Bonsor submitted on 30 May 1922 a draft on amalgamation procedure. A joint executive committee of twelve was to be set up, consisting of the chairman and three directors from each company, which would report back to the parent boards on questions of SR board and managerial appointments and compensation for loss of office. The committee would carry out joint decisions until the new SR board took over on 1 January 1923. The LSWR agreed with this procedure, except that it felt that the appointment of a general manager could not be carried out at the present time, and it again reiterated its opposition to schemes involving large capital expenditure being undertaken without joint approval. The LSWR conformed to this by submitting to its partners its proposals to build the floating dock at Southampton and to acquire and construct the Totton, Hythe & Fawley light railway.

The joint committee held its first meeting on 12 June and decided on 30 June to create a new committee of 21 directors—which would be a provisional SR board—on this the LSWR had eight seats. This first met on 26 July 1922, evidently accompanied by some dissent, as the LSWR challenged the accuracy of the minutes prepared by the LBSCR.

September saw the accountants reporting on the fusion of stocks. The capital structure was to be based in principle on 1913's gross earnings for each company, adjusted for current interest charges and for capital expenditure since 1913. To meet SECR wishes, the proposed capital of the new company was increased from £141,223,565 to

£144,846,797. Of this total the LSWR share was £52,740,374 or 36.41 per cent. The total capital of the pre-amalgamation companies was £152,500,000; their 55 classes of stock had been reduced to ten. In general terms, debenture and fixed interest stocks were exchanged to give the same annual income. Preferred and deferred ordinary shares were converted into similar SR stock, based on standard revenue expected to be earned by the grouped company. Undivided ordinary shares were converted into holdings of SR preferred and deferred stock equal to the original price.

The LSWR board approved the amalgamation scheme on 2 November 1922, and this was ratified by a special meeting of the proprietors on 17 November. The amalgamation and absorption schemes were examined by the Railway Amalgamation Tribunal at hearings on 11 and 12 December, and its approval was sealed on 23 December.

The joint committee decided on 5 December 1922 to continue the company boards temporarily as sectional committees, whose decisions would be confirmed by the SR main board. Only the finance and stores committees would be set up on an all-line basis. The South Western sectional committee was formed into two groups of four directors, each responsible for certain matters.

The Southern Railway board of 21 members included eight directors from the LSWR (of its board of twelve, two retired at Grouping and there were two vacancies). Being the largest constituent company, the LSWR chairman, Brigadier General Sir Hugh Drummond, assumed that office in the new company. Because of the lack of agreement on the future management of the company, the SR board on 4 January 1923 appointed the three existing general managers as joint general managers, and it was only a year later that Sir Herbert Walker obtained sole control of the Southern. The LSWR solicitor, W. Bishop, was appointed to the corresponding position on the SR. The LBSCR provided the secretary, J. J. Brewer; on his sudden death in April 1923 he was succeeded by Godfrey Knight of the LSWR. The remaining officers were not appointed until 7 June.

ELECTRICAL PROBLEMS—LBSCR

The difficulties between the LSWR and the LBSCR were primarily financial. The Brighton company had electrified some of its suburban lines on the 6,700 volt AC system in 1909–12 at a cost of £1 million and had commenced in 1913 a £2 million scheme to convert the rest of the network. Reliance on German equipment had brought work to a standstill soon after the outbreak of war. Due to inflation, the finance which had been raised before the war was no longer sufficient to cover the cost of completion. The Electrification of Railways Advisory Committee had agreed in 1920 to the work going ahead, although the AC system was not one of its recommended standards. Pending Grouping the railway capital market was depressed, and the LBSCR could not raise ordinary stock to finance its electrification. Instead, it decided in November 1921 to obtain Parliamentary powers for the issue of £1.5 million of debenture stock without any corresponding equity capital. Interest on this would have become a prior charge on the earnings of the Southern group. Opposition came first from City institutions representing Brighton preference and debenture stock-holders, but also from the LSWR. On 27 January 1922 Brigadier Drummond wrote to the LBSCR chairman, Charles C. Macrae, 'the exercise of such powers as are sought to be obtained by the Bill appeared to the board of the LSWR to be so prejudicial to the interests of the constituent companies of the Southern group when they become amalgamated that the question of opposing the Bill would have to be considered by that company.' The LSWR again emphasised that the constituent companies of the SR group should be in complete accord on electrification systems before substantial outlay was incurred.

The LBSCR therefore withdrew the offending clause from its Bill. The question of completing its suburban electrification was referred to the committee of experts already appointed by the Ministry of Transport to consider the system to be adopted for the SECR electrification. This committee ruled in March 1922 that the LBSCR could use £330,000 of existing authorised but un-issued debentures, which would produce some £300,000 cash—enough to complete electrification from Balham to Coulsdon and Wallington, on which considerable work had already been done.

The LBSCR still hoped to carry out the complete scheme, and even to make a start on main line electrification, so in April 1922 it applied to the Trade Facilities Advisory Committee for a Treasury guaranteed £5 million loan. However, a month later the Brighton withdrew its application, fearing that the LSWR might challenge the expenditure before the Railway Amalgamation Tribunal on the grounds of 'the doubtful prospective value to the Southern group of an unfructified capital commitment.' Brigadier Drummond told the Parliamentary Secretary to the Ministry of Transport on 23 June that the LSWR had no objection to the £300,000 scheme, but anything larger should be subject to agreement by the joint boards. Formal approval to the Coulsdon/Wallington electrification was given by the LSWR on 26 June 1922, the scheme eventually being completed by the SR in 1925.

ELECTRICAL PROBLEMS—SECR

The differences between the LSWR and the SECR were technical. The SECR Act of 1903 authorising electrification included restrictive clauses for the protection of Greenwich Observatory from electrical interference. The SECR electrical engineer, Alfred Raworth, had therefore devised in 1919 a unique 3,000 volt three-wire system employing two protected conductor rails at 1,500 volts positive and 1,500 volts negative respectively, which would neutralise any earth leakage, also having the economic advantage of needing only one sub-station at Lewisham to feed the entire inner suburban area. The Electrification of Railways Advisory Committee said in June 1921 that it did not recommend the system on technical grounds, unless there was financial advantage.

The encouragement given by the Ministry of Transport to the railways in 1921 to reduce unemployment through capital projects financed by government guaranteed loans, led the SECR to bring forward its electrification scheme. Its realisation would have saddled the Southern group with three incompatible systems of electrification. During the winter of 1921–2 meetings between the three companies were held but no agreement on electrical systems could be reached. Eventually, at a meeting on 18 January 1922 at the House of Commons between the chairman and A. Neal, Parliamentary Secretary to the Ministry of Transport, it was decided to appoint a committee of the three companies' consulting electrical engineers, under the chairmanship of Sir Philip Nash from the ministry. The LSWR's arrangement with Kennedy & Donkin had ceased at the end of 1919 and Sir Alexander Kennedy was now acting for the SECR, so Theodore Stevens was the LSWR consultant—the great AC protagonist, Sir Philip Dawson, represented the LBSCR.

The LSWR had emphasised to its partners the disadvantages to the new company of having three systems of electrification, but many people felt that there was no likelihood of interchange between LSWR and SECR. Here Sir Herbert Walker revealed to Sir Philip Nash on 14 February that now the LSWR suburban lines had been electrified and Waterloo rebuilt, the company was aware of the inadequacy of the Waterloo & City line and was thinking of building a full-size tube to take its electric trains into the City. Grouping now presented the opportunity to make this a loop, relieving the SECR termini in the City and joining the South Eastern main line near London Bridge, but for this a uniform electrical system would be essential. The underground project was serious enough for the London Electric Railway to have to leave room for it when extending the Hampstead tube to Kennington in 1923.

When Sir Philip Nash suggested that two different types of electric train should run over the LSWR, Sir Herbert said 'that the idea cannot be tolerated for two minutes.' Nevertheless the LSWR had proposed that the SECR inner suburban trains should operate at 600 volts DC and main line trains at 11,000 volts AC, which would have been the eventual voltage on the LBSCR. The two consultants, Kennedy and Stevens, had submitted irreconcilable cost estimates for the rival systems to the committee, which reported on 9 March 1922. It declared its inability to find a common system for the SR, and by a majority of three to one decided that the 3,000 volt three-wire electrification had peculiar advantages for the SECR. Stevens was the dissentient and issued his own minority report, setting out the disadvantages of such an untried system and minimising the additional cost of using 600 volt DC third rail traction.

There was a further meeting of the chairmen at the House of Commons on 16 March 1922. This was followed by a letter from Brigadier Drummond to Cosmo Bonsor on 23 March saying that the LSWR board did not contest the SECR right to proceed with its electrification scheme, but again repeated its objections on technical and economic grounds. The SECR was unable to make a start, as it had first to obtain the approval of the Trade Facilities Advisory Committee for the £6.5 million Treasury guaranteed loan it needed. Included in the project was the construction of its own power station at Angerstein Wharf, for which permission had to be given by the Electricity Commissioners, who were now reluctant to sanction privately-owned generating plant. The LSWR, as owner of its own station at Durnsford Road, supported the SECR in this application.

During this delay the LSWR's acquiescence turned again to hostility, and after meeting Drummond in June Ministry of Transport officials declared that the company was now determined to block the SECR scheme. In reply to a suggestion that the decision be referred to a meeting of the provisional SR board in October, the SECR told the LSWR on 9 August 1922 that 'if the decision of the Electricity Commissioners was in favour of the SECR scheme there can be no discussion at the October meeting as work will then have commenced.'

However, the Electricity Commissioners on 21 August refused consent for the SECR power station, and after some abortive negotiations between the railway and the supply companies they confirmed this decision on 27 September. The LBSCR had not supported the SECR's power station proposal and had hitherto been neutral in its attitude to the traction system, but by August certain members of its board were expressing opposition to the SECR scheme. The SECR now concluded a supply agreement with the London Electric Supply Corporation, and on 11 October told the LSWR that electrification work would commence as soon as this had been sealed.

With the question still open it could be raised at the October meeting of the provisional board, and the LBSCR reminded the SECR of the resolution of the joint executive committee on 12 June 1922, that no scheme involving large capital expenditure should be entered upon without the approval of the other companies. It was therefore decided to invite an American consultant, George Gibbs of New York, to advise and report. Meanwhile the SECR, which had now secured its finance for the scheme, would not conclude any contracts.

The Gibbs report was issued on 18 November 1922 and it pleased the LSWR by recommending 750 volts DC third rail for the SECR inner suburban area, and the LBSCR by favouring AC for any coastal extensions, while any expansion of the South Western system should be at 750 volts rather than 600 volts. On 21 November the provisional board adopted these recommendations by a majority vote. One of the first acts of the SR board on 1 February 1923, was to substitute the LSWR's 600 volts for the 750 volts system as the figure to be used for the South Eastern electrification.

To revert to Greenwich Observatory, Drummond tried to assure the Admiralty that there was no danger of serious interference from DC third rail. However, the First Lord, L. S. Amery, writing to the Prime Minister on 4 December 1922, had been briefed by the Astronomer Royal and other experts about the trouble at the National Physical Laboratory, and said that the third rail system would be fatal to the magnetic work of the observatory. The Southern Railway therefore had to pay the £34,000 needed to transfer the instruments to the country.

CHAPTER NINE

DOCKS AND MARINE

SOUTHAMPTON DOCKS

The railway had left the development of the port of Southampton in the hands of the independent Southampton Dock Company, which fell into increasing financial difficulties. The construction of the Empress Dock, opened on 26 July 1890, was only made possible by a £250,000 loan from the LSWR. It was apparent that the improvement and enlargement of the docks could only be carried out by a company with the South Western's financial resources. Purchase by the LSWR for £1,360,000 was agreed in December 1891 and was confirmed by its Act of 27 June 1892, becoming effective from 1 November 1892.

The first task was the rehabilitation of the existing docks (on which £81,868 had been spent by 1898), to be followed by the purchase of the mudlands between the rivers Itchen and Test as the site for extension. 3 August 1895 had seen the opening by His Royal Highness of the 745ft long Prince of Wales Graving Dock (No 5), then the largest in the world. Completion of building work on the new quays was marked on 12 October 1898 by the placing of the coping stone, with full Masonic rites.

It remained to equip the new quays with sheds, cranes, railway tracks and roadways, which was completed by 1902. The new facilities comprised the Itchen Quay, 1,642ft long with 28ft minimum depth of water, the short 425ft South Quay and the 2,227ft Test Quay, both with 32ft of water. Meanwhile, the old 1,756ft long Extension Quay of 1875 was widened to 50ft and dredged to 20ft to 32ft in depth. A coal barge dock on the River Itchen was completed in 1898–9 and land was acquired on the opposite bank at Woolston for future expansion.

The Test Quay was selected in 1898 as the site for a cold store intended to match arrivals of frozen meat to the market, with accompanying lairage and abbatoirs for the import of live cattle. A Southampton Cold Store & Lairage Co was formed to share the estimated £80,000 cost with the LSWR and to operate the storage. Planning was inadequate and construction costs escalated to a total of £272,113; the cold storage company was unable to raise the additional funds, leaving the railway to bear the cost of completion. A new International Cold Storage & Ice Co was formed in 1902 with LSWR financial support, but business was slow to develop. The LSWR only secured a return on its investment when the War Office used the store for victualling the armies overseas during the 1914–18 war.

During the Boer War the docks handled most of the military traffic to South Africa, totalling some 528,000 men and 28,000 horses. Invaluable were the 42 per cent increase in the length of quays and of 74 per cent in the area of dockside sheds achieved under LSWR ownership. In January 1902, T. M. Williams (the GCR harbourmaster at Grimsby) was appointed as docks and steam packet superintendent, being given managerial status in July 1909. The docks mechanical engineering department was brought under the locomotive superintendent, Dugald Drummond, with consequent redundancies in 1902–3. The dock company's varied stud of locomotives had been replaced by a uniform fleet of Adams B4 0-4-0Ts, which were allowed the distinction of names associated with France and the Channel Islands. Major construction projects were planned by the consulting engineer, W. R. Galbraith, and his staff. Execution was the responsibility of W. T. Foxlee, the new works engineer, but from 1903 reverted to the chief engineer and his resident engineer, F. E. Wentworth-Sheilds, who later became docks engineer for both LSWR and SR.

The need for more dry dock accommodation was felt in 1899, and with the growing size of ships the plans for the new dock were enlarged; the Admiralty also had to be consulted as Royal Navy vessels were sometimes docked at Southampton. In January 1900 J. Aird was given the contract for No 6 graving dock to be built on the western edge of the dock estate. The completion period was 27 months and the estimated cost £229,000. This entailed the excavation of 266,200cu yd of material to provide a dock 875ft long by 90ft wide and 33ft deep. Formal opening took place on 21 October 1905, the centenary of the great naval victory, so the new dock was appropriately named the Trafalgar Graving Dock.

The prospect of the Prince of Wales Graving Dock had brought the Inman Line (later the American Line) to Southampton in the 1890s. Now the existence of the Trafalgar Dock, as well as the possibility of gaining continental business, made the White Star line transfer its New York express service from Liverpool in June 1907. The 25,000-ton *Adriatic*, one of four vessels employed, arrived on 30 May 1907 to inaugurate the service. A number of improvements to quays

Aerial view of Southampton Docks in the 1920s, showing the floating dock installed in 1924 and the lengthening of the Trafalgar Dock to accommodate the *Berengaria*. *Commercial postcard, authors' collection*

The White Star Dock, Southampton, nearing completion in 1910–11. Union Castle liner *Carisbrook Castle* is at berth 46. *Southampton City Museum*

and buildings were made quickly to meet White Star requirements, while their shipbuilders, Harland & Wolff, erected repair workshops near the Trafalgar Dock.

This major increase in the port's traffic required a corresponding enlargement of dock accommodation. A new 16-acre wet dock was planned in the space between the Empress Dock and the Trafalgar Dock. On 9 October 1907 the tender of Topham, Jones & Railton for £492,231 was accepted for completion in 40 months. A thousand men and 85 machines were employed, and by early 1911 the dock was sufficiently complete to be used for laying-up ships during the winter. At the request of the White Star Line the dock was to be known as the White Star Dock, though available to other companies. The dock saw the first sailing of the new White Star liner *Olympic* on 14 June 1911 and of her ill-fated sister *Titanic* on 11 April 1912. The dock was 1,600ft long, 400ft wide, with a minimum 40ft depth of water, and it could accommodate five large ocean liners. Its 3,807ft of quays were provided with four large cargo and passenger sheds. Altogether the dock had cost nearly £750,000.

When it was known in 1908 that White Star was constructing the 46,000-ton *Olympic* and *Titanic*, which would exceed the capacity of the Trafalgar Dry Dock, the LSWR sought a site for an even larger graving dock. Lacking room within the existing dock area, it turned to the left bank of the Itchen below Woolston, which offered a virgin site with easy navigational access. The company's 1909 Bill included powers for a dock 1,000ft by 115ft, linked by rail to the Netley line by a 1 mile 55 chain branch. Once again this would have been the largest dry dock in the world and would have cost some £480,000. Despite opposition from Southampton Corporation and the Harbour Board the Bill was passed on 16 August 1909. After lengthy negotiations with the Chamberlayne Trustees the price for the land was fixed by arbitration in 1911.

However, the LSWR had now found that the Trafalgar Dock could be enlarged at a fraction of the cost of a new one, but the Woolston site should be retained for future use, and plans for its development were prepared in 1912. The site suffered from poor rail access, as a long detour would be necessary to reach the existing docks. During the 1914–18 war the Ministry of Munitions acquired part of the site for a steel rolling mill, and construction of the rail link was then considered. The LSWR renewed the powers of the 1909 Act in 1913 then annually until 1922, while the SR listed the project as being in abeyance.

The docks committee decided instead on 21 October 1909 to enlarge the Trafalgar Dock at an estimated cost of £185,000. Topham,

Jones & Railton again received the contract in May 1910 for completion within 500 days. The contractor took-over on 17 October 1910 and after excavating 30,000cu ft of material, the enlarged dock, now 897ft long and 100ft wide, was ready to accept the *St Louis* on 4 April 1913. The *Olympic* was able to use its facilities on 16 July 1913, while preparations were being made to accommodate the Hamburg Amerika Line's *Imperator*. However, she was not to enter the dock until 27 April 1922, when as the Cunard Line's *Berengaria* she squeezed in with 15in to spare. For her next visit in October a further 15ft had been cut away from the end of the dock to follow the shape of her bow.

The deep water approaches to the port were the responsibility of the Southampton Harbour Board. The LSWR had made loans and grants to enable it to dredge the channel to the 35ft depth needed for the new giant liners. Dissatisfaction with the performance of this body led to the formation of a new statutory board of 26 members representing shipping interests, official bodies (including the LSWR with three seats) and, a sign of the times, organised labour.

A strike in June 1911 won an increase from 6d [2¹/₂p] to 6¹/₂d per hour for casual workers and from 26s 0d [£1.30] to 27s 0d [£1.35] for weekly-paid men. A year later dockers who went on unofficial strike in sympathy with Thames men found their jobs quickly filled. 'The port had a bad reputation for labour disputes, the company had a small profit margin on cross-channel services and could not continue if costs rose.' These remarks were made, not by a ferry operator of the 1980s, but by Herbert Walker in April 1913.

During the 20 years of LSWR ownership the length of quays had increased from 12,054ft to 23,250ft, shed area from 554,718sq ft to 1,064,916sq ft and the mileage of railway tracks from 15 to 37. There were fast liners twice a week to New York by the American and White Star lines, while Cunard sailed weekly to Canada from the Itchen Quay. Union Castle had a regular Saturday mail steamer to the Cape from the Test Quay, as well as intermediate sailings serving both coasts of Africa. Royal Mail departed weekly from the Empress Dock to Brazil and the River Plate. From berth 50, tenders went out to meet the Atlantic services of Hamburg-Amerika and Norddeutscher Lloyd in the Solent, including the largest ships in the world, *Imperator* and *Vaterland*. Beside these liner services there were many other passenger and cargo sailings from Southampton to all parts of the world.

All the railway lines leading into the docks crossed Canute Road on the level, and as it was intending to lay additional tracks, the LSWR in 1901 opposed Southampton Corporation's electrification of the horse tramway along this road to the Floating Bridge. The electric tramcars were therefore diverted at Town & Docks station to go over Central

Bridge. In exchange for this concession the LSWR replaced at its own expense the level crossing at Dukes Road, St Denys, by a bridge. On 21 May 1914 an additional line from the Town station into the docks was approved—significantly, the War Office was to meet half the £2,645 cost.

This work was completed only in December 1914, so the bottleneck was still a hindrance to the despatch of the British Expeditionary Force in August 1914. Canute Road was barred to road traffic from August 1914 until July 1919, while it was 1917 before a pedestrian footbridge was erected. The closure had a drastic effect on takings at the South Western Hotel and other licensed premises nearby owned by the LSWR, and the company successfully claimed compensation from the government for loss of rent. The docks had been requisitioned as No 1 Military Embarkation Port, leaving the old Outer and Inner Docks for LSWR use.

The initial movement of the expeditionary force to France in August 1914 involved 118,454 men, 37,649 horses, 314 guns and 5,221 vehicles. This was only the beginning of a steady flow of men and material through Southampton to the fighting fronts, and of Dominion and US forces arriving in Britain. This reached its peak in 1918 with 2,207,084 men and 5,702 ships using the port. From August 1914 to December 1918 the docks handled 7,136,797 men, 822,160 horses, 13,403 guns, 153,810 vehicles and 3,381,274 tons of stores, all carried in 15,661 ships; sometimes as many as 30 ships sailed in one night.

Casualties in the 1914–18 war were heavy. The first reached Southampton on 24 August 1914, and the port received all those wounded in France during 1914 until Dover Marine was available in January 1915 to share the burden. The arrival of the hospital ship *Aquitania* from the Dardanelles in 1915 brought over 5,000 sick and wounded, enough to fill 20 ambulance trains. The heaviest traffic was during the bloody battle of the Somme in July 1916, with 68,492 casualties and 391 trains, no fewer than 6,174 men arriving on 7 July. The transfer sheds and the holding sidings for eight ambulance trains were provided with steam heating, and it was possible to complete disembarkation within 45 minutes. Altogether during the four years of war the port handled 1,234,248 casualties and despatched 7,822 ambulance trains.

A major wartime development was the inauguration of the train ferry to Dieppe on 13 November 1917, joined from 6 November 1918 by a Canadian vessel on a crossing to Cherbourg. The ferries had a capacity of 54 wagons each. Making three crossings per week, they conveyed to France a total of eight locomotives, 42 coaches and 6,763 wagons. The ferry berth was west of the Royal Pier, and was connected by a light railway alongside the West Shore Road to the main line on the down side of Southampton West station. There were seven sidings near the West station, two loops halfway, 20 marshalling and holding sidings near the ferry, as well as a connection to a barge berth near the Town Quay. War Department locomotives and personnel operated this line.

As the government gradually relinquished its use of the docks during 1919, negotiations were concluded with the Cunard Line for the transfer from Liverpool of its New York express service. The *Aquitania* sailed from Southampton in June 1919, but the first regular crossing was the arrival of the *Imperator* on 21 December 1919. Canadian Pacific also commenced using the port from 4 November. The name White Star Dock became inappropriate following growing use by other companies, and with White Star agreement the docks committee on 23 February 1922 chose the new title of Ocean Dock.

The White Star Line had been awarded as reparations the former German liner *Bismarck* of 56,000 tons, to be renamed *Majestic*. However, this vessel was too large for the Trafalgar Dock, and after considering the purchase of a government surplus floating dock the LSWR decided in 1922 to build a new floating dock able to take ships of up to 60,000 tons. A contract was placed in October 1922 with Armstrong Whitworth for a dock 960ft long, 134ft wide and 38ft deep, to cost some £375,000 for delivery in ten months. The dock was to be moored between the dock estate and the Town Quay; excavation of the site required the removal of 940,000cu yd of earth. The total cost of the project came to around £700,000, but any deficit on its operation was to be made up by the Cunard, White Star and Royal Mail lines. Powers for the dock were confirmed in the Southern Railway Act of 31 July 1923. It was opened officially by the Prince of Wales on 27 June 1924.

Additional wet dock accommodation was required, as sometimes the Ocean Dock was fully occupied by five of the largest liners in the world. The Woolston site was discarded in favour of the western mudlands, which offered ample room for expansion. In 1900 a private company had launched a Bill to reclaim the area. Southampton Corporation proposed in 1903 to find work for the unemployed on this task, but the LSWR declined to supply chalk for the filling. Spoil from the construction of the White Star Dock was dumped along the West Shore by means of a temporary railway, while the building of the train ferry installations in 1917 added to the reclamation.

G. S. Szlumper, the new docks and marine manager who had succeeded T. M. Williams in December 1920, outlined in May 1922

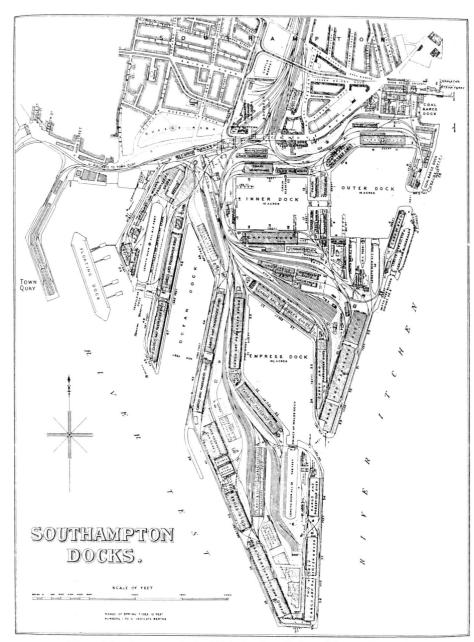

Plan of Southampton docks 1924 after installation of floating dock

the company's proposals for extension. 648 acres of mudland were to be reclaimed behind a two-mile bank enclosing 460 acres of land for development. Five 1,000ft by 300ft jetties would project from the wall, with two graving docks situated at the eastern end. Behind the quay and the dock warehouses would be a public park, a business district and housing estates. Rail access would be via a triangular junction with the main line between Millbrook and Redbridge. These plans differed in many respects from those authorised by the SR in 1924 and carried to completion during the ensuing decade.

Thirty years of LSWR ownership from 1892 to 1922 had seen Southampton Docks' annual traffic increase from 2,649 ships to 5,111, their gross tonnage from 2,369,698 to 21,524,606, cargo tonnage from 421,600 to 742,834 and passengers from 122,000 to 356,110, emphasising its position as the premier passenger port. As to finance, capital expenditure during the expansion period 1900 to 1913 had been at the rate of £166,653 per year, with the cumulative total reaching £5,216,875 at 31 December 1913. With the publication of accounts for railway ancillary activities, the docks net earnings for 1912 and 1913 of £110,145 and £122,525 respectively represented only 2.15 and 2.35 per cent on the capital then employed. In the difficult post-war conditions of 1922 the profit was only £69,741, giving a mere 1.34 per cent return. Southampton Docks were a better investment for the nation than for the LSWR shareholders.

CROSS-CHANNEL STEAMSHIP SERVICES

The close of the old century had been overshadowed by the tragic loss of the LSWR's ship *Stella* on 30 March 1899. She had sailed from Southampton at 11.20am on a Maundy Thursday extra service to the Channel Islands with 42 crew and about 140 passengers. Captain Reeks pressed on into thickening mist at the ship's full speed of 18 knots, relying on dead reckoning to tell him when he would be near the Casquets rocks. Suddenly the foghorn on the Casquets lighthouse was heard at close quarters, but avoiding action was too late to prevent the ship being ripped open on the concealed reefs—within eight minutes the *Stella* had gone down.

Five boats hurriedly launched were only partly filled and the large port lifeboat overturned as the ship sank, only eight of the 14 people who had been clinging to it surviving the night in the waterlogged boat. The other lifeboats were picked up the following morning by the LSWR's *Vera* and the GWR's *Lynx* on the overnight passage to the Channel Islands. Eighty-nine passengers and 23 crew were saved, but

CHERBOURG

11

For West Normandy.

Fast Steamers between Southampton & Cherbourg

FOR

VALOGNES, CARENTAN, BAYEUX, CAEN, ARROMANCHES, COUTANCES, AVRANCHES, ST. LO, &c.,

AS UNDER:—

SOUTHAMPTON TO CHERBOURG. Every TUESDAY, THURSDAY and SATURDAY, at 11.15 p.m. Boat Train leaves LONDON (Waterloo Station) at 8.15 p.m., but Passengers may travel by any previous Train.	**CHERBOURG TO SOUTHAMPTON.** Every MONDAY, WEDNESDAY and FRIDAY, at 11.0 p.m. (or as soon after as Tide and circumstances permit).

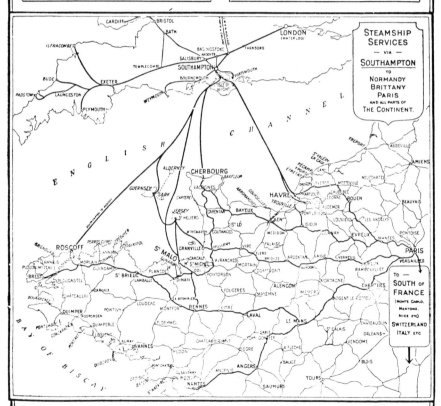

STEAMSHIP
SERVICES
— VIA —
SOUTHAMPTON
TO
NORMANDY
BRITTANY
PARIS
AND ALL PARTS OF
THE CONTINENT.

To —
SOUTH OF
FRANCE
(MONTE CARLO,
MENTONE,
NICE ETC)
SWITZERLAND
ITALY ETC

DIRECT CARGO SERVICES BETWEEN—

SOUTHAMPTON & ROSCOFF

AND

SOUTHAMPTON & HONFLEUR.

among the 19 crew and some 50 or more passengers who had been lost was Mrs Mary Rogers, one of the stewardesses, whose sacrifice in giving her lifejacket to a woman passenger is commemorated by a memorial on Southampton's Western Esplanade.

The LSWR made a grant of £3,000 to the dependents of the crew who had been drowned and its staff contributed generously to the relief fund. However, the board took action in the courts to limit the company's liability for damages to the statutory maximum of £15 per ton, which would total £15,885, but a provision of £25,000 was made in the accounts for compensation claims of £112,021, despite those from railway staff travelling on free passes not being accepted.

The Board of Trade enquiry blamed Captain Reeks for excessive speed in the weather conditions, also for not checking the log and making soundings as he approached the danger area. Press comment and counsels' questions accused the rival companies on the Channel Islands route of racing, but this was stubbornly denied by the LSWR witnesses. The enquiry recommended that to remove this possibility, simultaneous arrivals in the islands (as on 30 March) should not be scheduled.

This tragedy hastened to a conclusion negotiations between the LSWR and GWR which had been in progress for over a year. An agreement was reached between the two general managers in August 1899 and was sealed on 20 December. For a 15-year period from 1 October 1899 Channel Islands traffic receipts were to be pooled (after deduction for expenses) on the proportions earned by each company in 1897 and 1898, while return tickets were to be made interavailable. During the winter each company was to sail on alternate nights from either Southampton or Weymouth and return during the following day. Between May and September the LSWR would increase its service to run every night (except Sunday), while the GWR would provide a daylight service from Weymouth every weekday.

No time was lost in replacing the *Stella*. A tender from the Clyde-bank Engineering & Shipbuilding Co (later John Brown & Co) was accepted on 2 August 1899. The new vessel was named *Alberta*, and arrived at Southampton on 28 May 1900 to enter service on 1 June.

Two old steamers were disposed of during 1900. *Alliance* of 1855, a relic of the former South Western Steam Packet Company, was sold to breakers for £1,550 in February, followed in October by the remaining paddle steamer *Brittany*. Built in 1864, she had been used for the LSWR board's annual cruise round the Isle of Wight. A newer vessel sold in June 1901 was the *Dora* of 1889, stated not to meet the company's requirements, and with a reputation for rolling badly. She was purchased by the Isle of Man Steam Packet Company for £12,000.

The Channel Islands service employed three vessels during the summer months—*Alberta*, the newest ship in the fleet, *Lydia* and *Frederica*, which were extensively modernised in 1904–5 with more private cabins and larger dining saloons. The 104 nautical mile crossing to Guernsey took about six hours, Jersey being reached 2½ hours later. A traveller leaving Waterloo at 9.45pm arrived at St Helier at 9.15am.

The Southampton–Le Havre service was maintained by the popular steamers *Alma* and *Columbia*, with the *Vera* acting as the relief ship. Each carried 547 passengers and they were the first LSWR vessels to accommodate first class travellers in cabins. The third class steerage accommodation was often occupied by emigrants from Italy and Central Europe on their way to join the liners from Southampton to the USA. With a five-hour open sea passage, the LSWR Chairman, Sir Charles Scotter 'recommended this route to those who liked sea journeys, but he himself was not a good sailor and travelled by the short sea route.' Leaving Waterloo by the 9.45pm boat train, a guaranteed connecting train brought the traveller into Paris at 11.03am. From August 1906 the transfer at Le Havre was improved by running special tramcars between quay and railway station, for which the LSWR paid 15 francs per trip.

St Malo had a tidal service operated three times per week by the old steamers *Ella* and *Hilda*, which took 12½ hours on the voyage of 151 nautical miles. During the summer growing traffic had required the use from 1903 of the *Vera*, a larger and faster ship which made the crossing in ten hours, but the *Hilda* assisted as weekend relief boat. Southampton-Cherbourg, 83 miles, was not a popular passenger service; during the winter it was maintained by the small passenger/cargo steamers *South Western* and *Guernsey*, which spent seven hours on the crossing. In summer the *Ella* provided more passenger accommodation at the same thrice-weekly frequency.

Jersey was linked to the French ports of St Malo and Granville by a weekly service to each in winter and three times a week in summer, when there was considerable excursion traffic. The *Victoria* had been built for this service and after its transfer to Plymouth in 1904 was replaced by the *Laura*, while the *Honfleur* assisted and probably carried out the winter sailings on its own. In addition to these passenger services there were regular cargo sailings from Southampton to Honfleur, St Malo and the Channel Islands, performed by the small cargo vessels *Cherbourg*, *Maria* and *St Malo*.

To replace these old ships, orders were placed in October 1904 and May 1905 with Gourlay Bros of Dundee for two new cargo steamers. *Ada*, the first, made her trial trip on 20 April 1905 then worked her passage to Jersey with a cargo of Scottish coal on 29 April. Her sister, the *Bertha*, was launched on 9 November 1905 and arrived at Southampton with coal on 2 December. The life-expired *St Malo* was sold in May 1906 to J. Power for £300, and the *Maria* a year later to R. J. Campbell for £700.

Disaster struck the LSWR fleet again on 18 November 1905. On the tidal service to St Malo the *Hilda* was due to sail from Southampton at 8.15pm on the evening of 17 November. She carried 24 saloon and 86 deck passengers, with a crew of 28 commanded by Captain Gregory. Fog delayed the departure until 10.00pm and then compelled the captain to anchor off Yarmouth until 6.00am. During the Channel crossing a gale got up, and as the *Hilda* approached St Malo after dark snow squalls obscured the navigation lights essential to follow the safe course into the port. The captain held off, waiting for the weather to clear, but sometime late that evening the *Hilda* struck the Pierre des Portes rocks. She was wedged into a cleft in the rocks which prevented her main lifeboats being lowered. Passengers had been assembled on the quarter deck in an attempt to get them off in the two cutters, when waves broke over the ship, smashing the boats and sweeping many people into the sea. The rest retreated towards the bow of the ship, where next morning the *Ada*, setting off for Southampton after the storm had abated, found the six survivors (a seaman and five Breton onion men) clinging to the rigging.

A formal Board of Trade enquiry and a French investigation were held, but could throw little light on the cause. The ship was well found. Captain Gregory was an experienced and careful master; the surviving member of the crew had been off watch below when the ship struck and the Bretons could describe little of events. It could only be surmised that the weather cleared momentarily and Captain Gregory headed towards St Malo, but visibility deteriorated after he had passed the point of no return. The company donated £3,000 to the relief fund and soon placed an order with Gourlay Bros in January 1906 for a replacement vessel. The *Princess Ena* made her trials on 22 June 1906 and reached Southampton on 15 July; she was similar to the *Vera*, with berths for 140 passengers.

In February 1908 the steamship committee decided to remove the passenger accommodation from the *Guernsey*, rather than build or purchase another cargo steamer. A twice-weekly service from Southampton to Roscoff was introduced on 1 July 1909. One sailing was performed by a chartered cargo vessel and the other by one of the smaller ships with limited passenger accommodation, initially the *Honfleur*.

New ships were required for the Channel Islands route and the company decided to adopt turbine propulsion. Orders were placed in October 1909 with Cammell Laird for two 20-knot triple-screw steamers for delivery by 30 June 1910, in time for the peak summer traffic. The company's choice of names, *Anglia* and *Gallia*, was refused by the Board of Trade. The Roman names for the islands were substituted—*Caesarea* and *Sarnia*. Delays at the shipyard deferred the launch of the *Caesarea* until 26 May 1910 and she did not reach Southampton until 17 September, having missed the summer season. The *Sarnia* was launched on 9 July, but then became involved in a boilermakers' strike and was not delivered until 4 April 1911. The LSWR decided to enforce token late delivery penalties of £500 on each vessel.

From 1910 onwards a daylight sailing to Le Havre was provided from the end of July to mid-September, initially thrice-weekly, by the *Lydia*, with a connecting train from Waterloo at 8.55am and an arrival in Paris at 11.20pm. The same train from Waterloo also served a day sailing to the Channel Islands on August Saturdays, intended to eliminate duplication of the night boat.

Two more disposals took place in 1911. *Frederica* was sold to H. E. Moss for £9,000, who resold her to the Turkish government, and the *Honfleur* went to S. Galbraith of Glasgow for £900. Wireless telegraphy was installed experimentally in the *South Western* in 1910. An order was given to the Marconi company in April 1911 for its installation in four of the company's ships, including the *Caesarea* and *Sarnia*. However, equipment of the fleet was not completed until the First World War.

In 1909 the GWR had obtained an amendment of its 1871 shipping powers, extending its routes from Plymouth and Weymouth to French ports between St Malo and Nantes. Services were operated to Brest and Nantes from 1908 to 1910 without much success. As part of the LSWR/GWR agreement of 13 May 1910, the LSWR was to serve ports from St Malo eastwards, the GWR covering Brest and the west coast of France. The GWR could also run occasional excursions from Weymouth to Cherbourg, but bookings from London were not to be given. The LSWR had to withdraw its Roscoff service, which was declared to be unprofitable.

A similar pattern of events took place on the LSWR's other flank. The LBSCR had obtained additional powers in 1911 to serve continental ports between Ostend and Cherbourg, despite LSWR opposition. However, on 30 May 1912 the two companies signed an agreement for the LSWR not to serve ports east of Le Havre nor the LBSCR those west of Pourville, near Dieppe. There were clauses regulating existing commitments with third parties and provision for

LSWR Channel Islands steamer *Caesarea* among the warships at the 1911 Coronation Naval Review. *Southampton City Museum*

LSWR steamer *Hantonia* which served on the Southampton–Le Havre route from 1912 to 1952. *Southampton City Museum*

limited excursions within the other company's territory. The agreement involved the discontinuance of the Brighton's loss-making New-haven-Caen cargo service, and the LSWR bought the almost new steamers *Normandy* and *Brittany*.

It was now time to replace the *Alma* and *Columbia* on the Le Havre route and in April 1911 orders were placed with the Fairfield Ship-building Co for two geared turbine steamers for delivery by January 1912. The *Normannia* was delivered on 26 February 1912 and commenced service on 2 April; her sister was launched as the *Aurania* on 23 December 1911, but this name was changed to *Hantonia* before she reached Southampton on 31 March 1912. Accommodation was of a high standard with many cabins for first class passengers and a large dining saloon as well as a smoking saloon and ladies' lounge. The *Hantonia* was to spend most of the next 40 years on this route. In April 1912 the *Columbia* was sold to an owner in Algiers, while a month later the *Alma* went to the same destination.

The coal strike of 1912 severely reduced the company's services and many of the seamen were placed on half pay as their ships were idle. It became the practice at the end of September each year to withdraw the two large ships *Caesarea* and *Sarnia*, which had operated to the Channel Islands and St Malo during the summer season. After their annual survey and any necessary repairs, they were then laid-up for the winter in Southampton Docks, while the winter services were maintained by the older and smaller steamers, with the St Malo and Cherbourg routes reduced to twice-weekly sailings. The *Ella* became surplus in July 1913 and was sold to the Shipping Federation.

Despite the agreement with the GWR, cargo sailings to Roscoff were resumed on 2 January 1913 by the *Brittany*, but ceased at the outbreak of war. Calls at the small Breton port of Treguier were inaugurated by the *Normandy* on 20 May 1914.

The new steamers and accelerated train services enabled the London-Paris journey via Le Havre to be shortened by a 45 minute later departure from Waterloo at 10.30pm, with the arrival of the return service at 9.00am instead of 10.11am. Passenger traffic on the company's routes had increased substantially between 1900 and 1913; on the Channel Islands service from 54,811 to 81,434, Le Havre from 32,370 to 74,367 and St Malo from 8,636 to 27,405. Freight traffic always showed a preponderance of imports, mainly agricultural pro-duce from France, and it was usually necessary to charter four cargo steamers to bring over the early potato crop from Brittany. In spite of this growing traffic, financial results for 1912 and 1913 showed losses of £26,253 and £13,471 respectively.

Pay rates for seamen in 1910 were 28s 0d [£1.40] afloat and 26s 0d

[£1.30] ashore per week, while firemen received 31s 0d [£1.55] and 26s 0d respectively. The pay scale for captains was from £205 to £300 per annum, including a safe navigation bonus of £10 to £25, but it emerged from the *Hilda* enquiry that they had to buy their own charts to ensure that they were properly cared for.

The two major disasters have already been described, but there were many minor collisions and groundings for which masters could lose their bonus. Fog was a frequent hazard; for example, on 24 November 1906 the *Ella* and the *Princess Ena* were in collision off Cape de la Hague. The BoT enquiry blamed the *Ella*'s master for excessive speed and he was demoted to cargo service, losing £26 per year. Fog on 19 and 20 May 1908 brought a succession of accidents; the *Alma* grounded off Bembridge, the *Laura* went aground on the Shingles Bank by the Needles and the *Princess Ena* struck rocks off Jersey.

In 1905 the LSWR had offered to place its ships at the disposal of the Admiralty in time of national need. Soon after the outbreak of war in August 1914 the *Caesarea* and *Sarnia* were requisitioned as boarding vessels, the latter being torpedoed in the Mediterranean on 12 September 1918. The *Lydia* was engaged from 1915 onwards as a government transport on the Le Havre route, and survived two U-boat attacks. The *Princess Ena* was taken over for special service and sent to the Dardanelles in 1915.

The company's first casualty was the *Guernsey*, making a routine voyage from the Channel Islands on 9 April 1915, which struck a rock near Cape de la Hague due to the absence of the usual navigational lights and sank with the loss of seven of her crew. Her place in the fleet was taken by the *Granuaile*, a second-hand vessel purchased from R. E. V. James Ltd, which was renamed *Ulrica*.

Ships were transferred frequently between routes. During 1914–15 *Vera* and *Bertha* both worked from Weymouth for the GWR. War Risk insurance steadily increased. Crews' wages were swollen by War Bonuses and War Risk Allowances. In June 1917 the Admiralty provided the LSWR ships with defensive armament—six-pounder guns for the faster vessels and 12- or 13-pounders for the older and slower ones. The Admiralty also advised that funnels should be painted grey, though the company wanted to retain its own livery, but by the end of the war all the ships had been dazzle painted.

The Southampton-Le Havre service was still maintained by the *Normannia* and *Hantonia*; after the withdrawal of the Dieppe service from 17 April 1916 it became the only civilian route to France. Sunday sailings were added, and in 1916 the service carried a record total of 161,594 passengers. Sailing times were an official secret, but Bradshaw published approximate train times; in April 1918 the Waterloo departure was at 4.00pm with an arrival in Paris at 9.54pm next day. For a fortnight in March and April 1918 regular passenger sailings to Le Havre and the Channel Islands were suspended as the *Normannia*, *Hantonia*, *Vera* and *Alberta* had been requisitioned to rush reinforcements to France following the German breakthrough on the Somme.

The *Normandy* was fired on by the Portsmouth defences on 12 July 1917 and hit in 26 places, but on 25 January 1918 she fell victim to a German U-boat while on passage to Cherbourg; 18 passengers and 14 crew were lost out of the 45 on board. A second loss quickly followed on 16 March 1918 when the old *South Western* on the St Malo service was torpedoed only eleven miles south west of the Isle of Wight—29 of her complement of 35 were killed. In consequence, services were reduced from 1 May 1918. The Cherbourg route was suspended, St Malo had no direct service, and Channel Islands service operated only twice a week. Finally, regular Jersey to France services ceased in September 1918 when the Admiralty took over the *Victoria*.

Back in 1914 the company had ordered a new turbine steamer for Channel Islands services from Denny Bros for delivery in June 1915. Work on this had come to a standstill in August 1915 because of the priority given to naval construction, but the name *Lorina* (after Lady Walker) had been chosen. In December 1917 the Admiralty ordered work to be resumed for its completion as a transport, and the *Lorina* arrived at Southampton on 4 January 1919 to take her share of the flow of men coming home for demobilisation. The Southampton-Le Havre trooping service was brought under LSWR management from March 1919, employing the *Lorina*, *Lydia* and *Caesarea*.

In February 1919 the company decided not to restore the unprofitable Jersey-France service and the *Victoria* was sold to the James Dredging & Towage Co for £16,500. Cross-Channel services began to improve in July 1919 with the resumption of direct sailings to St Malo. The Le Havre boat train now left Waterloo at 7.20 pm with an arrival in Paris at 12.30pm; the route carried 152,561 passengers in 1919 as the short sea and Dieppe routes were only gradually being restored.

The LSWR had received £275,000 compensation from the government for its wartime losses. Much work was needed to restore the fleet to peacetime condition. In October 1919 the *Lorina* was sent to the Caledon Shipbuilding Co of Dundee for conversion and commenced LSWR service at last on 31 January 1920. The *Caesarea* was reconditioned by the same firm and was completed on 7 June 1920, while the *Princess Ena* was dealt with at Devonport dockyard. The *Vera*, which had remained in company employment, required major repairs at Cammell Laird, which finally cost £75,844.

The *Lydia* was 30 years old. Instead of refitting, the James Dredging & Towage Co offered to buy her for £20,000, in exchange for selling to the LSWR for £40,000 HMS *Peony*, a 1915-built escort vessel which was available at Malta. This was converted to passenger use by the Caledon company, and renamed *Ardena* she arrived at Southampton on 29 November 1920. After initial use on the St Malo service she re-opened the summer-only Cherbourg route on 4 July 1921. Services had then just recovered from the 1921 coal strike when cuts had included the suspension of LSWR sailings to the Channel Islands.

The *Alberta* had struck rocks in fog off Guernsey on 21 July 1920 and went to Dundee for repairs and a much needed refit, but was delayed there by strikes until 31 October 1921. To maintain services the LNWR steamers *Rathmore* and *Galtee More* were chartered for periods in 1920–1. There was a need for additional cargo vessels and the *Laura* was converted to full cargo use by company dockyard staff for £5,000. As the cost of building new ships was prohibitive, the 48-year-old *Cherbourg* was re-engined and re-boilered in 1921 at a cost of £12,000. To avoid the need to charter tonnage each spring for the potato traffic, the company bought two second-hand cargo ships, *Algethi* and *Algeiba* in June 1922, renaming them *Rina* and *Vena* respectively. Financially, 1922 saw the steamship services near to breaking even, with a loss of only £1,489.

LYMINGTON—YARMOUTH

The LSWR had acquired in July 1884 the fleet of the Solent Steam Packet Company which operated this route. To the two paddle steamers and various miscellaneous craft it had purchased the South Western added a new paddler, the *Lymington*, on 9 May 1893.

To replace the Steam Packet Company's vessel *Solent* of 1863, the LSWR ordered a new vessel in December 1899 from Mordey, Carney & Co of Southampton at a price of £8,300. Slow progress was made on her construction and she was apparently sub-contracted to a French shipbuilder. When delivery was eventually made in January 1901 it was found that the ship did not comply with the terms of the contract, an opinion confirmed in April by Professor Biles, the LSWR marine architect. Acceptance was refused, and after legal negotiations Mordey Carney offered to build a replacement vessel to Professor Biles' plans, for £9,000. The contract was sealed on 14 October 1901, and the new saloon paddler *Solent* was handed-over on 1 May 1902. Meanwhile the previous *Solent*, described as worn out, was sold for £225 in June 1901.

The other Steam Packet Company vessel, the *Mayflower* of 1866, was sold in June 1905 for only £50. Hitherto, barges with cargo had been towed by one of the paddle steamers, but the combined tug and cargo boat *Carrier* was purchased from J. Power on 6 February 1906; a 36-ton twin-screw vessel of wide beam she provided a large deck for motor cars, which were increasingly using the Lymington route as the easiest crossing to the Isle of Wight.

SOUTHAMPTON—COWES

This crossing to the Isle of Wight has long been operated by the Southampton, Isle of Wight & South of England Royal Mail Steam Packet Company (the Red Funnel Line). LSWR involvement in this route was the rail link between the Royal Pier, Southampton, and the main line at Town & Docks station. Passenger traffic over this roadside tramway had begun on 26 September 1871 with horse traction. Steam power had taken over in 1876 and the curves were successively eased to take firstly six-wheel stock and later bogie coaches. The service consisted of six or seven trains each way on weekdays and two or three on Sundays. The 50 chain journey occupied seven minutes—maximum speed allowed was 5mph, and frequent use of the whistle was prescribed. During 1912–13 a steam railmotor-car worked most of the services.

The pier service was discontinued and through bookings withdrawn from 6 August 1914 to allow clear passage into the docks for the BEF troop trains. In January 1922 the traffic committee decided not to restore the service; traffic had declined since the advent of electric tramcars at Royal Pier in 1911 and now the motor bus could provide a link with Southampton West, which was replacing Town as the principal station.

THE ISLE OF WIGHT JOINT SERVICES

The LSWR/LBSCR joint steamer service was managed by the Portsmouth, Southsea & Ryde Joint Railway & Steam Packet Committee, which met quarterly at either Waterloo, London Bridge or Portsmouth (aboard one of its vessels). Local management was exercised by a marine superintendent, but from January 1912 he came under the control of the LSWR docks and marine manager at Southampton. From April 1902 engineering supervision of the committee's fleet rotated between the owning companies, concurrently with that of the joint lines. Repairs to the ships were carried out at Newhaven or Southampton and activity at the committee's Portsmouth factory was much reduced. From January 1912 the LSWR took over the supervision of the fleet for a 10-year period, concentrating maintenance work at Southampton.

The joint committee had acquired in 1880 the fleet of the Portsmouth & Ryde Steam Packet Company. Its fleet was composed solely of paddle steamers, while two new ships had been delivered at the end of the old century: the *Duchess of Kent* in November 1897 and the larger *Duchess of Fife* in May 1899. The committee also operated the Stokes Bay to Ryde service, which offered the shortest sea crossing to the island, but the pier at Stokes Bay was exposed to the weather and rail connection to London via Eastleigh was circuitous. The LSWR and the joint committee agreed in October 1902 that the Stokes Bay service should be withdrawn for the winter, in future only operating between June and September. The service finally ceased on 30 September 1913 at the end of the summer season.

A deputation from the Isle of Wight in July 1908 expressed disatisfaction with the services, also with the accommodation provided for second and third class passengers. Accordingly, plans were prepared in 1909 for two new steamers, and D. & W. Henderson of Glasgow secured the contract for both. The *Duchess of Richmond* ordered in January 1910 was delivered on 15 July 1910. Her sister the *Duchess of Norfolk* was ordered in January 1911 for delivery in June (subject to strikes), but was not handed-over until 16 September 1911.

With these two new vessels, the 26-year-old *Duchess of Edinburgh* and *Duchess of Connaught* could be sold in October 1910 to Dutch shipbreakers for £900 each. Subsequently the *Alexandra*, a Steam Packet Company vessel of 1879, was sold in 1913 to P. W. Gilbert. For cargo traffic the firm of Mordey Carney supplied in 1903 a steam launch named *Ada*, which towed across to the island the horse boats and later the motor car boat built in 1912.

Navigation in the congested waters of Spithead and Portsmouth Harbour could be hazardous and numerous accidents were recorded. On 30 November 1900 the *Alexandra* managed to collide with the dockyard railway viaduct at Portsmouth because the ship's engineer had omitted to open the valve to the steering gear—he was duly demoted to shore labouring. A serious collision took place on 15 August 1903 between the *Duchess of Albany* and the steam yacht *Wintonia* causing £575 damage; the Board of Trade enquiry blamed the captain and mate of the joint committee's vessel and both were dismissed. Another nasty collision occurred on 3 September 1909 in Portsmouth Habour when the ss *Transporter* struck the *Duchess of*

Kent, requiring the latter to be beached and all her passengers to be taken off safely; the BoT held both parties to blame. More embarassing than destructive was the collision on 9 February 1912 between the *Princess Margaret* and HMS *Victory,* at that time still afloat in the harbour.

With the outbreak of war the entrance to Portsmouth Harbour was closed to civilian traffic during the hours of darkness. Evening sailings were made from Clarence Pier, Southsea. Although the committee had made arrangements with the Admiralty for the hire of its vessels during a national emergency the call did not come until 1916, when within three months the four newest ships in the fleet were requisitioned for minesweeping duties, leaving services to be maintained by the *Duchess of Albany* of 1889 and the *Princess Margaret* of 1893.

On 26 January 1917 the tug *Ada* and towboat No 5 were driven by a gale against Ryde Pier and sank with the loss of 12 cattle and 47 pigs. Temporarily a tug named *Bandit* was hired, but a permanent replacement for the *Ada* was not obtained until January 1920 when the tug *Adur II* was purchased from the James Dredging & Towage Co.

The return of the committee's vessels from war service was slow. The *Duchess of Kent* was reconditioned by Day, Summers of Southampton and resumed work on 23 September 1919, still incomplete. She was followed by the *Duchess of Fife* from Camper & Nicholson on 9 December 1919. The *Duchess of Richmond* had been sunk by a mine in the Mediterranean on 28 June 1919, while the *Duchess of Norfolk* was still in naval service at Gibraltar in January 1920. After a refit at Portsmouth Dockyard she rejoined the committee's fleet on 24 February 1921. To make up for the loss of the *Duchess of Richmond* the committee decided in April 1921 to repair the 32-year-old *Duchess of Albany* at a cost of £9,000. The coal-burning fleet was badly affected by the miners' strikes of 1920 and 1921, with only one vessel in steam making two return crossings daily.

STONEHOUSE POOL, PLYMOUTH

Plymouth was the first port of call for many liners coming up the English Channel. Passengers were transferred within Plymouth Sound to tenders based at the GWR Millbay Docks. When the American Line announced in the autumn of 1903 that its eastbound sailings would call at Plymouth en route for Southampton, the LSWR had to provide similar facilities for its valued customer.

Upstream from Millbay a small quay had been built at Richmond Walk, Devonport, by the Stonehouse Pool Improvement Company

(SPI). This was linked to the LSWR just east of Devonport station by a steeply-graded 1 mile 23 chain single line, which the LSWR leased and worked by an agreement of 30 May 1881 with the SPI. The branch had been passed for passenger use by the BoT in 1885, but since its opening on 1 March 1886, freight was the only regular traffic.

During 1903–4 the LSWR agreed with the SPI to rent more land and to erect a passenger terminal at its own expense. This comprised a 350ft island platform with one side for passenger traffic and the other for mails and baggage. Passenger amenities included two well furnished waiting rooms and a refreshment bar. Ticket, enquiry and telegraph offices and a customs and baggage hall occupied the rest of the building. The platforms were lengthened in 1907 and the roofing extended, so that two boat trains could be dealt with together.

The LSWR adapted as a tender its steamer *Victoria*, a 709-ton vessel built in 1896 for the Jersey–France service. The company applied for a contract to carry the mails brought by the American Line, but the Post Office refused to alter its existing arrangements with the GWR, whose route via Bristol gave good connections to the Midlands and North of England.

The first American Line vessel, *St Louis*, reached Plymouth on 9 April 1904. Between the weekly arrivals the *Victoria* was used during the summer months on popular excursion cruises to Torquay, Falmouth, Fowey and other West Country ports. More intensive traffic was foreshadowed by the intention of the White Star Line to transfer its New York express service to Southampton in 1907, with calls at Plymouth and Cherbourg en route.

The White Star traffic justified a purpose-built tender. In December 1906 a contract was placed with Gourlay Bros of Dundee for the *Atalanta* to be delivered in May 1907, in time for the arrival on 29 May of the *Adriatic* to open the new service. From the summer of 1908 the West African liners also called at Plymouth. Their arrival caused problems when they co-incided with the Transatlantic vessels, as the LSWR had only the one tender, the *Victoria* having returned to the Channel Islands.

The SPI company offered in May 1907 to transfer its undertaking to the LSWR in return for enough LSWR 3½ per cent preference stock to pay 2 per cent dividend on its £50,000 capital. Following agreement on 26 June 1907 and approval by LSWR shareholders, confirmation was obtained in the Act of 16 August 1909. However, the LSWR took over from 1 July 1907, paying the SPI £1,000 per annum until the purchase was completed at a final cost of £28,571.

The LSWR/GWR accord of 13 May 1910 brought an end to competition for the Plymouth ocean liner traffic and released the South

Western from its commitment at Stonehouse Pool. Services ceased from 28 May 1910, and the *Atalanta* was sold to the GWR for £24,500. She was sailed round to Fishguard and some of her crew signed on with the GWR. No more passenger trains were to use Stonehouse Pool, with the possible exception of naval specials. In 1912 the platform roofing was removed.

The Stonehouse Pool venture was certainly unprofitable for the LSWR; for example, on 18 February 1907 only eleven passengers disembarked from the *New York*, of whom three took the boat train to Waterloo. The question was raised at the February 1906 general meeting and the chairman replied that 'the company was duty bound to run the American Line boat train even with only five passengers.' Deprived of the mail traffic, the LSWR had to rely on those travellers in such a hurry to reach London that they were willing to transfer from liner to tender in Plymouth Sound at any hour of day or night. It was all part of the service provided for the South Western's good customers at Southampton.

CHAPTER TEN

TRAINS AND TRAFFIC

MAIN LINE SERVICES

The return of Sam Fay to the LSWR in 1899 as superintendent of the line was followed by the introduction of improved and accelerated train services. In June 1899 two new Waterloo to Bournemouth trains were added to the timetable, making the run non-stop in 125 minutes. It is said that Fay and Dugald Drummond wished to reach Bournemouth in two hours or less, but that this was vetoed by Sir Charles Scotter. The deputy chairman was probably right—the quadrupling of the main line was far from complete, and such a fast schedule would have been difficult to maintain.

In 1900 the down morning express was withdrawn and the best Waterloo–Bournemouth timings eased to 126 minutes. The LSWR had been reluctant to introduce corridor stock, and the only taste of luxury was the four Pullman cars which had run on the Bournemouth service since 1890 in the 12.30pm, 2.15pm, 4.55pm and (later) 6.55pm fast trains from Waterloo. The 2.15pm was non-stop to Christchurch, and was followed by a 2.20pm train which took the original route to Weymouth via Ringwood. The 4.55pm now called at Winchester, although until June 1900 it had served that city by slip carriage.

The LSWR's main line stock was composed of compartment vehicles with intermediate lavatories. Since 1898 some tri-composite coaches with two compartments and a lavatory for each class had been built to mitigate the rigours of long journeys to the West of England, but the standard vehicles provided only two lavatories between six or seven compartments. However, steam heating began to be installed in 1901, commencing with the West of England trains, while all new carriages were to have electric lighting. The principal trains to the west left Waterloo at around 9.00am, 11.00am, 1.00pm, 3.00pm and 6.00pm, time-honoured departures which have changed little over the years. During the summer months the 11.00am expanded into three divisions, respectively for Plymouth, North Devon and North Cornwall. Drummond's new T9 4-4-0s in 1900 worked the first division to Salisbury in 100 minutes (a 10-minute acceleration) and to Exeter in 215 minutes. The Portsmouth service was always the Cinderella; only four trains had any claim to be regarded as fast (the others stopped at all stations beyond Guildford) and even these took at least two hours to cover the 73¾ miles to Portsmouth Town.

Restaurant cars made their appearance on 1 July 1901; three five-coach sets were converted from the former 'American Eagle' boat train stock. Meals were served from a combined kitchen/van to passengers seated in second or third class open saloons or in first class compartments, but the corridors did not extend beyond the end of the set. More accelerations were carried out by Fay before his departure to the GCR at the end of 1901. Exeter was reached in 210 minutes and even Portsmouth in 111 minutes, although this was gradually eased out in subsequent years to the traditional two hours.

1903 saw a considerable acceleration of the West of England services, with the summer 10.50am from Waterloo reaching Exeter in 195 minutes and the former 3.00pm train being altered to leave Waterloo at 3.30pm with an unchanged arrival at Exeter. The LSWR chairman disclaimed any intention of racing the GWR—the accelerations only brought the West of England schedules into line with those to Bournemouth. There a new 10.15am train provided a much-needed morning fast service to Bournemouth and Weymouth. The accelerated trains to the West Country soon began to be worked by Drummond's new large 4-4-0s of the S11 and L12 classes.

At last orders were given in 1903 for the construction of ten sets of corridor coaches for general use on West of England and Bournemouth routes. The introduction of corridor trains on the Bournemouth line led to the gradual withdrawal of the Pullman cars as their patrons deserted them for the new vehicles. In 1905 restaurant cars appeared on the Bournemouth line, replacing a Pullman on the 12.30pm and providing both types of accommodation on the 6.55pm. The eight new 56ft dining cars were distinguished by the presence of a clerestory roof, unknown on the LSWR except for one of the Royal saloons. They seated 28 passengers in first class and lower class saloons, separated by a central kitchen.

West of England restaurant car services were increased from two to four daily, with through workings to Plymouth and during the summer to Torrington. Six trains each way were formed at least partly of corridor stock, although the 10.40am advance train to North Devon was still composed of lavatory stock, and its advertised non-stop run from Sidmouth Junction to Barnstaple Junction deprived passengers of the chance of relief at Exeter.

During 1906–7 more dining cars and corridor coaches were built, some existing brake thirds were provided with corridor gangways, while the remaining 'Eagle' stock was similarly converted for use on the West of England services. In 1907 a new 6.10am Waterloo–Exeter breakfast car train relieved the previous 5.50am to Weymouth and Exeter, which Bradshaw described as the 'News Express.' For residents of West London spending their holidays in the West Country, a curious train was introduced leaving Richmond (New) at 9.35am to head eastwards through Hammersmith and Kensington to Clapham Junction, thence via Wimbledon to Salisbury, where through coaches were attached to the 10.45am Waterloo–Ilfracombe.

In the summer of 1908 the LSWR had a 57.4mph run from Andover Junction to Vauxhall which, apart from a dubious 60mph sprint from Dorchester to Wareham in 1914, became the high water mark for its start-to-stop timings. At last something was done in 1909 for Portsmouth travellers; a new fast train from Waterloo at 6.40pm made the journey in 106 minutes and two other existing trains were accelerated, thanks to the transfer to this route of four of the S11 Class locomotives. The next landmark was the introduction on 3 July 1911 of two-hour schedules to Bournemouth by two up and one down trains. These expresses were initially worked by the T14 Class, the most effective of Drummond's 4-6-0s, but were soon replaced by his final 4-4-0 design, the large D15 Class. October 1911 saw the withdrawal of the last Pullman car working in the 7.50am ex Bournemouth West and the 4.50pm from Waterloo.

Although much corridor stock had now been constructed, its use was not general on the Bournemouth line, where only the restaurant car trains at 12.30pm, 4.50pm and 6.55pm from Waterloo were equipped. The other fast trains at 8.57am (introduced in 1912), 10.15am, 2.00pm, and the 4.10pm two-hour express were still formed of lavatory stock. Portsmouth enjoyed two restaurant car services daily from 1 October 1912, which brought some corridor stock to this route. To the West of England there were eight restaurant car corridor expresses daily during the summer season, when the 11.00am service was divided into trains at 10.50am for Plymouth, Sidmouth and Exmouth, 11.00am for Padstow and Bude and 11.10am for Ilfracombe and Torrington, all three arriving at Exeter within 15 minutes, with predictable possibilities of delay.

After the wartime service reductions described in Chapter 7, trains began to be restored in December 1918, but the post-war era really commenced on 1 June 1919 with a radical restructuring of the timetable. Sir Herbert Walker's principle of regular-interval services was adopted, with departures from Waterloo at 30 minutes past the hour to Bournemouth and at 50 minutes past the hour to Portsmouth, timings which became the peacetime standard for the next 60 years. Schedules were still slow with a 60mph maximum speed in force, and many carriages (mostly corridor) had yet to return from military use. Consequently, the usual summer duplications to the West of England were missing from the timetable, but the Urie N15 Class 4-6-0s were becoming available to work the heaviest trains. Restaurant cars were increased, although those on the Portsmouth line were only accessible from the two adjacent coaches.

Further substantial improvement had to await the end of the coal strike in July 1921. Schedules were cut but still did not match pre-war timings; the fastest run was a Basingstoke–Surbiton dash at 55.1mph. During the summer months trains for the Bournemouth line left Waterloo at hourly intervals from 8.30am to 7.30pm, while to the West of England departures were made systematically on the hour, from 8.00am to 1.00pm at hourly intervals, then at 3.00pm and either 5.00pm or 6.00pm. This avoided the previous concentration of departures around 11.00am. In the LSWR's final timetable of 1922–3 the weekly steam-hauled train mileage was 197,040, as against the pre-war equivalent of 216,000.

Surrey Warner, the LSWR carriage superintendent since 1906, now moved away from his pre-war traditional wooden-bodied designs by the construction in 1921 of four five-coach steel-panelled set trains for the Bournemouth line. More roomy than the pre-war stock, these coaches were among the first steam-hauled vehicles to be painted in the new livery of green with yellow lining. The set trains included a pantry third for serving light refreshments on mid-morning or mid-afternoon trains. Later these pantry sets were used on the Portsmouth line as more 'Ironclad' stock with restaurant cars became available for the Bournemouth services. However, at Grouping, lavatory stock was still being used for those trains without refreshment facilities, such as the 9.30am and 10.30am from Waterloo, and non-corridor vehicles were widely used for strengthening the normal formations.

In addition to the services in the published timetable there were the regular period excursions at reduced fares, which ran weekly to each advertised destination. Some left Waterloo before 8.00am; others departed for the West of England at around midnight. When period excursions were resumed in July 1921 after their wartime suspension, Friday became the day of departure with the 11.40am to North Devon and Cornwall, 12.04pm to Bournemouth (with nine non-corridor coaches), 2.04pm to Exmouth (with lavatory stock) and at 3.55pm to Bournemouth and 4.55pm to Portsmouth, each formed of 18 six-wheelers.

There were also the day excursions, many arranged by outside agencies—for example, Restalls ran an 11.30am to Weymouth on Thursdays in 1904 at a fare of 4s 3d [21p], which was nominally non-stop to Wareham in 185 minutes. The National Sunday League operated on the sabbath day, but sometimes its passengers were unwelcome at the more select resorts. Thomas Cook & Son catered for more up-market excursionists with (for instance) a special train to Salisbury for a tour by horse-drawn coach to Stonehenge and Wilton House.

SUBURBAN AND LOCAL SERVICES

A summary of suburban departures from Waterloo is given in Appendix 6. Progress on the reconstruction of the terminus and widening its approaches had enabled suburban services to be steadily improved in the years 1900–14. In place of the combined trains which ran (sometimes double-headed) as far as Surbiton, to divide there into main and New Guildford line portions, independent through trains could now be provided. The last LSWR slip coach workings at Walton (for Virginia Water) and at Feltham (for Ashford) ceased in June 1902, the former soon being replaced by additional through trains to the Chertsey branch. While suburban traffic was increasing on the main line and its branches (eg Epsom), inner suburban departures on the Windsor Line were decreasing. It was still necessary sometimes to change at Wimbledon, Surbiton or Twickenham for the branches, and one of the benefits of electrification was the provision of regular through trains.

Services ran approximately hourly within the inner suburban area, but their timings were irregular. While there were additional fast trains during the rush hours to such destinations as Hampton Court and Leatherhead, their departures were not evenly spaced. On Sundays the morning church interval was abolished on 6 October 1901, most services ran to a regular-interval pattern, usually hourly but from July 1912 increased to half-hourly where necessary to cater for summer riverside traffic. The introduction of electric trains at regular intervals on the inner suburban routes in 1915–16 enforced similar timings on the remaining steam services to Woking, Guildford, Leatherhead, Windsor and Reading.

Construction of six-wheel stock for suburban services had ceased around 1900, and in 1902 there began to appear the standard four-coach bogie block trains which eventually numbered 145 sets. These close-coupled sets, accommodating all three classes, were used singly in the off-peak and coupled in pairs (sometimes with additional vehicles) during the rush hours. The LSWR's 1921 *Appendix* laid down that they were not to run more than 30 miles non-stop or to exceed 40mph. By 1914 there were few six-wheel coaches to be seen at Waterloo, and most of those remaining were some nine-coach sets of elliptical-roofed stock built before 1904. These arrived on commuter trains during the morning rush hour, but had no rostered duties afterwards, enabling them to be used for race specials or excursions; two pairs of these sets remained in use until after Grouping on trains from Epsom and Hampton Court. Most suburban trains were hauled by the Drummond M7 Class 0-4-4Ts, although some of the Adams 4-4-2Ts remained in the London area until electrification.

Tender engines were used on the longer runs to Woking and Guildford, while intermediate stations on the main line were served as well by trains bound for Basingstoke, Alton or Portsmouth. These were invariably formed of lavatory stock, usually in four-coach sets, although there was a five-coach variety which coupled a six-wheel van to four bogie carriages. Some of these sets made long slow journeys on 'Parliamentary' type services; the 10.35am from Waterloo eventually terminated at Swanage at 4.05pm, after detaching an Ascot portion at Woking. The four-coach set on the 11.15am from Waterloo ran semi-fast to Exeter, whence it formed the 4.29pm to Torrington, and it was followed by a similar set on the 11.20am which reached Exeter at 6.23pm after calling at almost every station beyond Surbiton.

The pioneer steam railmotor venture on the Southsea branch was quickly extended (as already described), but as the limitations of the steam cars became apparent Drummond introduced some small 2-2-0Ts and 0-4-0Ts to work with pairs of saloon trailers. When these locomotives were found to be underpowered, they were replaced in 1914–15 by Adams 0-4-4Ts in push-and-pull working. Many services were successively operated by all three methods. The self-propelled steam cars were converted from 1916 onwards into open saloons for push-and-pull operation, and (for example) many of these saloon cars continued to maintain the local services in the Plymouth area. Other two-coach push-and-pull trains were formed by splitting four-coach bogie block sets, and this type could be found in the London area.

CROSS-COUNTRY SERVICES

The first through links with the GWR were made at Salisbury, where two trains in each direction between Portsmouth and Cardiff were introduced on 1 July 1896. With the reconstruction of Salisbury station, two pairs of Portsmouth–Bristol trains were added to the timetable in the summer of 1903.

Basingstoke was the other exchange point with the GWR, but it was GCR enterprise which removed the necessity for all north to south passengers having to change there. On 1 July 1902 a Bournemouth–Newcastle through service formed of GCR stock was introduced. Initially this was attached to trains to and from Waterloo, but in July 1903 the southbound service ran independently from Basingstoke, and a GWR through coach from Birkenhead was added.

From 1 July 1905 the northbound service also became a separate train leaving Bournemouth West at 11.20am with four GWR coaches for Birkenhead and GCR vehicles for Manchester, Bradford and Newcastle (including a buffet car).

From 1 July 1910 the Birkenhead service was accelerated and ran separately; departing from Bournemouth West at 10.15am, it ran non-stop from Eastleigh to Oxford behind a LSWR locomotive. The Birkenhead portion was formed of LSWR stock with restaurant car, while the GWR provided a section for Manchester, detached at Birmingham. During the 1914–18 war, the Newcastle train was withdrawn between 1915 and July 1922, but the Birkenhead service was suspended only from January 1917 until May 1919. The 1910 accord between the LSWR and the GWR also led to the introduction of three trains daily from Reading to Portsmouth, with one of the return services starting from Stokes Bay.

Two through services to the north via the London junctions commenced on 1 July 1905. A Midland train left Portsmouth Town at 10.30am with through coaches for Nottingham and Bradford, at Eastleigh a Southampton–Nottingham carriage was attached, and the three vehicles then ran via Staines and Richmond to Hendon, where they joined a train from St Pancras. This service ceased in October 1908. Little more successful was a combined service to the LNWR and GNR which left Weymouth at 9.55am for Clapham Junction, where the single LNWR carriage continued to Willesden Junction en route for Liverpool or (later) Manchester. The three GNR coaches then ran via the Widened Lines to King's Cross, where passengers transferred to the afternoon trains for Scotland and the north. This service was finally withdrawn in October 1910.

There was also a flow of traffic between the South Coast and the West Country. From 1 July 1907 a Brighton–Plymouth service was inaugurated, and the LSWR provided seven dual-fitted carriages for this; the through coaches leaving Brighton at 11.20am were attached at Salisbury to the 1.00pm from Waterloo. From July 1908 through coaches from Brighton to Bournemouth West were added to this train as far as Southampton; the LSWR locomotive took over from the LBSCR one at Cosham.

After wartime withdrawal of cross-country services, a Portsmouth–Plymouth train was restored in July 1920. The approach of Grouping led to some innovations in July 1922 between the companies of the future Southern Railway. A 10.15am from Ilfracombe formed of LSWR stock attached GWR or LSWR through coaches from Cardiff at Salisbury, then continued via Eastleigh to Portsmouth, where it picked up a portion from Bournemouth (LSWR or LBSCR vehicles) and the combined train reached Brighton at 5.42pm. The other new service left Bournemouth West at 10.30am via Havant to Guildford, where its through coaches were attached to the SECR Birkenhead to Dover train.

BOAT TRAINS

For the American Line traffic the first class 'Eagle' stock had been built during the 1890s. Their liners sailed on Saturdays, with special trains leaving Waterloo at 8.30am and 10.00am. The working timetable laid down schedules of about 95 minutes between Waterloo and Southampton Dock Gates, but American Line passengers sometimes found themselves rushed up to Waterloo in as little as 76 minutes. The Union Castle Line also sailed on Saturdays, and there were trains from Waterloo at 10.02am, 10.35am and 11.35am as well as a last-minute special for mail and specie at 11.57am. The White Star Line sailed for New York from 1907 onwards on Wednesdays, with specials from Waterloo at 8.30am and 9.45am formed of new corridor stock.

The 19th Century outflow of emigrants from the United Kingdom had required the LSWR to house and feed them in its premises at Nine Elms, but during the 1900s the emigrant traffic originated in Eastern or Central Europe and merely passed through Britain in transit to the USA. Groups of migrants would cross on the LSWR steamers from Le Havre; on 25 March 1906 four hundred arrived at Southampton aboard the *Vera* but only 120 could be accommodated on the liner to New York, and the rest were despatched by special train to Liverpool for the next sailing to the USA. For such eventualities the LSWR built between 1905 and 1908 three sets of (mainly) third class carriages, which were dual-fitted and constructed to a restricted loading gauge, able to convey emigrants to any port in the country.

Passengers for the overnight sailings to the Channel Islands and Le Havre usually left Waterloo in carriages attached to the 9.50pm

Dorchester mail train, being worked forward from Basingstoke to Southampton Docks. During the summer months the boat train ran separately from Waterloo at 9.45pm, accelerated in July 1914 to leave at 10.30pm. Refreshment facilities were introduced in July 1913, and a new 29-seat elliptical-roofed dining car was provided a year later. For the inward Le Havre service during the summer a special train left the Docks between 7.00am and 7.30am, but at other times of year passengers made their way to the 7.45am ordinary train from Southampton Town, arriving Waterloo 10.11am. Similarly, Channel Islands travellers in winter joined the 5.15pm from the Town station; if either boat were late a special train would be worked round to Southampton West and attached there to an up Bournemouth train.

American Line passengers disembarking at Stonehouse Pool were conveyed to Waterloo in one of the converted 'Eagle' stock restaurant car sets. It seems that meals were served at whatever time the train ran (rather in the manner of airlines today) and some of the survivors of the Salisbury disaster described the meal they had just taken after midnight as either lunch, tea or dinner. More comfortable overnight travel was provided for White Star passengers from Plymouth in the four sleeping cars built in 1908; these 56ft vehicles each provided seven single and two double berth compartments and were unique in accommodating single berth passengers in brass bedsteads. When the Plymouth service ceased in 1910 the car bodies were sold to the GWR. The original running time of the specials between Devonport and Waterloo was 4 hours 20 minutes including a stop at Templecombe to change locomotives, but after the Salisbury disaster the schedule was eased to 4 hours 28 minutes, with the customary stops at Exeter and Salisbury. In addition, the GWR enforced a brief halt at Exeter St David's.

SPECIAL TRAFFIC

Race meetings were an important source of business for the LSWR, a popular meeting at one of the London courses (Hurst Park, Kempton Park and Sandown Park) attracting as many as 14,000 racegoers. On Easter Monday 50 or more specials would run to Kempton Park, with a similar number on Whit Monday to Hampton Court for Hurst Park races. Race specials carried headcodes to distinguish members' and first class non-members' trains from those carrying ordinary racegoers.

The Royal Ascot meeting in June was the most important fixture in the racing calendar for the LSWR, bringing it some £20,000 revenue.

On Gold Cup day up to 40 specials left Waterloo at four-minute intervals, many hauled by express locomotives to ensure strict punctuality. Inevitably, ordinary passengers on the Windsor line suffered some interference with their train services. During the Edwardian years the company noted with concern the increasing number of motor cars to be seen at Ascot and other racecourses, which was having its effect on the first class traffic, but in August 1906 Sir Charles Scotter expressed the opinion that business would recover 'when people tired of motor cars.' After the drab years of war Ascot races in 1919 attracted a record 37,900 passengers; the LSWR had to institute a system of regulated bookings as there was insufficient rolling stock despite borrowing coaches from other companies.

The LSWR was always termed the military line. Every summer saw great activity transporting the army to and from its field manoeuvres. Besides the Regular Army, the Volunteer and Territorial forces had their annual camps, which were usually held at Bank Holiday periods, when the railway was at its busiest with civilian traffic. In 1909 the LSWR ran 170 special troop trains during the week preceding the August Bank Holiday. Ninety of these were for Territorial units, with 29 trains during the weekend leaving Waterloo and nine departing from Nine Elms, conveying a total of 22,000 men, 1,700 horses and 32 guns to Amesbury.

Manoeuvres were only a practice for real war, and during the Boer War the LSWR had the task of carrying most of the expeditionary force for embarkation at Southampton. Between August 1899 and January 1900 the company ran 464 special trains, formed of a total of 1,818 passenger carriages, 249 horse boxes (for officers' mounts), 1,189 cattle trucks and 1,366 other goods vehicles. During this period 118,177 troops were conveyed to the port, with 124,507 reinforcements following during the first half of 1900. Many of the troop trains were hauled by Drummond 700 Class 0-6-0s; these locomotives worked through to Tilbury and the Royal Albert Docks on specials carrying those units which sailed from the Thames.

The despatch of the troops to South Africa was accomplished punctually, except for the departure of the Brigade of Guards from Waterloo in October 1899. This attracted large crowds, who by climbing on to carriages and swarming across the tracks delayed the special train's departure. Subsequent contingents left from the seclusion of Nine Elms. When the victorious troops and commanders returned from the Cape, many of the specials from Southampton were diverted to Paddington, better equipped than Waterloo to cope with patriotic enthusiasm.

Queen Victoria's last rail journey was made on 18 December 1900,

T9 Class 4–4–0 No 307 leaving Waterloo with a special for Southampton Docks – possibly one of the trains for the 1902 Coronation Naval Review. *National Railway Museum*

T14 Class 4–6–0 No 446 on the Bournemouth West portion of an express from Waterloo, passing the railmotor halt at Meyrick Park. *L&GRP*

when T9 Class 4-4-0 No 706 worked the royal train from Windsor to Gosport for her Christmas stay at Osborne. The LSWR played only a minor part in the Queen's funeral arrangements, but the country soon began to prepare for the spectacle of the coronation of King Edward VII in June 1902. The three days of ceremonies culminated from the railway's angle in a naval review at Spithead on 28 June. Every effort was made to complete the main line widenings in progress, five temporary block posts were installed between Woking and Winchester and additional sidings and platforms were provided within Southampton Docks. On the Saturday morning of the review 49 specials with official guests and spectators were to leave Waterloo at four-minute intervals; the empty trains were to be assembled nose-to-tail on both up lines between Clapham Junction and Wimbledon. All down main line traffic was to be suspended until after 10.00am. At the last moment the King developed appendicitis, the coronation had to be postponed and the naval review took place on 16 August, but on a reduced scale requiring only 17 special trains.

The LSWR royal train was composed of two nondescript but internally ornate saloons dating from 1885; plans in 1910 for three new vehicles were never carried out. Sometimes the GWR train was used, as on 8 July 1903 when President Loubet of France accompanied the King from Victoria to Farnborough. The funeral of King Edward VII on 20 May 1910 involved the LSWR in running 97 specials to Waterloo, Nine Elms, Addison Road and Windsor for the troops lining the route.

The coronation of King George V followed in June 1911. The Spithead naval review on 24 June called for the despatch from Waterloo between 6.16am and 9.25am of five military and 33 civilian specials; in addition a train from Addison Road conveyed the LNWR directors to the ss *Scotia* (the 9.25am from Waterloo took the LSWR board and its guests to the *Sarnia*). Improvements and widenings of the main line since 1902 enabled a limited service of ordinary trains to be maintained while the specials left from the new South station at Waterloo. The LSWR chairman at the August 1911 meeting said that the coronation traffic had been disappointing: 'the public had been frightened away by the security precautions and London prices.'

THE FREIGHT BUSINESS

The LSWR derived only about a third of its revenue from freight traffic. Thus its loaded freight train miles in the years 1900–11 of about 4.5 million per annum contrasted with passenger train miles of up to 15 million. During the ensuing years, peacetime freight traffic declined while the passenger business continued to increase. Much of the freight tonnage was inwards traffic of bulk commodities, such as coal, and originating business was only about one-third of the total. Some of the most important freight movements were meat and produce for the London markets. There were three fast goods trains nightly from Exeter to Nine Elms and three corresponding departures: in 1913 these left at 10.45pm for Plymouth (long known as the 'Tavy') and at 11.00pm and 12.25am for intermediate stations to Exeter.

From Southampton Docks there was a considerable traffic in perishables. Special trains brought to Nine Elms new potatoes from Brittany, tomatoes and flowers from the Channel Islands. Chilled meat from overseas was despatched from the docks by a regular train at 1.30pm, which carried the meat in road vans mounted on flat trucks, to ensure quick transfer to Smithfield market after arrival at Nine Elms at 7.05pm. In 1913 there were six freight trains a day between Southampton Docks and Nine Elms, the fastest taking just $4^{1}/_{2}$ hours.

London's milk traffic was also considerable, with five trains daily from the West Country during 1913. As described in Chapter 3, much of this milk was handled at Vauxhall, but some was unloaded at Wimbledon, Clapham Junction and Waterloo itself. The empty churn trains were assembled at Waterloo, and in 1920 the two principal departures comprised 40 vans for 31 different destinations on the West of England and Somerset & Dorset lines. In contrast to the 1980s prejudice against milk imports, 1913 loadings included empty churns for Cherbourg.

Modernisation of freight handling was starting. In 1922 the company devised the 'demountable flat,' a kind of large pallet on wheels which could be rolled on or off a flat lorry from a trolley stand alongside the goods loading platform. It was said to improve the productivity of motor vehicles by making up to six trips per day possible. Motor vans had been in use in the London area for parcel traffic since 1912, four small auto-carriers being ordered in June 1914 for light deliveries in the Kingston and Surbiton district. In the post-war period the company had 40 lorries on loan from the government, but decided in May 1921 to buy 45 new vehicles to replace deliveries by horse and cart in the London, Southampton and Bournemouth areas. By this, 40 motor drivers and their mates would replace 175 carters, 167 horses and 118 vans at an annual saving of £1,600.

OPERATIONS, ACCIDENTS AND INCIDENTS

Published punctuality figures showed that Waterloo arrivals during October 1903 and October 1910 both averaged 90 per cent on time or less than five minutes late. However, October was usually a good month for the traffic department, being midway between the summer holiday rush and the bad weather of the winter. The first meeting of the traffic officers' conference described the results for December 1912 as unsatisfactory: only 51.41 per cent of trains were punctual and average lateness was 2.63 minutes. The holiday traffic of August 1913 must have caused congestion as punctuality had fallen to 44.10 per cent and average delay to 5.34 minutes. August 1922 saw an improvement; 60.16 per cent of trains were punctual and lateness averaged 2.86 minutes, perhaps due to easier schedules and regular-interval departures.

Punctuality suffered every winter from the 'pea-souper' fogs which used to afflict London and the Thames Valley. Fog was the cause of most of the LSWR's accidents. On 23 November 1901 the 10.35pm train from Kingston to Waterloo, hauled by M7 Class tank No 42, passed a signal at danger and collided outside Malden with the 5.15pm Brent to Wimbledon freight, killing the guard of the goods train and injuring 45 passengers. On 22 January 1904 the 9.30pm from Windsor ran into the rear of the 9.32pm from Kingston at Clapham Junction West home signals, because the fog signal detonator had not been securely placed on the rails at Point Pleasant Junction.

Four years later, on 23 January 1908, the double-headed 1.55pm train from Southampton over-ran signals and detonators at Raynes Park and collided with the 4.18pm from Leatherhead standing on the through line at Wimbledon West; twenty-four passengers were hurt and compensation payments totalled £2,250. The night of 3 February 1921 must have been dreadful. At 6.59pm the 6.04pm from Waterloo to Chertsey (M7 Class 0-4-4T No 374 and eight coaches) ran into the rear of the 5.54pm to Woking (L11 Class 4-4-0 No 161 and ten coaches), halted at Queen's Road East home signal, injuring 47 passengers and the guard of the Woking train. The Chertsey driver had mistaken the Vauxhall West signals and had missed those at Loco Junction, but fortunately he was only travelling at about 15mph. Later that evening there was a collision between two electric trains on the Windsor line outside Clapham Junction, but damage this time was slight.

Waterloo was the scene of several minor collisions. On 5 May 1905 the 1.45pm from Reading struck an outgoing empty milk train, one passenger being killed and twelve injured. This accident was held to be due to a signal linesman's error during renewal work. On 26 March 1919 the 7.17am steam train from Leatherhead over-ran Waterloo 'A' box home signals and collided with the departing 8.10am electric to Claygate; five passengers and two staff were hurt and £500 damage done. The signalman in 'A' box was in error by accepting two conflicting movements, while the steam train driver admitted mistaking the road he was on. A more serious instance of mis-reading signals occurred at Vauxhall on 29 August 1912. T9 Class 4-4-0 No 312 set off on the through line from Nine Elms to Waterloo to work a boat train. However, the driver was reading the signals for the up local line, and the light engine crashed into the rear of the 6.37am from Aldershot standing in Vauxhall station while tickets were being collected. One passenger was killed; two staff and 50 passengers were injured.

Three very destructive accidents took place on the West of England main line, happily not accompanied by serious casualties. On 4 July 1914 the 10.25pm freight from Exeter to Salisbury broke away at Sutton Bingham, and before the leading portion could be diverted into the loop at Yeovil Junction, the runaway vehicles collided with it 200yd from Yeovil Junction West signalbox, wrecking 22 wagons and demolishing part of the box.

At 12.47am on 13 October 1914, new H15 Class 4-6-0 No 488 with 39 wagons on the 8.10pm market freight from Exeter to Nine Elms passed all signals approaching Andover Junction at danger and collided with the 10.00pm up goods from Salisbury, which was standing in the platform. The full speed collision caused great destruction, involving wagons in the down siding and a MSWJ freight on the other side of the island platform. Seventy wagons were destroyed and many cattle were killed and injured, while normal traffic was not resumed for two days. This was an instance where the extreme penalty of dismissal was inflicted on the driver of No 488; lesser offences were usually dealt with by down-grading or a period of suspension. By a strange coincidence on 5 October 1916 sister locomotive No 490 was approaching Andover Junction on the same train with 58 wagons when some trucks ran back during shunting and fouled the up line; another destructive collision ensued which wrecked 38 wagons.

After 17 years during which only one passenger among 1,270 million had been killed, the LSWR suffered its worst accident at 1.57am on 1 July 1906. The Salisbury disaster was one of the three unexplained major accidents of 1906–7 and was marked by the high proportion of casualties among those on board the American Line boat express from Stonehouse Pool. Of the 43 passengers and six staff on the train, 24 passengers, and the driver and fireman of its locomotive (L12 Class 4-4-0 No 421) lost their lives, while seven pas-

sengers and four staff were injured. Also killed was the guard of a
down empty milk train entering the station and the fireman of a
Beattie goods engine in the Bournemouth bay, which were struck by
the derailed express locomotive.

Much has been written about the Salisbury disaster. Why did
Driver Robins take his train around the sharp reverse curves at the
east end of the station at twice the permitted speed of 30mph? In the
early days of the Plymouth ocean liner expresses some very fast
running had been made, but Dugald Drummond quickly issued strict
instructions that the specials must run to the schedule times and as
recently as February 1906 the passing times at Salisbury had been
revised to allow for reduced speed through the station. At the Board of
Trade enquiry, Henry Holmes, the superintendent of the line, said
that the boat train schedules were based on normal sectional timings
and no excessive speed was required to keep time. However, the train
had made a slow start from Templecombe and Driver Robins may
have been trying to regain lost time. Major Pringle could only sum-up
his enquiry with the conclusion that the accident was due to the
excessive speed of the boat train.

Whatever the cause, a considerable number of affluent Trans-
Atlantic passengers had been killed and injured. Claims for compensation quickly rose to £137,901. To meet these the LSWR diverted
£20,000 from the Steamship Renewal Fund and made a special provision against profits of £30,000, which knocked a point off the year's
dividend. Meanwhile, the company's lawyers set to work and by May
1909 they were able to announce that all claims had been settled for a
total of £60,421; added to the material damage (the 'Eagle' stock on
the boat train had been shattered) the final bill for the disaster came to
£70,648.

Vandalism is not a recent phenonemon, and numerous attempts to
damage or derail LSWR trains are recorded. The most serious took
place between St Budeaux and Tamerton Foliot on 30 July 1917,
when the 4.55pm from Plymouth Friary to Tavistock was derailed by
stones placed on the line; one of its carriages turned over on to the
foreshore, injuring five passengers. It was reported that two lads from
a nearby industrial training ship had been arrested.

Early on the morning of 26 April 1913 a patrolling policeman
noticed flames coming from carriage No 280 of bogie block set No
85B, berthed since the previous evening in the sidings near Fairfax
Road, Teddington. By the time the fire brigade had arrived, three
second class compartments had been burned out. Evidence was found
of attempts to start fires elsewhere in the train, while abusive post-

Clearing the line after the Salisbury disaster, July 1906. *Commercial postcard, courtesy G. Gundry*

The new locomotive works and offices at Eastleigh. *National Railway Museum*

cards addressed to the Prime Minister and Home Secretary indicated that the arson had been the work of suffragettes.

At about 11.45pm on the night of 17 June 1921 five or six men armed with revolvers entered Barnes Junction signalbox and tied up the signalman. The intruders proceeded to set fire to the building and then disappeared. Fortunately, the flames were seen by the station porter, who released the signalman and called the fire brigade to extinguish the fire while it was still confined to the roof. Similar attacks on signalboxes were made simultaneously on the lines of several other companies, and it was assumed that they were linked with the troubles in Ireland.

CHAPTER ELEVEN

MANAGING THE RAILWAY

NINE ELMS TO EASTLEIGH

The 45 acre works site at Nine Elms had become inadequate for the construction and maintenance of the company's locomotives and rolling stock. Already in 1890–1 the carriage and wagon works had moved to Eastleigh, allowing some enlargement of the locomotive works, but any further extension and modernisation would require a larger site, while the land at Nine Elms was needed for traffic purposes. Powers were obtained in 1898 to acquire some 200 acres of the Chickenhall Farm estate at Eastleigh, situated between the main and Portsmouth lines, and it was decided in principle during 1899 to move the locomotive works to this site. It was also intended to build a new locomotive depot there to replace the old shed at Northam; the combined cost of the two projects was estimated at £277,000.

Work started on the locomotive depot in November 1900, and the transfer from Northam took place in January 1903. The decision to start construction of the locomotive shops was taken in December 1902, but progress was slow as each stage was subject to separate authorisation. By the summer of 1909 machinery was running, and before the end of that year 350 men were at work on locomotive repairs, while the main transfer from Nine Elms took place during January 1910. The move was completed by 31 January, except for the chief mechanical engineer's staff, whose office block (deferred for a year) was not ready until September 1910.

The old Nine Elms locomotive works had employed around 2,400 men with a weekly payroll in 1901 of £3,600, largely based on piece-work rates. Due to reduced traffic revenue the men were placed on a short-time 40-hour week during the 1901–2 and subsequent winters. The normal annual output of the works was 30 new locomotives and more than 400 repair jobs. During its existence Nine Elms built 832 locomotives, the last one being completed on 24 June 1908, while Eastleigh turned out its first new locomotive on 12 September 1910.

Part of the structure of the boiler shop which dated only from

1892–3 was re-erected at Eastleigh, and many of the machine tools were transferred. The new works at Eastleigh were laid out with wide bays for easy movement and efficient production, with room available for future expansion. Their layout had been planned by Dugald Drummond, who visited the site frequently to supervise progress in his special saloon, 'The Bug.' Following the end of World War I the opportunity was taken to acquire government surplus machinery for the works. At the same time some extension and modernisation was made to the carriage works.

When the men of the carriage and wagon works moved to Eastleigh in 1890–1, the quality of the housing provided for them by local builders was so poor that a public enquiry had to be held, while a local board of health was set up in 1892. The transfer of the enginemen from Northam to Eastleigh was delayed by the lack of housing. The company then agreed in January 1903 to build 54 cottages in Campbell Road (a new road named after the chairman) costing £255 each, which were completed at the end of 1904.

The locomotive works move involved 1,500 men and their families, but in 1908 the company had expressed the view that it was not desirable for it to undertake the work of house building, as the needs of the transferred staff would be better provided through the medium of private enterprise. Inevitably, land prices rose sharply and no speculative building was carried out. When men began to arrive at Eastleigh during the autumn of 1909 they spent their weekends vainly searching for accommodation; many of the workforce were compelled to take lodgings in surrounding towns and commute daily to the works. On Saturday mid-day a special train ran to Waterloo, returning on Sunday evening, to enable them to visit their homes in London for the weekend. At the urgent recommendation of the locomotive committee, the board then approved in January 1910 the construction of 100 more cottages on company land in Campbell Road, to be let at rents of 5s 6d [27½] per week; these were eventually completed in November 1912 at a total cost of £30,758.

There were other aspects of welfare at Eastleigh. Within the works was a large dining hall for 600 men, and a clerical staff dining room which served a hot meal for 6d [2½p]. The LSWR Institute at Eastleigh had been established in 1891, providing a large meeting room and educational and recreational facilities for its thousand members. The influx of LSWR employees and their families required additional provision for their spiritual needs. The company contributed £500 towards the enlargement of Eastleigh parish church, with donations of £50 to each of the nonconformist chapels.

TRACK

In December 1901 the engineering committee decided to increase the standard weight of rail from 87lb/yd to 90lb/yd, raised again in 1905 to 95lb/yd, with 100lb/yd rails to be used on the very busy section between Waterloo and Clapham Junction. The committee's annual renewal programme was budgeted to cover about five per cent of the track mileage, equal to about 80–90 miles per year. At the start of 1907, 1,211 miles of the total running line mileage of 1,715 were laid with heavy rails of 87lb/yd or above, and only 21 miles were formed with rails of less than 80lb/yd. A major programme of bridge strengthening was launched in May 1914, but was soon interrupted by the war, with the difficulty of obtaining manpower and materials for track maintenance. At the end of 1919 arrears of track renewals amounted to 251 miles, but most of this backlog was cleared during 1920, enabling train speeds to return to normal in 1921.

In 1905 the chief engineer, J. W. Jacomb-Hood, had instituted a system of premium gradings for track maintenance. The three engineers' districts were divided into 36 inspectors' divisions, which competed for prizes, with challenge cups, medals and cash bonuses awarded to the inspectors, foremen and platelayers whose sections obtained the highest marks in the competition. The permanent way was judged on rail joints and alignment, ballasting and general appearance; the judging committee sat on tiers of seats in a four-wheeled inspection car (thus feeling the rail joints), propelled slowly by a locomotive.

The company had acquired in 1897 a large quarry at Meldon on the northern slopes of Dartmoor, which was estimated to contain 3 million cu yd of rock suitable for track ballast. Its output in 1913 was 125,200 tons; the war reduced this to 84,060 in 1919 but it recovered to 121,827 tons in 1920. In 1905 sixteen 40-ton bogie hopper wagons were purchased to convey the Meldon ballast to relaying sites: similar vehicles are still employed 80 years later. A small community grew up around the quarry. There was a staff platform where the pay clerk alighted each Friday, while the quarrymen's wives joined a train each Saturday for their weekly shopping trip to Okehampton.

SIGNALLING AND COMMUNICATIONS

The LSWR was responsible for the introduction to Britain of low-pressure pneumatic signalling. This had been developed in the USA by the International Pneumatic Railway Signal Co of New York, which in conjunction with the British Pneumatic Co formed in 1900 the British Pneumatic Railway Signal Co to exercise its rights in the UK. Considerable claims for the system's labour-saving advantages had been made in the USA, but in British conditions the principal benefit was the saving in space needed for interlocking in large signal-boxes, such as Clapham Junction. There was also a relaxation of the stringent Board of Trade limitations on the maximum distance facing points could be worked from a signalbox. The pneumatic system did enable the LSWR to instal automatic signalling on its main line at a time when electric operation of signals was in its infancy. Initially criticisms were made by the inspecting officers of the lack of overlap beyond automatic signals and at the transition from automatic to controlled sections, and various modifications had to be made. Compared to similar mechanical signalling, the pneumatic system was more costly to instal and proved to be more expensive to maintain.

Fog was a serious problem to the LSWR. A series of fogs in October and November 1903 cost the company £3,200 for the extra wages paid to fog signalmen. To ease their hazardous task of placing detonators on the line, the company adopted in 1906 the Clayton mechanical fog signalling apparatus for general use on multiple track sections.

Another approach to safety in fog was through automatic train control. Dugald Drummond in 1911 devised an apparatus employing mechanical contact between locomotive and track ramp. When the signal was at danger the apparatus emitted a warning whistle in the cab and applied the brakes. Some trials were carried out near the LSWR's signalling works at Wimbledon, but the physical contact involved in this system caused practical difficulties. An alternative offered by a private inventor was the Prentice 'wireless' signalling system: 'wireless' here refers to its inductive link between wires on track and train, rather than to any use of radio. A signal at danger cut the current in the track wire, causing a warning to sound in the locomotive cab and applying the brakes; the driver could only proceed by holding off the brake valve. Initial trials on the Hampton Court branch in 1913 were encouraging, and further experiments were being conducted at company expense when war broke out.

The LSWR was one of the companies which used the Coligny-Welch lamps to distinguish its distant signals. Among the devices developed by its signalling superintendent, J. P. Annett, were plat-form route indicators to simplify terminal signalling. A demonstration was made in 1920 of position light signals, based on a Pennsylvania Railroad system. Four white lights arranged horizontally, diagonally or vertically indicated danger, caution and line clear respectively, and in conjunction with route indicators both speed and direction signalling was provided. The signals were mounted on the gantry outside Waterloo 'A' box, but were not used operationally.

The new buildings at Waterloo included a modern semi-automatic telephone exchange. In 1921 a general improvement of communications was authorised in the London area and between Waterloo and Southampton to replace the old needle telegraph system by telephone circuits.

REFRESHMENTS AND SERVICES

It was LSWR policy not to operate catering services itself, but to lease its refreshment rooms to outside contractors, principally Spiers & Pond Ltd. This firm's contract was renewed for seven years from 1 January 1902. Under the contract's terms, the firm undertook to pay the LSWR 15 per cent of gross receipts, with a minimum of £19,000 per annum. The LSWR asked for tea and coffee prices to be reduced from 4d [2p] to 3d per cup, and tea baskets to be supplied for 1s 6d [7½p] instead of 2s 0d [10p]. Meals in the newly-introduced dining cars were to be at the same tariff as on the GWR. In 1913 £41,238 of Spiers & Pond's year's turnover of £137,876 was derived from the 36 restaurant car services operated each weekday. The Spiers & Pond contract was renewed annually from 1909 to 1919, when a seven-year contract was again granted.

The exception to the LSWR's practice of non-involvement in catering was the South Western Hotel, Southampton. Its lease by E. H. Rand expired on 29 September 1899, the contract with Spiers & Pond was nearing its conclusion, and the LSWR had plans for extensive enlargement and re-decoration of the hotel. The board therefore decided to take the management into its own hands, and authorising powers were obtained in the Act of 30 July 1900. Maple & Co contracted in January 1900 at £29,932 to modernise the hotel.

Meanwhile a Swiss manager had been appointed at a salary of £400 including his wife's services as housekeeper. The board decided that in view of the hotel's location, the members of the docks & steamships committee should form the hotel committee. The manager was given full authority to obtain provisions, but the purchase of wines and spirits was to be subject to the approval of the directors—in practice, the hotel committee limited its function to the choice of champagne. In November 1910 an accountants' report recommended that the manager's services should be terminated. An offer by Spiers & Pond was accepted to work and manage the hotel for 12½ per cent of gross receipts, with a minimum annual rental of £3,000. The LSWR also owned the Junction Hotel at Eastleigh, but this had been leased to Spiers & Pond since 1899.

In its dealings with its tenants and concessionaires the LSWR anticipated today's airport authorities in seeking to obtain a maximum share of the takings rather than a fixed rent. Onerous demands were made when Faulkner's moved into its new hairdressing saloons at Waterloo, and the rental accounts for 1922 showed that the LSWR took one-third of the receipts. From telephone call boxes the railway collected 20 per cent of the takings from both the National Telephone Co and its successor, the Post Office.

· Automatic machines were widely installed, to sell sweets or cigarettes or to amuse waiting passengers, who could try their strength or experience an electric shock for their penny, one third of which usually went to the LSWR. Similar machines were supplied by the manufacturers to the railway to issue penny tickets for short terminal journeys, such as Kew Gardens to Richmond and Thames Ditton to Hampton Court, where the booking office was on the opposite platform. Then in May 1913 the first platform ticket machines were installed at Waterloo and spread rapidly to other important stations. Before leaving the subject of pennies in the slot, the traffic officers conference was told in July 1913 that station lavatories had made a gross profit of £309.

STAFF RELATIONS

At the start of the century few companies recognised the railway trade unions, although the LSWR was not among those which still victimised union activists. Men humbly petitioned the directors for wage increases and gratefully accepted whatever was offered. In October 1899 LSWR platelayers were granted an increase of 1d on daily wage rates of between 2s 10d [14p] and 3s 9d [18p]. Clerical staff were placed in 1902 on a salary scale of £60 to £110 per annum, while increases were granted individually at the discretion of management and the board.

Sir Charles Scotter said at the company's general meeting in August 1907 that only five per cent of LSWR staff were members of the Amalgamated Society of Railway Servants, although some belonged to other unions, and there was no need for a third party in staff negotiations. This was in reply to union demands for recognition and improved conditions of service which, under the threat of a strike, led to the Liberal government setting up in November 1907 a system of conciliation boards to consider staff applications to which management could not assent. The LSWR was one of the first companies to reach agreement with its staff within the new framework, and among other benefits its traffic employees were granted overtime and Sunday payments at time-and-a-quarter from May 1909.

Significantly, the LSWR in 1907 had ceased to subscribe to the National Free Labour Association, an anti-trade union body which had supplied strike-breaking labour on such occasions as the Taff Vale dispute. The unions were not satisfied with the working of the conciliation boards, widespread unrest in August 1911 culminating in the calling of an official railway strike. Only two men on the LSWR came out. The company's main role in the dispute was to rush 17,855 troops into London to protect the capital from the disorders which accompanied this strike in many parts of the country. The strike was ended by the appointment of a Royal Commission to examine the conciliation system, which led to the trade unions being included in negotiations between the companies and their employees, although Herbert Walker felt that recognition of the unions would cause a lowering of standards of discipline.

The ASRS organ, *The Railway Review*, admitted that the unions were weak on the LSWR where the staff relationship was 'feudalistic but friendly.' A recruitment campaign was launched, and by November 1913 even members of the railway police had joined the National Union of Railwaymen (as the ASRS had now become), alarming the directors at the possible conflict of loyalties in the event of a strike. In May 1912 the clerical staff petitioned for improved salaries, and a new pay scale for employees earning less than £200 per year was introduced in January 1914. Wages staff had achieved a minimum rate of £1 per week in 1912, while working hours had been reduced— signalmen to ten hours and guards to eleven hours per day. The effect of these concessions was an increase in average wages from 24s 6d (£1.22$^{1}/_{2}$] per week to 26s 3d [£1.31] between December 1911 and January 1914, costing the company £60,000 a year.

The normal weekly wage was always liable to reduction by short time working due to either a decline in traffic or outside causes. The coal strike of 1912 led to the immediate dismissal of casual permanent way staff and to Eastleigh works being placed on short time. The reduction of 50 per cent in main line and 25 per cent in local train services meant that many men were put on half pay, but in these cases the company waived half the rent on their company cottages or paid them a rent allowance.

The troubled story of labour relations during the First World War and its aftermath has already been told in Chapters 7 and 8.

The LSWR was in the forefront of employers providing for staff pensions. Its staff superannuation fund had been set up in 1864 and improvements were made to the scheme in 1900 and 1909. The company paid £8,000 a year into its funds; members were assured of a pension of one-fiftieth of their final seven years' salary for each year of membership. For the uniform staff there was a pension fund which had run into deficit in 1900, but the company then agreed to meet its outlay from revenue. Locomen had a separate contributory fund. The pension fund paid out retirement allowances of between 6s 0d [30p] and 10s 9d [53p] per week. To assist instances of individual hardship due to sudden death, sickness or accident the Chairman's Fund could make small grants of £5 or £10.

Consideration was shown to staff in other ways. Signalmen over 60 years of age employed in signalboxes between Waterloo and Clapham Junction were allowed to transfer to quieter suburban cabins without losing pension rights and the whole of their service increments. Similarly, drivers demoted for reasons of health or eyesight could retain their existing pay and holiday entitlements. During the Boer War the dependents of reservists were granted half pay and the men's absence was counted as leave for pension purposes; of 171 men called to the Colours, 161 returned to the company's service. Leave was granted for employees to attend Territorial Army camps and an LSWR Rifle Club was formed in 1901, to promote readiness to defend the country in time of war.

Railway work was dangerous, and many children were left fatherless. In 1885 the South Western Railway Servants' Orphanage had been established at Clapham, and additional premises for girls were added in 1900 at Lambeth. Larger and more convenient accommodation was required, and with the help of a large bequest 7½ acres of land at Woking were purchased from the London Necropolis Co, where a new orphanage building housing 150 children was erected at a cost of £24,000. The foundation stone laying in October 1907 and the ceremonial opening on 5 July 1909 were both performed by HRH the Duchess of Albany, a regular traveller by the LSWR from Esher station. Maintenance costs of the orphanage were met by staff contributions, windfalls from money found on stations and by the contents of the collecting boxes carried by the well-loved dogs at some of the principal stations.

The habit of saving was encouraged by the LSWR Friendly Society, to which the company made an annual contribution from 1907 onwards of up to £1,500. London area employees had the benefit of the Vauxhall Institute & Club, while serious topics of railway interest were discussed at the Main Line & Metropolitan District Debating Society, established in 1901, which soon had 1,000 members. From

1904 onwards the LSWR guaranteed £100 a year towards the fees of railway students at the London School of Economics. One of the last actions of the company in 1922 was to purchase 13½ acres of land at Raynes Park for a sports ground. The general manager asked the board for £10,000 towards its cost, which would be met from the profit on the sale of platform tickets. Finally, the South Western railwayman could go to his last resting place in Brookwood cemetery, where company employees were offered plots at the reduced charge of 15s 0d [75p].

The long hours on duty often required train crews to lodge away from home. Small dormitories for locomen were provided at the principal depots, sometimes at the base of the water tank. A hostel for guards was opened in February 1919 in some houses near Southampton Terminus station.

At Grouping the LSWR owned 1,544 staff cottages and houses, many being primitive and remote. In April 1904 the Seaton Junction signalman was granted £10 towards medical fees for typhoid contracted by his daughter, due to bad drainage. At Liss the station-master was given £13 18s 0d [£13.90] to pay his doctor's bill for blood poisoning caused by impure water from the station well. The staff cottages at Portcreek Junction could only be reached by walking along the line, so the joint committee had to issue track passes to the vicar, doctor, district nurse and school attendance officer. The board in October 1913 approved plans and funding for new and better staff cottages, but ruled that these were to be let at rents which would provide a five per cent return on capital. In June 1920 the LSWR agreed to advance £30,000 from the Locomen's Pension Fund to Guildford Town Council, to finance the provision of 20 houses for enginemen on the Guildford Park estate.

Staff housing of a different standard was to be found on the down side of Surbiton station, where a number of substantial houses had been acquired by the company during the 1880s in connection with the Kingston & London project. These were rented to private tenants on short leases, but proved difficult to let and often stood empty for long periods. It was decided in 1902 to offer them to company officers at reduced rents. Among these South Bank Lodge, overlooking the station, was appropriately occupied by Henry Holmes, the superintendent of the line at a rent of £80 per annum; its neighbour, No 2 South Bank, went to Dugald Drummond for £100 a year, and he named it Morven.

DIRECTORS AND OFFICERS

The chairmanship of the LSWR in 1900 was held by Lieut Colonel the Hon Henry Walter Campbell. Born in 1835 and a veteran of the Crimean War, he joined the LSWR board in 1872, being elected chairman in 1899. He was uncle of Earl Cawdor, chairman of the GWR, but there was little evidence of family affection between the two companies. Colonel Campbell retired from the chairmanship in 1904, but remained on the board until his death in 1910.

The soldier was succeeded in the chair by a professional railwayman. Sir Charles Scotter, born in Hull, started his career on the MSLR, leaving that company in 1885 to become a very successful general manager of the LSWR. Retiring in 1898, he immediately joined the board and became deputy chairman in 1899 then chairman in 1904. He had immense knowledge and experience of the railway, but he was already 69 when he took office. Public duties also claimed his time and energy, notably the thankless task of chairing the Vice-Regal Commission on Irish Railways during 1906–9. He was rewarded with a baronetcy in 1907. His absence through indisposition from various company functions was noted during 1909–10, but he successfully completed his negotiations for agreement with the GWR before his last illness led to his death on 13 December 1910.

The LSWR's final chairman was Hugh Henry John Williams Drummond. Although born in Devon, he was a Scot and a professional soldier who had left the army on his marriage to a member of the Rolle family, the principal landowners in East Devon. Having become a partner in the Exeter Bank and living then at East Budleigh, he was active in the promotion of the Budleigh Salterton and Axminster & Lyme Regis Railways. On the sudden death of Michael Williams, he was invited in 1900 to become the Devon member of the LSWR board and was elected deputy chairman in 1904.

Hugh Drummond succeeded Sir Charles Scotter to the chairmanship in 1910. At the age of 51 he brought new vigour to the task, expediting the completion of Waterloo and making the choice of Herbert Walker as general manager. During the early days of the 1914–18 war he returned to the army and raised new cavalry regiments in Devon for Kitchener's Army, for which he was given the honorary rank of Brigadier General. He was created a baronet in June 1922. One of his greatest services to the railway was his steady support of Sir Herbert Walker during the difficult negotiations prior to Grouping and during the early traumatic months of the SR's existence, when he had become chairman of the new company. The path to the future success of the Southern Railway had been assured when he died in August 1924.

The deputy chairman from 1910 until Grouping was Sir William Portal, Bt, a member of the paper-making family, whose father, Wyndham S. Portal had been chairman of the LSWR from 1892 to 1899. He had succeeded his father on the board in 1902 and retired at Grouping.

From time to time individual shareholders would apply to be considered for election to the board, but its members were carefully chosen to represent the various territorial, industrial and financial interests which would benefit the company. This is illustrated in Appendix 10 which lists the members of the board just prior to Grouping.

Sir Charles Scotter had been succeeded as general manager in 1898 by Charles J. Owens, who had spent his entire career on the LSWR, mainly in the goods department. He was knighted in June 1902, said to be in recognition of the LSWR's efforts during the Boer War, and he retired on 31 December 1911 after nearly 50 years in the company's service.

To find his successor the company went 'head hunting,' offering the post to Herbert Ashcombe Walker, goods manager of the LNWR and one of that company's bright young men, who saw better prospects of advancement south of the Thames. He was appointed as General Manager on 1 January 1912 at the age of 43 and went on to become one of the greatest of railway managers, whose achievements have already been described in these pages. He was knighted in January 1915 and advanced to KCB in 1917.

The LSWR had not previously had a full-time solicitor, as the work was carried out by the firm of Bircham & Co whose head, Sam Bircham, became solicitor and chief of the company's legal department from 1 January 1900. He retired on 30 June 1910 and was succeeded by W. Bishop, who had joined the company from the LNWR in 1903 and who suggested Herbert Walker to the LSWR chairman when the vacancy as general manager arose.

The traditional railway organisation concentrated extensive powers for commercial as well as operating matters in the hands of the superintendent of the line. When G. T. White died suddenly on 17 March 1899, Sam Fay returned from the MSWJR to take over at a salary of £1,500. After three years of enterprising activity he left for the general managership of the GCR, the post going to one of the unsuccessful candidates of 1899, Henry Holmes, at a salary of only £800. He was a competent but conventional railway officer who was reputed not to have agreed with some of Herbert Walker's innovations, while Walker's management changes reduced the scope of his office. He retired abruptly on 31 October 1916 at the early age of 53, with none of the customary references to ill health. He was succeeded by his assistant, G. F. West, who served until Grouping, when acknowledged ill health led to his immediate retirement from the SR.

Civil engineering affairs were subject to dual control. W. T. Galbraith had been appointed as consulting engineer in 1887, and his office was responsible for most of the company's new construction projects. In regard to electrical matters, Sir William Preece became consulting electrical engineer in 1899. The full-time head of the engineering department was the confusingly-titled resident engineer, E. Andrews. He was succeeded on retirement from 1 March 1901 by J. W. Jacomb-Hood at a salary of £1,000. After the two offices of consulting engineer had been abolished in 1904, the latter was termed chief resident engineer in 1905. Jacomb-Hood died suddenly on 6 March 1914 while riding in Devon. The office, now that of chief engineer, was taken by A. W. Szlumper at £1,400 per year.

Much has been written about the company's locomotive superintendent, Dugald Drummond. He had succeeded William Adams on the LSWR in 1895 and had provided the company with large numbers of reliable locomotives in the best traditions of Scottish engineering practice. However, his innovations with large four-cylinder 4-6-0s and steam railmotors were less successful. He was a stern disciplinarian but became well-liked by his staff. On his tragic death at the age of seventy-two on 7 November 1912 his coffin was carried by a party of engine drivers from his house to Surbiton station nearby, where a special train hauled by No 463, one of his latest 4-4-0s, conveyed him on his last journey to Brookwood cemetery.

Drummond was followed as chief mechanical engineer (as the office had been known since 1905) by R. W. Urie, the Eastleigh works manager. To him is due the credit for the first modern mixed-traffic locomotive; his H15 Class of 1914 featured rugged construction and a large boiler, with two outside cylinders and a high running plate for easy maintenance. These locomotives were a godsend to the company during the First World War. Orders were placed in 1916 for express (Class N15) and freight (Class S15) versions, but because of wartime difficulties these did not emerge from Eastleigh until September 1918 and March 1920 respectively. Urie also improved the already competent Drummond designs by the provision of superheaters.

The advent of Herbert Walker as general manager was not accompanied by any drastic purge of existing officers. Advantage was taken of the retirement in January 1912 of Alfred Malby, the goods manager, to split the office between indoor and outdoor managers.

Following the death of Dugald Drummond, the function of locomotive running superintendent was detached from the chief mechanical engineer's department. The district superintendents' offices for
the Main Line and Metropolitan districts were both situated at Clapham Junction, and it was decided in May 1912 to amalgamate them as
the London district, with offices at Waterloo. At the same time, the
district superintendents were given more authority to make local
decisions, and assistant superintendents were appointed.

An advertising and publicity department was formed in 1913
within the general manager's office, this being expanded in 1914 by
the formation of a continental section. The publicity department
published free booklets such as *Charming Residential Districts Within
Easy Reach of London, Quiet Holiday & Seaside Resorts in Normandy*
and *The Royal Road*, the latter a guide to resorts on the LSWR. The
department produced some very effective publicity to inform the
public about the new electric suburban services. In 1918 the company
took over the *South Western Magazine* from its previous private owner;
the head of the LSWR publicity department, F. V. Milton, became its
editor.

Herbert Walker exercised his influence over the railway through
the general manager's office. He first had as assistant J. H. Vickery,
then G. S. Szlumper (the son of the chief engineer) from January
1914. The office was run by the chief clerk, W. Buckmaster, who
brought the knowledge derived from 40 years' service. Under him
were experienced section heads, who kept in touch with the districts
and departments, bringing matters of importance to the notice of the
general manager; they also acted as secretaries at the regular meetings
of the company's officers. The statistical clerk had the task of furnish-
ing the newly-appointed general manager with full details of the
LSWR system, which thereafter remained in Walker's retentive
memory.

Another means of managerial control was the traffic officers conference introduced in 1913, which was held monthly three days prior to
the board meeting. The conference was composed of the general
manager, his assistant, the superintendent of the line, the district
superintendents, the goods managers and the locomotive running
superintendent. Regular items on the agenda included train service
changes, fare alterations, new works and the investigation of accidents
and irregularities. Where board approval was necessary, the conference made recommendations to the appropriate committee.

In addition, statistical reports were submitted monthly or at longer
intervals on such matters as passenger train punctuality, freight train
loadings, locomotive failures, train mileages (with emphasis on light

and assisting locomotive working), excessive hours worked by staff, men called in for special Sunday duties, cartage costs, bad debts and the periodic examination of staff on the company's rules. Additional reports were provided on new aspects of the company's business, such as road motor operation and platform ticket receipts. The system was designed to reveal poor performance, waste and slackness within the operating and commercial organisation.

FINANCIAL MATTERS

The LSWR valued its second class traffic. In May 1896 it had reduced second class fares from 1¹/₂d to 1¹/₄d per mile in the belief that this small premium would be attractive to commuters and others seeking to escape from the company of their social inferiors. In 1901 4,753,000 of its 61,973,000 passengers travelled second class. After 1905 there was an apparent sharp decline in LSWR second class bookings when MDR electrification of the lines to Wimbledon and Richmond eliminated second class travel on District trains. Second class passenger numbers slowly diminished to about two million a year, equal to first class traffic. Despite the abolition of second class on the GWR, certain South Western directors and officers still felt that it was of value to long-distance travellers. Gradually, second class disappeared from railmotors, push-and-pull trains, then the suburban electrics, but it was the exigencies of war which led to its final abolition in 1918.

Workmen's traffic was heavy in the London area; 4,500,000 tickets were issued in 1901 and 136 trains were run daily. From the end of 1901 third class season tickets began to be issued, and steadily the use of season tickets was encouraged by their issue for shorter periods and without the necessity for advance notice. Between 1901 and 1912 the number of season tickets issued more than doubled from 56,000 to 116,000 a year. Considerable alternative availability was offered to season ticket holders in the London area, and there were substantial reductions for several members of a family who took out identical seasons. The instruction 'All Season Tickets to be Shewn' was not made mandatory until 1 January 1917. To avoid delays caused by commuters fumbling within their voluminous clothes for their tickets, Mr Buckmaster designed a new type of season ticket in a metal mica-covered holder which could be attached to watchchain, wrist or handbag.

The decrease in pre-electrification suburban traffic was offset in total by more long-distance business; 61,973,000 passengers in 1901 had increased to 65,815,000 in 1912. Traffic was stimulated by the issue of day and market returns, weekend and tourist tickets, as well as period excursions. Most of these cheap facilities were withdrawn during the war. To assist wartime temporary staff the company introduced a simplified ticket system in 1918, which reduced 250 types of ticket to 24, printed in four colours. As the abnormal traffic of the war and early post-war years receded the LSWR began making efforts to attract passengers again, and cheap day returns were resumed in July 1921.

There had always been keen competition between the LSWR and its western neighbour the GWR. Tentative approaches had been made by the LSWR for an agreement in the early 1900s, but apparently it hoped to base any apportionment of traffic receipts on the existing situation before the GWR could gain any benefit from its new cut-off routes to the west. Completion of these in 1906 opened the way to more realistic negotiations, and the LSWR chairman signified his willingness for agreement at the company's general meeting in February 1908. Serious negotiations started in December 1909, the heads of agreement being signed in February 1910 by the respective chairmen, Sir Charles Scotter and Viscount Churchill. The final 90-year agreement was concluded on 13 May 1910. This provided in essence that competitive traffic was to be worked in such a way as to yield the greatest revenue to the two companies jointly, and that receipts were to be pooled and then divided on the basis of 1908 volume. The LSWR was to withdraw from the Plymouth ocean liner traffic. The companies expressed the intention to co-operate in securing economies at their junction stations and to promote through services between their systems.

The story of the LSWR's road motor services has already been told, but these were not carried on under any statutory powers. In common with other railway companies the LSWR sought to obtain Parliamentary authority for its bus services, but a clause in its 1906 Bill was opposed by the London Master Carmen and Carter Paterson, and was accordingly withdrawn. Another attempt was made in the 1913 Bill, but this met with 48 objectors, including local authorities and the Aldershot & District Traction Co—again the clause had to be withdrawn. The LSWR was not prejudiced against new forms of transport; in 1922 it agreed to offer through bookings for proposed air services from Southampton to France and the Channel Islands.

The start of the 20th century found the LSWR board faced with many competing claims for capital investment: the rebuilding of Waterloo, the widening of the main line, the new branch lines, station reconstruction and the continual expansion of Southampton Docks. As a result the board sometimes found difficulty in committing itself to capital expenditure.

During 1901 there was a downturn in traffic receipts and an increase in coal prices, so that net earnings fell by £60,000 and the dividend had to be reduced. To meet existing capital expenditure commitments, £760,000 had to be raised on the stock market before February 1902, at a time when the price of the company's shares was depressed. The board ruled on 10 October 1901 that capital works were to be divided into three categories:

A – to be carried on to completion
B – to proceed gradually as convenient
C – to be held over until further instructions.

The main victim under category C was the Eastleigh to St Denys widening, which was never revived, but only a few urgent and self-financing works were accorded A class priority.

More financial difficulties occurred in 1904, and the finance committee asked the board for a reduction of £45,000 in approved capital expenditure. The February meeting was told of the difficulty in raising capital and that no new works were contemplated. It was repeated at the August meeting that it was company policy to reduce capital outlay until better times. The shareholders at the meeting in February 1908 were told that it was a matter for congratulation that there was no company Bill (involving further expenditure) before Parliament that year.

This shortage of funds and the reluctance to raise additional capital when the market was unfavourable does much to explain the apparent slow progress on many of the company's projects, notably the reconstruction of Waterloo. It was the company's practice, after being authorised to raise additional capital, to issue it to the market in small quantities through the company's stockbrokers. In this way the price was not depressed by a sudden large issue of stock. Frequently the LSWR shareholders complained of not being allowed to get in on the ground floor through a 'rights issue,' but the directors held to their view that this method would not secure the best price for the company.

When large amounts of capital were required for electrification the company included in its 1913 Act powers to raise £1.5 million by the issue of redeemable preference stock, an innovation in railway finance. It was intended to issue this stock in August or September 1914 at a time when contractors' bills for the electrification work would be due for payment. However, the outbreak of war brought a financial panic, and for a few days even the routine credit facilities needed to pay the half-year dividend were in doubt. There was certainly no possibility of a public share issue as the stock exchange was closed, so on 11 August the board ordered that all avoidable work on current contracts was to cease and that no new contracts were to be made. After the panic had subsided somewhat, a finance house, Boulton Bros & Co, came to the LSWR's rescue and took £1 million of the new five per cent redeemable preference stock at a price of 97½. It soon sold £440,000 of it at a price of 99¾ and the rest was probably disposed of at a premium after the stock exchange re-opened in January 1915. With funds now assured, work on the suspended contracts was resumed on 29 October.

Herbert Walker made a number of reforms in accounting practice in regard to capital expenditure. Over the years assets had been charged to capital account and some of these were no longer being used. The general manager instituted a review of such redundant buildings, track and signalling which could be removed. Their cost was then taken out of capital and charged to a capital works disused and displaced suspense account, their residual value to be written-off over a period of years. To prevent the problem recurring, new rules for capital investment were laid down; items costing less than £300 and all rolling stock were to be charged to revenue. Works designed to save revenue were to be charged to a new works revenue suspense account, and this was to be credited annually with the actual savings, chargeable to the user department. A fund for betterment works was set up for the cost of improvements not properly chargeable to capital, and another suspense account was created for some of the cost of electrification. Thus of the £50,753 cost of the Hampton Court Junction flyover, only £35,896 was charged to capital and the balance was either debited to revenue immediately or charged to these various improvement accounts, where it would be written-off within 20 years.

Because of the LSWR's function as primarily a passenger line serving many holiday resorts, in the days of half-year accounting the results of the second half were always better than the first half of the year. Throughout the period 1900–1916 there was a continual outlay on capital expenditure; between 1 January 1900 and 31 December 1913 £10,436,490 had been spent, an increase of nearly 27 per cent on the assets at the end of 1899. Issued capital and debentures likewise increased by 29 per cent, but net earnings only rose by £254,000, an increase of 13 per cent. To compare with other 'blue chip' companies, the LNWR over the same period improved its earnings by 15 per cent for an increase in capital expenditure of 12 per cent, while the GWR had corresponding increases of 32 per cent and 25 per cent respectively.

In consequence the LSWR ordinary share price which in 1900 had been one of the highest in the market, exceeding that of the LNWR and GWR, was by 1913 equal to the GWR and below that of the LNWR; by 1922 it was the lowest of the three. During the years of government control these companies were able to maintain a higher rate of dividend than the LSWR, but for 1919 the South Western was able to increase its dividend by $1/8$ per cent, due to improved revenue from refreshment rooms and rents. In 1921 the LSWR's six per cent dividend was only maintained by the inclusion of a £250,000 government compensation payment. The company's final dividend for 1922 was boosted to eight per cent by the payment from the Treasury of four per cent interest due on capital expenditure since 1913; this was the only return the LSWR shareholders received from the investment in electrification and the increase in traffic it generated.

The company's investment since 1900 had created a more efficient railway, but before the benefits could be realised war had broken out and government control prevented the LSWR shareholders receiving their reward: only as part owners of the Southern Railway did they share in that company's prosperity, which was based on the LSWR's investment and the leadership of its general manager, Sir Herbert Walker.

ABBREVIATIONS

A&LR	Axminster & Lyme Regis Light Railway
ASLEF	Associated Society of Locomotive Engineers & Firemen
ASRS	Amalgamated Society of Railway Servants
BEF	British Expeditionary Force
B&W	Bodmin & Wadebridge Railway
BoT	Board of Trade
BSR	Budleigh Salterton Railway
BTH	British Thomson Houston
CLR	Central London Railway
CSLR	City & South London Railway
DNSR	Didcot, Newbury & Southampton Railway
E&CH	Easton & Church Hope Railway
FYNR	Freshwater, Yarmouth & Newport Railway
GCR	Great Central Railway
GER	Great Eastern Railway
GNR	Great Northern Railway
GNCR	Great Northern & City Railway
GWR	Great Western Railway
H&C	Hammersmith & City Joint Line
IoMSP	Isle of Man Steam Packet Co
IWCR	Isle of Wight Central Railway
IWR	Isle of Wight Railway
L&B	Lynton & Barnstaple Railway
LBSCR	London, Brighton & South Coast Railway
LCC	London County Council
LCDR	London Chatham & Dover Railway
LER	London Electric Railways
LNC	London Necropolis Company
LNWR	London & North Western Railway
LSWR	London & South Western Railway
LUT	London United Tramways
Met	Metropolitan Railway
MDR	Metropolitan District Railway
MR	Midland Railway
MSLR	Manchester Sheffield & Lincolnshire Railway
MSWJR	Midland & South Western Junction Railway
MoT	Ministry of Transport

NSWJ	North & South Western Junction Railway
NUR	National Union of Railwaymen
NCR	North Cornwall Railway
NLR	North London Railway
P&D	Plymouth & Dartmoor Railway
PDSWJ	Plymouth, Devonport & South Western Junction Railway
REC	Railway Executive Committee
S&DJR	Somerset & Dorset Joint Railway
SER	South Eastern Railway
SECR	South Eastern & Chatham Railway
SMAR	Swindon Marlborough & Andover Railway
SPI	Stonehouse Pool Improvement Company
SR	Southern Railway
SW&IOWJ	South Western & Isle of Wight Junction Railway
W&C	Waterloo & City Railway
WD	War Department
WLR	West London Railway
WLER	West London Extension Railway
W&S	Wimbledon & Sutton Railway

LSWR CROSS-CHANNEL FLEET 1900-1922 HISTORY

Name	Builder	Launched	To LSWR Service	Disposal
Alliance	Ditchburn & Mare, London	1855	1855	Sold 2/1900. Scrap
Brittany (I)	J. Ash & Co, Cubitt Town	1864	1864	Sold 10/1900. Scrap
St Malo	Aitken & Mansel, Glasgow	8/1865	1865	Sold 5/1906 Scrap
Maria	H. Murray & Co, Port Glasgow	1871	1871	Sold 4/1907
Cherbourg	J. & R. Swan, Dumbarton	1873	1873	To SR. Scrapped 1930
Honfleur	Aitken & Mansel, Glasgow	1874	1874	Sold 2/1911
Guernsey	J. & W. Dudgeon, London	1874	1874	Wrecked 9/4/1915
South Western (II)	J. & W. Dudgeon, London	1874	1874	Torpedoed 16/3/1918
Ella	Aitken & Mansel, Glasgow	1881	1881	Sold 7/1913
Hilda	Aitken & Mansel, Glasgow	1882	12/1882	Wrecked 18/11/1905
Laura	Aitken & Mansel, Glasgow	20/3/1885	18/5/1885	To SR. Scrapped 1927
Dora	R. Napier & Sons, Glasgow	2/3/1889	4/1889	Sold 1901 to IoMSP Co
Frederica	J. & G. Thomson, Clydebank	1890	1890	Sold 6/1911 to Turkey
Lydia	J. & G. Thomson, Clydebank	16/7/1890	1890	Sold 2/1920—later to Coast Lines
Columbia	J. & G. Thomson, Clydebank	1894	10/1894	Sold 4/1912 to Algiers
Alma	J. & G. Thomson, Clydebank	1894	12/1894	Sold 5/1912 to Algiers
Victoria	J. & G. Thomson, Clydebank	1896	1/8/1896	Sold 5/1919 to James Dredging
Vera	Clydebank Engineering & Shipbuilding	4/7/1898	9/1898	To SR. Scrapped 1933
Alberta	John Brown & Co, Clydebank	3/4/1900	1/6/1900	To SR. Sold 1930
Ada	Gourlay Bros, Dundee	1905	29/4/1905	To SR. Scrapped 1934
Bertha	Gourlay Bros, Dundee	9/11/1905	20/11/1905	To SR. Sold 1933
Princess Ena	Gourlay Bros, Dundee	25/5/1906	15/7/1906	To SR. Burnt 3/8/1935
Caesarea (II)	Cammell Laird, Birkenhead	26/5/1910	23/9/1910	To SR, later to IoMSP Co
Sarnia	Cammell Laird, Birkenhead	9/7/1910	4/4/1911	Torpedoed 12/9/1918 on RN service
Normannia	Fairfield Co, Govan	9/11/1911	26/2/1912	To SR. Sunk 5/1940
Hantonia	Fairfield Co, Govan	23/12/1911	31/3/1912	To SR/BR. Scrapped 1952
Normandy (II) (ex LBSCR)	Earle & Co, Hull	12/5/1910	31/5/1912	Torpedoed 25/1/1918
Brittany (II)(Ex LBSCR)	Earle & Co, Hull	9/7/1910	3/6/1912	To SR. Sold 1936
Ulrica (Ex Granuaile)	Ailsa Co, Troon	1895	6/1916	To SR. Sold 1928
Lorina	Denny Bros, Dumbarton	12/8/1918	31/1/1920	To SR. Sunk 5/1940
Ardena (ex HMS Peony)	A. MacMillan, Dumbarton	1915	6/12/1920	To SR. Sold 1934
Vena (ex Algeiba)	Scott & Sons, Bowling	1902	6/1922	To SR. Sold 1926
Rina (ex Algethi)	Adrossan Dry Dock Co	1902	6/1922	To SR. Sold 1926

LSWR CROSS-CHANNEL FLEET 1900–1922 DETAILS

Name	Propulsion	Speed knots	Gross tons	Length ft	Beam ft	Draught ft	Cost £
Alliance	Paddle	—	400	175	24	15	—
Brittany (I)	Paddle	—	678	236	26	13	—
St Malo	S/Screw	—	309	161	22	12	—
Maria	S/Screw	—	272	156	21	11	—
Cherbourg	S/Screw	12	386	166	23	12	—
Honfleur	S/Screw	—	410	176	24	12	—
Guernsey	S/Screw	—	545	195	26	13	—
South Western (II)	S/Screw	—	657	222	27	13	—
Ella	S/Screw	13¹/₂	820	235	29	14	28,850
Hilda	S/Screw	13¹/₂	849	235	29	14	33,000
Laura	S/Screw	13	617	207	27	13	—
Dora	S/Screw	—	813	240	30	14	32,800
Frederica	T/Screw	19	1,059	253	35	15	62,980
Lydia	T/Screw	19	1,059	253	35	15	60,800
Columbia	T/Screw	19	1,145	270	34	15	50,800
Alma	T/Screw	19	1,145	270	34	15	49,300
Victoria	T/Screw	16¹/₂	709	220	28	16	26,200
Vera	T/Screw	19	1,136	270	35	14¹/₂	54,000
Alberta	T/Screw	19	1,240	270	36	15	67,000
Ada	S/Screw	12	529	175	28	12	13,200
Bertha	S/Screw	12	528	175	28	12	13,600
Princess Ena	T/Screw	19	1,198	251	33	15	45,000
Caesarea (II)	Turbine	20	1,505	285	39	16	69,280
Sarnia	Turbine	20	1,498	285	39	16	69,280
Normannia	Turbine	20	1,560	290	36	15	69,000
Hantonia	Turbine	20	1,560	290	36	15	69,000
Normandy (II)	S/Screw	12¹/₂	618	192	29	14	16,750
Brittany (II)	S/Screw	12¹/₂	618	192	29	14	16,750
Ulrica	S/Screw	11	383	150	24	8	10,430
Lorina	Turbine	19	1,457	291	36	15	135,971
Ardena	S/Screw	16	1,092	250	33	17	151,994
Vena	S/Screw	—	565	170	27	11	⎱ 15,650
Rina	S/Screw	—	548	170	27	11	⎰

LSWR LYMINGTON AND PLYMOUTH VESSELS 1900–1922 HISTORY

Name	Builder	Launched	To LSWR service	Disposal
Solent (I) (ex Solent SS Co)	Inman, Lymington	3/11/1863	7/1884	Sold 6/1901. Scrapped.
Mayflower (ex Solent SS Co)	Marshall Bros, Newcastle	6/7/1866	7/1884	Sold 6/1905. Scrapped.
Lymington	Day Summers, Southampton	6/4/1893	9/5/1893	To SR. Sold 1929
Solent (II)	Mordey Carney, Southampton	1902	3/1902	To SR/BR. Sold 1948
Carrier (Tug & cargo)	Holland	1904	6/2/1906	To SR. Converted to barge 1931
Plymouth Tenders: Victoria (see Appendices 2A and 2B)		1904–7		
Atalanta (III)	Gourlay Bros, Dundee	25/4/1907	27/5/1907	Sold 6/1910 to GWR

LSWR LYMINGTON AND PLYMOUTH VESSELS 1900–1922 DETAILS

Name	Propulsion	Speed knots	Gross tons	Length ft	Beam ft	Draught ft	Cost £
Solent (I)	Paddle	12	61	94	16	7	
Mayflower	Paddle	12	69	98	16	7	
Lymington	Paddle	11	130	120	18	8	6,000
Solent (II)	Paddle		161	133	20	8	9,000
Carrier	T/Screw		98	61	21	8½	2,750
Atalanta (III)	S/Screw	13	577	170	32	15	25,500

LSWR AND LBSCR JOINT ISLE OF WIGHT FLEET 1900–1922 HISTORY

Name	Builder	Launched	To Joint service	Disposal
Alexandra	Scott & Co, Greenock	1879	1879	Sold 2/1913. See note
Duchess of Edinburgh	Aitken & Mansel, Glasgow	9/4/1884	27/6/1884	Sold 10/1910. Scrap
Duchess of Connaught	Aitken & Mansel, Glasgow	29/4/1884	8/7/1884	Sold 10/1910. Scrap
Duchess of Albany	Scott & Co, Greenock	7/11/1889	26/12/1889	To SR. Scrapped 1928
Princess Margaret	Scott & Co, Greenock	17/4/1893	23/5/1893	To SR. Scrapped 1928
Duchess of Kent	Day Summers, Southampton	1/7/1897	15/11/1897	To SR. Sold 1933
Duchess of Fife	Clydebank Engineering & Shipbuilding	1899	22/5/1899	To SR. Scrapped 1929
Ada (Launch and tug)	Mordey Carney, Southampton	1903	1903	Sunk 26/1/1917
Duchess of Richmond	D. & W. Henderson, Glasgow	11/6/1910	15/7/1910	Mined 28/6/1919 on RN service
Duchess of Norfolk	D. & W. Henderson, Glasgow	25/7/1911	16/9/1911	To SR. Sold 1937
Adur (II)	South Shields (ex James Dredging)	1912	1919	To SR. Sold 1925

Note: P/S Alexandra was sold to the Bembridge & Seaview Steam Packet Co and was then purchased by Cosens of Weymouth in September 1914.

LSWR AND LBSCR JOINT ISLE OF WIGHT FLEET 1900–1922 DETAILS

Name	Propulsion	Gross tons	Length ft	Beam ft	Draught ft	Cost £
Alexandra	Paddle	235	171	20	8½	8.900
Duchess of Edinburgh	Paddle	342	191	26	9	18,400
Duchess of Connaught	Paddle	342	191	26	9	18,400
Duchess of Albany	Paddle	256	170	22	8½	11,300
Princess Margaret	Paddle	260	171	22	8½	10,000
Duchess of Kent	Paddle	399	195	26	9	17,000
Duchess of Fife	Paddle	443	215	26	9½	26,000
Ada	S/Screw					1,860
Duchess of Richmond	Paddle	354	190	26	9	16,500
Duchess of Norfolk	Paddle	381	190	26	9	18,400
Adur (II)	S/Screw	54	70	16	7	3,500

FASTEST TIMINGS BETWEEN WATERLOO AND PRINCIPAL STATIONS SUMMER SERVICES 1900–1922

Year	Salisbury 83³/₄ miles Minutes	Exeter Queen Street 171³/₄ miles Minutes	Southampton West 79¹/₂ miles Minutes	Bournemouth Central 108 miles Minutes	Portsmouth Town 73³/₄ miles Minutes
1900	100	215	105	126	121
1901	100	210	98	126	111
1902	100	210	98	126	110
1903	91	195	101	126	110
1904	91	195	100	126	115
1905	91	195	98	126	117
1906	91	195	98	126	122
1907	92	194	98	126	122
1908	91	194	98	126	122
1909	91	192	97	126	106
1910	91	192	97	126	106
1911	91	192	97	120	106
1912	91	198	98	120	106
1913	91	198	98	120	106
1914	91	198	98	120	111
1915	91	198	98	126	111
1916	91	198	103	126	116
1917	91	198	103	155	127
1918	103	237	110	159	132
1919	103	238	103	151	118
1920	103	236	103	151	120
1921	95	205	92	135	118
1922	93	200	92	135	117

SUBURBAN SERVICES

Waterloo departures (Monday to Friday)   Electric Services

	1900	1914	1922	Headcode	Trains per hour	
	Trains per day				Weekday	Sunday
Main Line						
Woking Slow	20	21	21			
Chertsey	4	6	3			
Guildford via Cobham (a)	5	8	20			
Epsom	17	23	21			
Hampton Court	22	25	67	H	4	3
Shepperton via Kingston	–	1	34	S	2	–
Kingston Roundabout	30	34	78	V	4	3
Others	2	2	–			
Total Main Line	100	120	244			
Windsor Line						
Ascot & Reading	10	14	18			
Windsor	17	16	19			
Hounslow via Brentford	30	30	44	O	2	1
Hounslow via Richmond	–	2	33	Ō	2	1
Shepperton via Richmond	10	11	7	Š	Peak only	1
Kingston roundabout	28	32	74	V	4	3
East Putney (b)	16	21	22	P	1	–
Kensington	15	–	–			
Others	11	4	–			
Total Windsor Line	137	130	217			
Total Departures	237	250	461			

Notes
(a) Claygate electric trains ran twice hourly during 1916–19, headcode I.
(b) East Putney electric trains ran three times an hour until May 1918.

APPENDIX 7A

RUNNING POWERS EXERCISED BY THE LSWR

Company	Section	Miles	Chains	Traffic
LBSCR	Streatham Junction – Tulse Hill			
	Junction	2	12	Passenger
	Cosham Junction – Farlington Junction	0	45	All
	Havant Junction – Portcreek Junction	3	61	All
	Longhedge Junction – Battersea Wharf	0	75	Freight
SECR	Tulse Hill Junction – Ludgate Hill			
	station	5	20	Passenger
	Lavender Hill Junction – Loughborough			
	Junction	3	3	Passenger
	Wokingham Junction – Reading	6	75	All
	Aldershot Junction – Ash Junction	1	48	Passenger
WLR	Addison Road (WLER boundary) –			
	Kensington Junction	0	58	Passenger
NSWJR	Old Kew Junction – Willesden Sidings	3	66	Freight
MR	Acton Wells Junction – Brent Sidings	3	62	Freight
GWR	Winchester (Bar End) – Winchester			
	(DNSR)	0	9	All
	Dorchester Junction – Weymouth	6	73	All
	Yeovil Town – LSWR Goods Yard	0	10	Freight
	Exeter St David's – Cowley Bridge			
	Junction	1	31	All
	Devonport Junction – Friary Junction	2	60	All
	Devonport Junction – Keyham	1	50	Dockyard only

RUNNING POWERS EXERCISED BY OTHER COMPANIES OVER THE LSWR

Company	Section	Miles	Chains	Traffic
LBSCR	Peasmarsh Junction – Guildford	1	57	All
SECR	Aldershot Junction – Aldershot station	2	4	All
	Shalford Junction – Ash Junction	6	54	All
	Reading SEC Junction – GW Junction	0	3	All
	Lavender Hill Junction – Clapham Junction	0	49	All
GNR	Lavender Hill Junction – Clapham Junction	0	49	All
MR	Lavender Hill Junction – Clapham Junction	0	49	All
	Acton Junction – Studland Road Junction	1	78(a)	Freight
NSWJ	Kew Curve East Junction – Kew Bridge station	0	25	Passenger – (LNWR/NLR)
NLR	Acton Junction – Richmond	3	3	Passenger
Met	Hammersmith Junction – Richmond	4	70(b)	Passenger
MDR	Putney Bridge Junction – Wimbledon	3	35	Passenger
	Studland Road Junction – Richmond	4	25(c)	Passenger
GWR	Hammersmith Junction–Richmond	4	70(b)	Passenger
	Barnstaple Junction – station	0	16	All
	Boscarne Junction – Wadebridge	4	51	All
	Cattewater Junction – Plymstock Junction	0	54	All
MSWJR	Red Post Junction – Andover Junction station	1	37	All
	Red Post Junction – Southampton Town & Docks station	29	25	All
S&DJR	Broadstone Junction – Bournemouth West	7	71	All
	Wimborne Junction – Wimborne station	0	25	All

Notes:
(a) From 1911, 1 mile 66 chains westbound.
(b) Powers ceased 1914.
(c) From 1911, 4 miles 13 chains westbound, 3 miles 65 chains eastbound.

JOINT LINES

Partner	Section	Miles	Chains	Operation
LBSCR	Epsom and Leatherhead	3	42	Both companies
	Tooting, Merton and Wimbledon	5	51	Both companies
	Portsmouth and Ryde (mainland)	7	27	Both companies
	Portsmouth and Ryde (Isle of Wight)	0	96	Worked by trains of IWR and IWCR
LBSCR/ LNWR/ GWR	West London Extension (including Chelsea Basin branch)	5	24	All companies
MR	Somerset & Dorset Joint	97	69	Joint committee
GWR	Weymouth Harbour	1	8	Worked by GWR
	Weymouth and Portland	4	63	

(Passenger traffic operated by each company alternately for five year periods – freight traffic operated by both companies)

Yeovil Town	Joint station		
Chard Junction and station	0	41	
Plymouth North Road	Joint station		

LEASED AND WORKED LINES

Worked Jointly

Line	Miles	Chains	Remarks
Bridgwater Railway	7	56	Worked by S&D Joint Committee
Easton & Church Hope (including Admiralty line)	3	57(a)	Worked by LSWR and GWR jointly

(a) Extended by 31 chains to Sheepcroft Sidings 1917–19

Worked by LSWR and shown on RCH maps as LSWR mileage

Line	Miles	Chains	Remarks
Exmouth Dock	0	40	(approx)
Lee-on-the-Solent	3	9	
North Cornwall	50	14	Halwill to Padstow
Plymouth, Devonport & South Western Junction	22	28	Lydford to Devonport
Plymouth & Dartmoor	3	64	Turnchapel and Cattewater branches
Sidmouth Railway	8	23	
Salisbury Railway & Market House company	0	20	(approx)

LSWR MILEAGE AT 31 DECEMBER 1922

	Miles	Chains
Route mileage		
Owned	862	17
Share of joint lines	10	1
Leased or worked	89	23
Share of lines leased or worked jointly	57	57
Total	1,019	18
Track mileage		
First track	1,019	18
Second track	695	30
Third track	78	56
Fourth track	65	31
Over four tracks (on single track basis)	36	44
Sidings etc	486	20
Total	2,381	39
Lines authorised but not built	15	66

THE LSWR BOARD IN 1922

Chairman
Brigadier General Sir Hugh W. Drummond, Bt, CMG. London SW1 and Churt, Farnham, Surrey. Joined board 1900. Banker and company director.

Deputy Chairman
Sir William W. Portal, Bt. London W1 and Laverstoke, Whitchurch, Hampshire. Joined board 1902. Member of family firm making banknote paper. Retired at Grouping.

Directors
Colonel Sir Robert Williams, Bt, MP. Bridehead, Dorchester. Joined board 1892. Chairman of stores and locomotive & carriage committees. Retired at Grouping.

The Rt Hon Sir Evelyn Cecil, GBE, MP. London SW1 and Lytchett Heath, Poole, Dorset. Joined board 1902. Chairman of the finance committee. Member of family of the Marquess of Salisbury.

Colonel the Hon Sir Henry Crichton, KCB, ADC. London SW1 and Netley Castle, Hampshire. Joined board 1903. Chairman of docks & marine committee, also supervised purchases of company horses. Died May 1922 – seat left vacant.

The Rt Hon Viscount Pirrie, KP. London SW1 and Witley Park, Godalming, Surrey. Joined board 1907. Chairman of Harland & Wolff.

The Rt Hon Lord Clinton. Heanton Satchville, Dolton, Devon. Joined board 1907. Chairman of engineering & estates committee.

Sir Owen Philipps, GCMG,MP. London SW1. Joined board 1910. Chairman of Royal Mail and Union Castle shipping lines.

Robert Holland-Martin, CB. London SW7 and Tewkesbury, Gloucestershire. Joined board 1911. Member of the Martins Bank family.

The Rt Hon Sir George H. Murray, GCB, GCVO. London SW1. Joined board 1912. Former Permanent Secretary to the Treasury.

Sir Charles J. Owens, CB. London SW15. Joined board 1912. Former LSWR general manager.

The Rt Hon Frederick Huth Jackson. London SW7. Joined board 1916. Merchant banker and director of the Bank of England. Died December 1921 – seat left vacant.

Dugald Drummond, chief mechanical engineer 1895–1912. *National Railway Museum*

J. W. Jacomb-Hood, chief engineer 1901–14. *National Railway Museum*

Sir Herbert Walker, KCB, general manager 1912–1922. *National Railway Museum*

Brigadier-General Sir Hugh Drummond, Bt, CMG, chairman 1910–22. *National Railway Museum*

LSWR PRINCIPAL OFFICERS 1900–1922

General Manager:	(1898)	Sir Charles J. Owens, CB
	1912	Sir Herbert Walker, KCB
Secretary:	(1898)	Godfrey Knight
Solicitor:	1900	Sam Bircham
	1910	W. Bishop
Superintendent of the Line:	(1899)	Sam Fay
	1902	Henry Holmes
	1916	G. F. P. West, GBE
Goods Manager:	(1898)	Alfred Malby—office divided 1912 into:
Indoor Goods Manager:	1912	Joseph Smeal, CBE
Outdoor Goods Manager:	1912	G. T. Hedge, OBE
Accountant:	(1890)	F. Hartnell
	1913	A. E. Newhook
Treasurer:	(1894)	G. G. Currie
	1909	W. T. Olding
Resident Engineer/Chief Engineer:	(1887)	E. Andrews
	1901	J. W. Jacomb-Hood
	1914	A. W. Szlumper, CBE
Locomotive Superintendent/CME:	(1895)	Dugald Drummond
	1912	R. W. Urie
Electrical Engineer:	1912	Herbert Jones
Carriage & Wagon Superintendent:	(1890)	W. Panter
	1906	Surrey Warner, OBE
Estate Agent:		A. V. Haines—office divided 1902:
	1902	S. B. Saunders
	1918	W. T. Selwyn
Rating Agent:	1902	J. C. Mortimer
	1914	H. E. Judd
Storekeeper:		G. R. Barrell
	1909	C. Alexander
	1920	C. Francis, CBE
Docks & Marine Manager:	(1892)	J. Dixon
	1902	T. M. Williams
	1920	G. S. Szlumper

FINANCIAL SUMMARY 1900–1922

Year to 31 Dec	*Capital issued* £	*Debentures issued* £	*Capital expenditure* £	*Net earnings* £	*Consol. Ord. Stock* *Dividend* %	*Middle price*
1899	26,240,540	13,161,912	39,116,437[a]			
1900	500,000	129,046	1,235,867	1,936,036	$6\frac{1}{8}$	$195\frac{1}{2}$
1901	810,000	235,793	1,271,412	1,876,199	$5\frac{3}{8}$	176
1902	1,224,014	350,829	1,274,734	2,055,818	6	176
1903	252,012	105,434	985,605	2,058,474	6	162
1904	590,580	231,000	847,160	2,088,703	6	$156\frac{1}{2}$
1905	349,998	100,967	451,447	2,116,344	6	$163\frac{1}{2}$
1906	250,000	1,000	440,619	2,118,820	$5\frac{3}{4}$	153
1907	821,306	167,813	393,124	2,092,349	$5\frac{7}{8}$	144
	526,360		721,528	W&C and A&LR	purchases	
1908	150,000	201,134	462,613	2,067,129	$5\frac{1}{2}$	$139\frac{1}{2}$
1909	50,000	101,176	469,707	2,113,470	$5\frac{3}{4}$	$134\frac{3}{4}$
			5,025	P&D purchase		
1910	228,531	1,255	510,088	2,196,212	$6\frac{1}{8}$	$136\frac{7}{8}$
			32,638	SPI purchase		
1911	673,999	151,331	646,098	2,227,659	6	$141\frac{1}{2}$
1912	503,187	364,465	384,835	2,118,157	$5\frac{3}{8}$	$128\frac{5}{8}$
			63,520	BSR purchase		
1913	280,000	101,580	230,470	2,190,502	$5\frac{7}{8}$	$117\frac{3}{4}$
1914	1,000,000	1,663	398,155	2,195,454	$5\frac{5}{8}$	116
1915		1,727	619,922	2,193,321	$5\frac{1}{2}$	$97\frac{1}{4}$
1916	3,000	1,748	225,517	2,209,268	$5\frac{1}{2}$	81
1917		1,887	97,554	2,207,829	$5\frac{1}{2}$	$82\frac{5}{8}$
1918		1,932	86,549	2,264,755	$5\frac{7}{8}$	$84\frac{1}{2}$
1919			152,177	2,298,664	6	80
1920			216,816	2,293,499	6	$70\frac{1}{8}$
1921			172,003	2,323,264[b]	6	58
1922			98,864	2,623,879[c]	8	81

Notes:
(a) Excludes £3,679,560 on consolidation of stock.
(b) Includes £250,000 government compensation payment.
(c) Includes £100,000 government interest received on capital expenditure made since 1913.

AUTHORS' NOTE

This book is a combined effort incorporating the detailed research carried out by R. A. Williams for Volume 2 and the projected Volume 3 of the LSWR History. However, its appearance would not have been possible without the assistance of others, of whom we would like to thank: Alan A. Jackson for his encouragement and for the benefit of his extensive knowledge of London's railway development; H. V. Borley for contributions from his store of precise information; Denis Cullum for the provision of much authoritative detail on track and signalling changes; Mike King of the South Western Circle for his expert knowledge of LSWR rolling stock; and Reg Randell at Waterloo for his advice.

Among publications, we are indebted to those of the late D. L. Bradley on LSWR locomotives which have enabled us to ignore mechanical matters; G. A. Pryer for compiling the series of track diagrams of the LSWR system (from which our sketch maps are derived); and to R. H. Clark for his Southern Region Chronology, to which readers are referred for such details as station re-namings. We are grateful to the many authors who have dealt with local and specialised facets of the LSWR, listed in the Bibliography.

For facilities in research the authors are appreciative of the Trustees of the British Museum and the newspaper library at Colindale; the Clerk of the Records at the House of Lords; the Public Record Office at Kew; the libraries of the Chartered Institute of Transport, the Institution of Electrical Engineers, and the Railway Club.

Illustrations have been provided by courtesy of the Keeper of the National Railway Museum, the Trustees of the Imperial War Museum and the Curator of the City of Southampton Museums. We also thank our friend George Gundry for the use of picture postcards from his collection. Finally, the completion of this book owes much to Mrs Phyllis Faulkner.

Dates quoted in relation to stations and train services normally refer to the day on which public traffic commenced, and in the case of closures, to the day when trains ceased to run. In comparison with some of its neighbouring companies, LSWR minutes are relatively brief, and to add to the difficulties of the historian many of the company's records were destroyed during the war. Accurate dating of some developments has not been established, but here the best estimates have been given. For reasons of space many minor changes to stations and track facilities, and some references to projected but unauthorised schemes have had to be omitted.

The authors have made every effort to ensure accuracy, but apologise if they have included any errors.

BIBLIOGRAPHY

COMPANY RECORDS

LSWR	Reports and accounts
	Minutes of directors and board committees
	Minutes of traffic officers' conference
	Miscellaneous papers and agreements
	Working and public timetables; special traffic notices
	Appendix to the working timetable
	Operating instructions (yellow notices)
LSWR/LBSCR	Minutes of joint committees
LBSCR	Minutes of board
SECR	Minutes of managing committee
SR	Annual reports
	Minutes of directors and board committees
	Working and public timetables
	Appendix to the working timetable
	Southampton Docks handbook

OTHER RAILWAYS MINUTES

Axminister & Lyme Regis Light Railway
Bishop's Waltham Railway
Easton & Church Hope Railway
Lee-on-the-Solent Railway
Plymouth & Dartmoor Railway

Plymouth, Devonport & South Western Junction Railway
Stonehouse Pool Improvement Company
Windsor & Ascot Railway

PARLIAMENTARY/GOVERNMENT

Deposited plans for new lines
Acts of Parliament
BoT/MoT Reports on inspection of lines
Reports on railway accidents
Light Railway Orders
Miscellaneous papers and reports
BoT   Reports on shipping casualties
Railway Clearing House maps and junction diagrams

CONTEMPORARY PUBLICATIONS

Bradshaw's Railway Guide & Timetables
Bradshaw's Railway Manual & Shareholders' Guide
Railway Gazette
Railway Magazine
Railway News
Railway Times
Railway/Transport & Travel Monthly
South Western Gazette/Magazine
Tramway & Railway World
The Times
Railway Year Book

BOOKS, ARTICLES & SUPPLEMENTS

Bagwell, P. S. *The Railwaymen*. Allen & Unwin, 1963
Barker, T. C. & Robbins, R. M. *History of London Transport* Allen & Unwin, 1974
Bradley, D. L. *Locomotives of the LSWR* Railway Correspondence & Travel Society, 1967
Brown, G. A., Prideaux, J. D. C. & Radcliffe, H. G. *Lynton & Barnstaple Railway*. David & Charles, 1964
Cheesman, A. J. *Plymouth, Devonport & South Western Junction Railway*. Oakwood Press, 1967
Clark, R. H. *Southern Region Chronology & Record 1803–1965*. Oakwood Press, 1964

Clarke, J. M. *The Brookwood Necropolis Railway*. Oakwood Press, 1983

Clinker, C. R. *Register of Closed Passenger Stations*. Avon–Anglia, 1978

Connolly, C. *London United Tramways – Short History*. Tramway & Light Railway Society, 1964

Course, Edwin *Southampton & Netley Railway*. Southampton Record Office, 1983

Crombleholme, R., Stuckey, D. & Whetmath, C. F. D. *Callington Railways*. Branch Line Handbooks, 1967

Cummings, John *Railway Motor Bus Services in the British Isles*. Oxford Publishing Co, 1980

Dendy Marshall, C. F. *History of the Southern Railway*. (Revised by R. W. Kidner) Ian Allan, 1963

Duckworth, C. D. & Langmuir, G. E. *Railway and Other Steamers*. Shipping History Ltd, 1948

Fairman, J. R. *Netley Hospital and its Railways*. Kingfisher Books, 1984

Fay, Sir Sam *The War Office at War*. Hutchinson, 1937

Gale, P. R. (compiler) *The GWR* Reprinted Avon-Anglia, 1986

Griffith, E. C. *Basingstoke & Alton Light Railway*. 1970

Howard Turner, J. T. *History of the LBSCR*. Batsford, 1979

Jackson, A. A. *London's Termini*. David & Charles, 1985

Jackson, A. A. *London's Metropolitan Railway*. David & Charles, 1986

Jackson, A. A. *Wimbledon & Sutton Railway, Railway Magazine*, December 1966

Jackson, A. A. *Horton Light Railway, Railway Magazine*, October 1981

Jackson, A. A. & Croome, D. *Rails Through the Clay*. Allen & Unwin, 1962

Karau, P., Parsons & Robertson *Didcot, Newbury & Southampton Railway*. Wild Swan, 1981

'Kennington' *London County Council Tramways Handbook*. Tramway & Light Railway Society, 1970

Klapper, C. F. *Sir Herbert Walker's Southern Railway*. Ian Allan, 1973

Lucking, J. H. *The Great Western at Weymouth*. David & Charles, 1971

MacDermot, E. T. *History of the Great Western Railway*. (Revised by C. R. Clinker) Ian Allan, 1964

Maggs, C., *Railways to Exmouth*. Oakwood Press, 1980

Maggs, C. & Paye, P. *Sidmouth, Seaton and Lyme Regis Branches*. Oakwood Press, 1977

Paye, P. *The Lymington Branch*. Oakwood Press, 1979

Plumridge, J. H. *Hospital Ships and Ambulance Trains*. Seeley Service, 1975

Pratt, E. A. *British Railways in the Great War*. Selwyn & Blount, 1921

Pryer, G. A. (and Paul, A. V.) *Track Layout Diagrams of the SR*. Published 1980–6

Pryer, G. A. & Bowring, G. J. *Historical Survey of Selected Southern Stations*. Oxford Publishing Co, 1981

Robertson, K. *The Southsea Railway*. Kingfisher Books, 1985

Railway Gazette Supplement 15 November 1940: Rejuvenation of the Waterloo & City Tube.

Railway Gazette Supplement 12 May 1922: *Feltham Concentration Yard*.

Ronald, D. W. & Carter, R. J. *Longmoor Military Railway*. David & Charles, 1974

Shipbuilding & Shipping Record Supplement 27 July 1933: *Southampton Docks Extension*.

Simmons, J. *The Railway in Town and Country 1830–1914*. David & Charles, 1985

Simmonds, R. *Park Prewett Hospital Railway*. British Railway Journal, issue No 2

Stone, R. *Meon Valley Railway*. Kingfisher Books, 1983

Whetmath, C. F. D. & Stuckey, D. *North Devon & Cornwall Junction Light Railway*. Oakwood Press, 1963

INDEX

Note – numbers in *italic* refer to illustrations and maps